Platform for Change

Platform for Change

The Foundations of the Northern Free Black Community, 1775-1865

Harry Reed

Michigan State University Press
East Lansing
1994

All Michigan State University Press books are produced on paper which meets the requirements of American National Standard of Information Sciences—Permanence of paper for printed materials ANSI Z23.48-1984.

Printed in the United States of America

Michigan State University Press
East Lansing, Michigan 48823-5202

02 01 00 99 98 97 96 95 94 1 2 3 4 5 6 7 8 9 10

Library of Congress Cataloging-in-Publication Data

Reed, Harry A. (Harry Atwood), 1934-
    Platform for change : the foudations of the northern free Black community, 1775-1865 / Harry Reed.
        p.   cm.
    Includes bibliographical references and index.
    ISBN 0-87013-341-1
    1. Afro-Americans—History—To 1863. 2. Afro-Americans—History—1863-1877. I. Title.
E185.18.R44 1994
973'.0496073—dc20   93-37526
                                                                          CIP

Contents

Acknowledgments

In the summer of 1977 when I started the research for this volume I envisioned a lightning-like process of work resulting in a published manuscript within two years. Now more than a decade later I have confirmed not a speedy resolution, but that my original estimate of two years' work was accurate. As I immersed myself in teaching, articles were being written but less and less time was given to *Platform for Change*. The topic, the material, the people whose lives I was touching, continued to excite me but it was difficult to find time to work on the manuscript.

During two summers I managed with the assistance of small grants from the College of Arts and Letters, Michigan State University, to continue collecting data. Once into the term, however, I would find only a day, occasionally a week, to work on the book. Finally, a colleague, David Bailey, responded critically but favorably to one of my draft chapters. Other colleagues (named below) also read the drafts and encouraged me to continue writing. Their confidence and interest encouraged me further and the result is this monograph.

Any work that takes such a long time to complete incurs numerous debts and kindnesses that cannot be fully repaid. Among my academic colleagues I wish to thank especially Douglas T. Miller, Peter Levine, and Richard Thomas. Not only did they read parts of the manuscript but they encouraged me in other substantial ways. Doug and Peter share my interest in sports and helped me find time to relax when duties became too pressing. Richard continues to make claims for my work being a significant guide to his own research in urban history. All three of them have given, I fear, a great deal more than they received.

Although he did not read any of the manuscript, David Loromer has acted as a cheerleader throughout the entire process. My good friend and former colleague, Robert Paul Duggan, has always been supportive of me as a historian despite the meager evidence I presented to justify such a claim.

To David Smith and Janet Campbell my thanks for many favors including sharing their home during various stages of my work. My appreciation also goes to my research assistant Anita Herald. Julie Loehr, my editor, has substantially enhanced this work through her support, insights, and humor.

Last, and most important, thanks to my daughters Gillian and Jordan. Throughout the period we have maintained our special relationship. Gillian assisted at various times by running down leads and checking bibliographical material. Jordan cheered me at basketball games, designed my favorite gym shirt, and wondered, many times, aloud, when I would finish. All of the persons mentioned here have helped make this a better manuscript. The errors of ommission, interpretation, and style are, of course, my own.

1

Background

This work is an attempt to articulate the beginnings of community consciousness among northern free blacks in America. It is also meant to shed light on black life in the years from the Revolution to the Civil War. Part of the task is to describe certain responses which, in part, still characterize black actions and reactions to life in America. For this investigation I have used the cities of Boston, New York, and Philadelphia because they set the trend in organizing a black voice to accompany their obvious but discriminated against visibility.

While the narrative of events explains how and why things were different in the three cities, no attempt is made to follow a strict comparative framework. Instead, it is argued that the three cities were representative of the growing trend toward self-determination on the part of blacks in the North. Each city was representative of northern black life in terms of population, organizations, black leaders, and black aggitation. Collectively, the cities represent the burgeoning awareness of the black community that it could fashion political, social, and economic responses and find methods to express itself. Moreover, blacks in Boston, New York, and Philadelphia took the lead in designing and carrying out actions to relieve certain disabilities in their lives.

Thus, they are representative because they were part of the rapidly urbanizing pattern of black life individually and collectively. The three cities were the major northern centers of black population. They each contained a critical mass of blacks that could organize around significant issues. By 1800, Boston, New York, and Philadelphia were among the few cities in America with a free black population in excess of one thousand people. Like white Americans at the same time, blacks were flocking to urban centers to take advantage of the proliferation of services and opportunities that existed there.

Because of the available resources, in addition to population, the cities were also major arenas of black activity: churches were formed, newspapers were founded, organizations flourished, and ideas were transformed into actions within their confines. While such activities were not absent from black rural areas only the urban populations developed a visible, viable tradition of organized protest.

Even among cities the primacy of Boston, New York, and Philadelphia can be noted. A case in point is the growth and development of black activities in Newport and Providence, Rhode Island. Because of its early and aggressive involvement in the slave trade, Rhode Island had the largest black population of any New England colony. Moreover, blacks in Newport organized one of the earliest civic associations in America: the Newport African Union in 1774. Neither large populations nor early entry into political activity, however, assured that Newport or Providence would emerge as trendsetters of black American political activity.

Finally, the pre-eminence of these three northern cities was acknowledged by black leaders who made them the sites of conventions, sources of financial and moral support, the centers of national organizations, and places where they spent considerable time pursuing personal and professional goals. Again, we note the representative position of the three cities. The most popular black leader in antebellum America, Frederick Douglass, resided in Rochester, New York. From that venue he owned and edited the most popular black newspaper of the period. Yet his presence and the newspaper's high profile did not create the platform for change that characterized Philadelphia, New York, and Boston.

Despite the prominent focus on groups and associations, this is not a study of organizations and organizational behavior. It is instead an examination of the interplay between individuals, institutions, and ideologies. This interplay reveals that black people sometimes sought particular solutions to their own problems and at other times sought universal solutions to problems faced by all Americans.

The major focus is on how blacks, in the three cities investigated, achieved voice and visibility through a set of structured activities. This platform for change was designed, in part, to help black people lead purposeful lives while facing particular disabilities. No rational human being can ignore the specter of American racism, but given its existence and its intransigence the more pressing concern illuminated here is how blacks constructed methods and instruments to pierce the battlements when possible, and to keep going when it was impossible to crack the barriers. This work confirms my assumption that neither blacks, nor any other group, can survive only through reaction.

In recent years there have been a number of critical and sharply drawn studies of black life in the three cities examined here. While all note the connections between the cities, each study makes a claim for the uniqueness of blacks in a particular locale. Here the three cities are drawn together to reveal a conscious nexus of individuals, institutions, and ideologies working to establish a national sense of purpose: the platform for change. This national agenda informed the work and thought of nineteenth-century northern black leaders and to a large extent is still part of the black platform for change.

One purpose of this work is to challenge the wisdom of some of the existing scholarship on nineteenth-century black Americans. Much of this work notes cooperation between blacks and whites but also assesses black activity as just another exercise in powerlessness. My work demonstrates that blacks discovered their power, organized it collectively, and achieved some incremental triumphs. The very act of objecting to their oppression was empowering. It can also be argued that early black activists went beyond objecting and began constructing a platform for change that would ultimately benefit them as well as other Americans. By no means has the empowerment been complete, but Richard Allen, Peter Williams, Jr., Prince Hall, Mary Ann Shadd Cary, Jacob C. White, Jr., and a host of others set in motion a growing political consciousness and structures for its exercise that continue to inform black political activities into the last decade of the twentieth century.

I

The late eighteenth century witnessed changes in American perceptions of their British connections, while blacks began consciously and self-consciously to define themselves and to erect the parameters of their own community. Particularly during the revolutionary war period there were direct cause and effect relationships between black and white rhetoric. While American patriots argued, sometimes persuasively yet always vociferously, for their rights as Englishmen, black Americans organized to argue for their rights as human beings. Afro-Americans did not imitate their white contemporaries but rather echoed the universality of the ideas being espoused at the time: liberty, tyranny, representation, self-determination, and slavery. Although lacking American political experience, blacks proved to be skilled at generating critiques of their own circumstances. Moreover, they became adept at turning patriot and later American arguments around for their own use.

Throughout the revolutionary and early national periods black Americans began generating and circulating the ideas and institutions of a political community. In addition, the individuals who formulated and promulgated the ideologies and led organizations were becoming recognizable personalities within the community. On the eve of the Civil War the five activities illuminated in this work—the founding of independent churches, the creation of organizations, the emergence of newspapers, the convention movement, and the philosophy of emigration—gave legitmacy to the political awareness and competence of black America.

Throughout this work these five areas of activity address the issue of black community consciousness, which is the central theme of the book. Far more than a geographic setting of racially or culturally identifiable humans sharing certain traits, the community paradigm employed here describes a process of self-determination. It encompasses the awareness of difference and exclusion but, more important, generates procedures for change. For the analysis contained herein change and interrelatedness are necessarily crucial. Perhaps more than any other single element the interrelated networks resulting from the nexus of the five movements provide eloquent testimony of the vision of antebellum black leaders. One can see black leaders clearly perceiving their value to the contemporary scene while understanding their effect on future generations of blacks. The growth of church, organizations, the black press, the black convention movement, and the ideology of emigration helped black activists chart their platform for change.

The ability to depict the pattern and the interrelatedness of efforts does not suggest that the route to community consciousness followed a smoothly banked progression. Instead, like most human endeavors, black community consciousness proceeded by fits and starts. Throughout the periods of conflict, cooperation, continuity, and change the black leadership exhibited an underlying unity that is impossible to ignore.

First, the independent black church provided the initial institutional structure. Later it became the most important institution in the black community. For varying periods of time it provided needed community services until more specialized agencies came into being.

Second, self-help, women's, and fraternal organizations provided institutional support and took over many of the responsiblities that had been performed by the early churches. Although such agencies started with the limited scope of servicing exclusively their membership, most expanded to assume a communitywide role. This expansion of services and responsiblities triggered a process of institutional differentiation within the community. On a broad basis the variety of organizations provided social outlets, financial counseling, resource protection, sick and survival benefits, and helped to stimulate education and business aspirations.

As with the early churches, black newspapers intitially had a dual responsibility. Beyond building a communications network to service a range of black needs, this third movement also helped to shape cultural tastes, teach about the black past, and to circulate black opinion for the benefit of whites as well as blacks. Black newspapers provided an outlet for intellectuals, activists, and the masses to read about and speak to a variety of issues ranging from education to women's liberation.

The fourth activity that gave substance and shape to political development in the community was the black convention movement. During these deliberations issues of national importance were discussed and acted upon. Leaders who had ordinarily only a regional constituency were given a national platform. Never as exclusive as the convention titles would suggest, whites were inivited as participants/observers, if not voting members. The direction, scope, and decisions were black-oriented and black-dominated. In addition to providing a national forum to discuss black problems and solutions, the convention movement also acted as a system of closure for the fledgling community.

Fifth and finally, the ideology of emigration contributed overwhelmingly to the growing political aggressiveness within the community before the Civil War. It must be acknowledged that the back- to-Africa movement was a minority philosophy. Its prominence, as an analytical unit here, can be attributed to the single-minded activists who advocated its acceptance as an answer to black political impotence. Although it advocated leaving America, emigrationism ranks as a foundation of the free black community. This is so because emigrationists emphasized political assessment, power, and economic competition with slave produced goods, and ultimately formed the beginning thrusts of black nationalism in America.

Taken all together the five activities demonstrate black political awareness in its formative stages. That it was self-conscious and political can be seen not only by the overlapping leadership but also from the targets it chose to attack. Richard Allen, founder of the African Methodist Episcopal Church, was also a leader and organizer in the early convention movement. Peter Williams, Jr., a leading clergyman, organized the financial backing for *Freedom's Journal.* A former newspaperman turned doctor, Martin R. Delany, became the leading advocate of the back-to-Africa idea prior to the Civil War. All activists, even those opposed to separate racial enclaves, attended the conventions. Their rationale was simple: to maintain credibility and currency one had to be where the action was.

II

In short, the years 1770 through 1865 traced through the five activities reveal the growing political awareness of black Americans. Moreover, these ideas, institutions, and ideologies have continued to be utilized by the black community during periods of political crises. Far from an arbitrary assigning of importance, the chronology here reflects currents in American politics that provided an atmosphere in which black aspirations could achieve fruition. Prior to, during, and immediately after the revolutionary war an overwhelming concentration on American liberty legitimized a resort to petitions to legislative bodies that called for redress of the petitioners' grievances.

The first such black American petitions appeared in 1772. In March of that year the representatives of the Massachusetts General Court received a petition containing one signature. The following month the same body received a petition signed by five blacks calling the legislature's attention to their status in bondage. Both petitions noted the patriots' utilization of the word slavery to describe their own status vis-a-vis Britain. Black petitioners gently pointed out that the word more correctly described their state and hoped the legislature would act to end black bondage while pursuing their own liberation.

While the slaves struck the first blow for their freedom, the New England colonies, caught up in the fury of the political discussions, began a slow movement toward the first emancipation. Although in the case of New Hampshire the process was not completed until 1857, the first steps taken in the 1770s signaled a new attitude about black bondage. Certainly, the colonies were not seized with a unanimous spirit to free enslaved blacks nor were the ecomonic forces which had an effect on emancipation elsewhere absent in the New England case. Nonetheless, even gradual emancipation plans allowed for more discusssion about black American status, and although not invited to take part in the dialogue, blacks inserted themselves slowly into the process. Insinuating themselves into the process reflects the simplest manifestation of black community consciousness. Blacks began a conscious, sometimes self-conscious manipulation of visibility and voice. Certainly, black visibility had existed since the earliest days of the colonies. As slaves, "servants," and free people they provided labor, a different set of cultural values, occasional problems for political and religious authorities, and seemingly always served as the outsider to be pilloried in word, song, legislation, and popular usage.

Although a distinct minority, the black presence was always felt and generally commented upon. The value of blacks in the colonies seemed to outweigh their actual numbers. Before the revolutionary period, however, what was missing was their own voice giving circulation to a unique black view of being resident in America. Revolutionary America with its chaos provided an arena where blacks could combine visibility and voice as the initial step in the process of building a sense of community consciousness. Once the two were welded together it gave black leaders the opportunity to establish specific, concrete signs of the platform for change. That process of initiation, maturation, and acceptance is what concerns us here.

The fullest expression of black community consciousness is revealed in the activities attendant upon establishing churches, organizations, newspapers, conventions, and the ideology of emigration. All of these actions coupled visibility and voice and contributed to a growing awareness within and outside the community. Too often the combination of forces was viewed negatively by outside observers. Black dissatisfaction with the status quo was usually attributed to their creation of separate churches, educational societies, newspapers, and other community vehicles. The degree to which black empowerment was connected to the activities and institutions is seen in the attacks on those examples of black independence during race riots throughout the period. Moreover, the constant use of cartoons or editorials lampooning black actions suggests strongly that black community building activities posed a siginificant potential threat to white domination.

These activities beginning in the 1770s highlight a shift in fortunes for blacks. Prince Hall, a free Massachusetts black, received permission from British officers to organize an African Masonic Lodge. Although not an area of concentration in this volume, another series of events signals the 1770s as the genesis of black community consciousness. In the course of the war approximately fifteen thousand blacks made a decision to accept the British government's inducements to join the British army. The decision to join the British forces involved the assessment of the chances of getting to the British lines; feeling that the the British would deliver on their promises of freedom, relocation, and provisions; the probability that they would survive the war; and the hope of better prospects for freedom, justice, equality, and the right to pursue their own political and cultural designs.

III

Another shaping influence of the platform for change was locale. Individually and collectively Philadelphia, New York, and Boston represented centers of black opinion and to a certain extent took the lead in producing a national black political agenda. While Richard Allen and Absalom Jones were giants of the black church movement they represent only the tip of the iceberg. A remarkable number of outstanding black churchmen served important parts of their careers in Philadelphia: Samuel Cornish, Daniel Alexander Payne, William T. Catto, Robert Douglass, John Gloucester, and Alexander Crummell. On a continuing basis black clergy from other locales had intimate and frequent contacts with Philadelphia including Henry Highland Garnet, Charles B. Ray, Daniel Coker, Theodore Wright, Thomas Paul, and others. These examples alone clearly establish Philadelphia as a national trendsetter for black consciousness in antebellum America. When combined with similar actions in Boston and New York the result is a new synthesis of black community awareness.

The three cities represent the axis of identity of purpose and action combined with a plan to attack the twin evils in black life: slavery and discrimination. Moreover, the process of action forged in the three cities was consciously imported and copied by other leaders and institutions across America. Although each process was modified to meet local circumstances, the broad outline remained committed to the same basic five activities: church, newspapers, organizations, conventions, and emigration. What emerges is a clearly discernible self-determined pattern that assisted blacks in living creative, purposeful lives within the midst of oppression. No attempt is made herein to construct a comparative model. The more important exercise is to illuminate how consciously and unconsciously the three cities complemented and sustained each other and the entire black population in the drive to find and maintain the platform for change.

IV

The present volume challenges prevailing ideas about black passivity and instead asserts that the community was not institutionally weak, philosophically confused, or adhoc in its organizational techniques. For example, the church has been the single most important institution in black American history. The present work affirms that conclusion while clarifying and redefining the black church's position in antebellum America. In each of the communities (thus nationally) the church experienced a relative decline in its hegemony. Simultaneously the church maintained its importance in ways not recorded by existing scholarship. The church was the incubator for other organizations in the community. Thus the church became the central force generating a communitywide institutional infrastructure. Ironically this process of institutional specialization and differentiation helped speed the secularization of the community, while secularization enhanced the church. The interdependence of the institutional structure meant that generally after the mid 1830s the church was *primus inter pares* rather than the sole community organization.

By juxtaposing the church and interrelatedness of purpose with emigration we can discern the vitality of the present analysis. It will be demonstrated that black American perceptions about leaving America changed over time, from a slave corollary to revolutionary rhetoric, to reform/religious utterance, to bitter frustration, and finally to nationalist assertion. More important, this evolution of ideology was vitally assisted by the other four activities central to this study. Churchmen were in the forefront of both generating and restricting interest in leaving America. Newspapers, frequently devoting primary coverage to discussions of emigration, were of overwhelming importance to the ideology. Conventions of at least two persuasions, the reformist/religious and nationalist, were utilized to promote interest in emigration. Finally, old and new organizations were pressed and sometimes pressured into the service of convincing black Americans to consider relocation. Within this discussion of emigration an attempt will be made to make a clear distinction between colonization and emigration. In this study colonization is seen basically as a white scheme and emigration as a self-determined black approach to relocation. It must be noted, however, that blacks sometimes employed the term colonization and simultaneously acted for and against the idea.

While the present study is confined to the years 1770-1865, the efficacy of viewing the five elements as the platform for change clearly extends beyond the stated chronological boundaries. Black Americans have continued to use these same arenas to deal with the problems of being black in America. Thus the present work affirms clearly the tenacity of the platform for change idea in black American consciousness to the present day.

Clearly, the years 1770-1865 did not represent a golden age for northern free blacks. Nor is it implied that blacks responded as a monolithic entity to the areas of activity examined here. What is demonstrated explicitly is that a group of black spokespersons developed ideologies, built institutions, and served as individuals who represented the best hopes for the community. Moreover, as will be demonstrated, the individuals, ideologies, and institutions became fixed symbols of racial progress that blacks learned, shared, valued, and passed on to future generations.

V

A compelling interest in this work is to demonstrate that black responses were not solely reactions to racism. Although more difficult to illuminate than responses to oppression, blacks were also motivated by a series of human needs that largely have remained unexplored or unexplained by historians. Any human group, it would seem, would find it necessary to come together for mutual support, sustenance, and relating to their kinsmen. It is within the resulting interactions that individuals and ethnic groups could relax and be themselves. Blacks in America began the tentative steps toward collective cultural identity as they simultaneously attacked the remnants of slavery in the North and the entire institution of slavery in the South. While at this same time blacks attacked the more virulent growth of discrimination in the North, this activity cannot be clearly understood through the narrow prism of black desires to achieve integration with white America. More important goals for black activists were acceptance by white America and the ability to pursue the equality of opportunity that America ideally promised.

Throughout the present study an attempt will be made to analyze black activities in terms of their fight against slavery and racism as well as the simple human task of building a community to cope with a world not entirely of their making.

There were two compelling needs driving the desire to create a sense of community. The first stimulant is easy to discern for both the black experience in America and the historical concentration on racial conflict have arrested our view sometimes to the exclusion of other considerations. To be sure, racial prejudice was a clear and present danger especially for the northern free black community, and will be given proper focus here. The second stimulant, not as clearly seen but equally as compelling, was the cultural factor and the not easily definable human need to work, play, and live with people similar to oneself. This choice, if taken to its extreme, of course, results in racism and sometimes the separatism advocated by some black activists. A cautionary word on racism. I categorically reject the sometimes fashionable notion of black racism. I believe that racism embodies a power dimension and too often an authority dimension that black people simply do not possess. I can entertain black ethnocentrism and black chauvinism, but not black racism.

Even a cursory exploration of language, religion, and power reveals several independent cultural foci that drove the urge to community consciousness as surely as racial injustice did. No aspect of Afro-American life is totally independent of racism's imprint. With that in mind we can examine how language, religion, and power provided a cultural subtext for black community consciousness that was as important as the more obvious stimulant of American racism.

Despite the complexity and the multiplicity of African groups making up the slave and free black American population, they shared more among themselves than they did with their European counterparts. All Africans had to adapt to and learn a European language, sometimes several within a brief span of time. The ease with which one obtained fluency in one of the new languages often directly affected the life chances of a bondsman or bondswoman. Fluency in the new language differentiated between leaders and followers. While that categorization worked to the whites' advantage, language acquisition also had advantages for Africans. Language was not only the key to communicating with Europeans but also speeded one's understanding of the new society's cultural norms. Rather than being used for assimilation the familiarity with European language and customs was a prime tool in the escape and maintenance of a fugitive slave. Gerald Mullins and Lorenzo J. Greene have brilliantly demonstrated that a significant percentage of fugitive slaves possessed more than a passing acquaintance with European languages. Whether they disdained European languages or not, all blacks' lives were to some degree controlled by a foreign language. Existence outside the native language was a powerful magnet to community building. It was among people of similar language background that the new African could feel at ease from the pressures of language/cultural domination.

Although African languages were as complex and different as European languages they had enough in common to act as stimulants to community building. Most African captives from the Guinea Coast south to Angola came from the Niger-Congo Bantu language complex. While the languages making up the Niger-Congo complex are differentiated by structure, syntax, grammar, and usage, the differences are more easily negotiated by a native speaker than the problems involved in moving from Ibo to Spanish. In addition, on the African coast and during the middle passage, captive Africans fashioned pidgins to help them bridge the gap between themselves, as well as between themselves and Europeans. In the antebellum period, where this study is grounded, language was still a strong molder of community needs.

By the antebellum period blacks were second-sometimes third-generation Americans and their language acquisition was far superior to what it had been during the colonial period. In the revolutionary and antebellum periods the power dimension of language was still operative but language symbolism and manipulation became more accessible to black Americans. Black language manipulation in the revolutionary period embraced collective need rather than being utilized by individual slaves seeking to escape or to increase their mobility within the slave system.

Several factors made black language manipulation different from what it had been earlier. First, their experimental basis for using the language had been in process about 150 years. Second, and probably the most important factor, the topics in vogue during the revolutionary period, while not consciously applied to black status by whites, could be appropriated for black usage. Every phrase and symbol of revolutionary rhetoric could be molded to serve a black end. Political debate was rife with the words slavery, representation, tyranny, and corruption. Not only were the words part of the American political scene but in the preceding 150 years blacks had watched colonists define themselves opportunistically in or out of the English orbit.

The important factor was that the revolutionary period allowed blacks to test their 150-year apprenticeship. Revolutionary America provided an opportunity and an arena in which to demonstrate their new ability. The fact that blacks took advantage of the opportunity to engage in public dialogue and manipulate the language for their own benefit was a harbinger of the newly emergent black community consciousness.

Writing works such as petitions, broadsides, poetry, and eulogies, allowed blacks to directly utilize the power of language. These writings indicted American society in terms that American patriots noticed, even when they failed to act on the suggestions put forward by blacks. Unlike the patriots who arraigned the English system, blacks called attention to the same forces operating in America. It was a fantastic debut: an unlettered, unhistoricized people defending the rights of their oppressors and simultaneously noting their oppressors' own weaknesses in a manner that did not create a backlash. The petitions and other means of agitation were placed so conspicuously, too, that the oppressor had to at least acknowledge if not act on them. The self-affirming quality of the black petitions during the revolutionary period is unmistakable. Contained in the petitions is the beginning process of self-identity and naming the people. Petitions spoke of Africans and disadvantaged Africans, thereby creating a conception of a people but also a community of common interest and the potential for united action. Moreover, the petitions reveal a people firmly rooted in the present but with visions of the future. Present and future consciousness placed them squarely alongside the patriots. The petitions note the struggle of Americans to define their political autonomy and display black awareness of the significance and universality of the political currents swirling around them. Deftly manipulating the language the petitioners align themselves with the ideals of the patriots. The subtlety inherent in this act is worthy of brief explanation.

The petitioners never call down the wrath of God on Lord North or Parliament but instead give credence to natural law and higher authority. As men, and law-abiding men, the petitioners will respect laws made relative to their position. They thus affirm the need for a government but also affirm the idea of consent. The petitions attempt to inform and influence opinions about black status and, significantly, try to force a redefinition of black status and a resolution to black problems on favorable terms for blacks. The petitions may be the earliest political documents containing what black literary critics refer to as encoding in black language. Two aspects of this language concern us here. One, the petitions seem to say little while speaking volumes. Two, the enterprise, the language of the petitioners, is in part cultural and is a sign of the movement toward a sense of community among northern free blacks. That sense of community is invoked in at least two ways. In part, the petitions sound as though there is an existing black community that has unanimously endorsed the sentiments of the petition. More accurate, however, is the observation that the petitioners were speaking from their own personal assessment of black status in America and hoped to influence other blacks to join them in a show of unity. What is apparent without question is the assertion of both an individual and collective self on the part of black Americans during the revolutionary period.

If language performed this powerful office for blacks as they came to grips, publicly and collectively, with their status in American life, religion must have served in a similar capacity. Whether one embraces it or abhors it, religion remains one of the fundamental cultural constructs of the human psyche. As with religion in most preindustrial societies, we know that religion in precontact sub-Saharan Africa permeated every aspect of life. It would have been impossible in precolonial sub-Saharan Africa to make the sharp distinctions between sacred and secular that inform our contemporary existence. Like other preindustrial people, black slaves were "preconditioned" to a religious life as an expression of community. Within the environs of bondage slaves were able to construct their invisible institution. As soon as they were given a chance to make public manifestations of their religious feelings they joined white denominations. They did not, however, embrace white religions because of a desire to be white, to be necessarily Christian, or to worship with white people. Nor did this movement result in the extinction of African-related religious practices or the invisible institution. Most blacks desired a public outlet for their religious manifestations. For some slaves the act of public worship may have been preferrable because practicing the invisible institution could be dangerous, even life-threatening. For free blacks the motivation for public worship was simply an expression of the liberty they possessed. In both cases, worshiping in white churches may have been uncomfortable and dissatisfying on many levels, but not life-threatening.

African practices survived tenaciously despite black attendance at white churches. Even into the last decade of the antebellum period some worshipers in northern free black churches were clinging to African emotionalisms, as they were labeled by disapproving black and white clergy. Apparently small in number, the African-oriented parishioners continued to influence daily worship services of the African Methodist Episcopal (AME) Church up to the Civil War. To his consternation, Bishop Daniel Payne Alexander was still trying to stamp out the heathenisms in the Philadelphia AME Church. Granted these Africanisms may have been dimly remembered, but their form and content were significantly different from integrated or white services to impress the observer. Getting the spirit, moving in a trancelike state, doing a version of the ring shout, losing control of one's limbs, and engaging in a call/response pattern with the preacher were observed in free black churches before the advent of the Reconstruction phenomenon, when Southern black churches moved north and brought with them a tone that was more emotional than the desired norm in more sedate northern churches.

Even when the practices were not extreme they were different enough to be remarked upon. Unfortunately, the surviving observations are from sources who questioned not only the Christianity but also the propriety of the African related practices. Still their disapproval provides eloquent testimony about the emotional content of black worship as well as the uniqueness of black religious activity. Thus, the cultural need for religion, quite apart from the racial or cultural oppression of whites, was a stimulant to black community growth and an assertion of black community consciousness.

Finally, we need to view power, free of the need to confront white oppression and equally free of invidious comparisons with white power, as a positive contribution to community consciousness. Power, charisma, and authority were prized in the community and could be attained without reference or little reference to white power. Obviously, Richard Allen and Absalom Jones understood both the symbols and realities of their leadership. Allen and Jones were different personality types: Jones was older, more retiring; Allen, was younger, more ambitious and, perhaps, even pugnacious.

Allen did not retire gracefully when the AME order, mistakenly from his perspective, chose Daniel Coker as its first bishop. He refused to confirm Coker or even to consider an arrangement of two equally powerful bishops. Instead, he forced the council to reconsider its vote and Coker to reject the offer of authority and Allen emerged as the first bishop of the AME Church. Whatever role personal pique may have played in Allen's behavior, it is evident that he thought he deserved the position but also had the power to hold out for his results. Moreover, those who remained within the AME order continued to respect the power and authority of Bishop Allen. Although Allen was not able to muscle the Wesley Church into his denomination, the fact that he braved the dissidents at Wesley indicates a man well aware of his power. We need to note that this was power exercised within the community and without a white reference point. Perhaps Allen's decision to invest Morris Brown as second AME bishop in 1825, a half-dozen years before his death, is a good illustration of his concept of power and authority and its necessity with blacks or black activities. By appointing Brown, Allen thus avoided the trauma of disrupting the continuity of office that ruptured so many black churches in antebellum America. Upon Allen's death in 1831 Morris Brown assumed the leadership of the AME Church.

The more than two decades of strife that plagued African Baptists (Boston) and African Presbyterians (Philadelphia) following the deaths of their charismatic leaders was not repeated partly because of Allen's insight and his power. That power was part of the equation in the AME decision not to dissent from either of Allen's decisions. His power and authority were respected within the church even after his death. This analysis in no way detracts from Morris Brown's own qualities that fitted him for the office. It is clear, however, that able men were ready to assume a leadership role in African Baptist and African Presbyterian churches and factionalism prevented their investment. That dissidents were in evidence in Allen's church is well established, but they were either unable to consolidate their own power or to diminish the power of Richard Allen.

Richard Allen's case is a more straightforward exercise of power within the community but the Peter Williams, Jr., case is also instructive. Although roundly criticized for bowing to white Bishop Onderdonk's call for his resignation, Williams continued to wield some influence and power in the community.

He was still sought out by those who wished to emigrate to Haiti and Africa and he used his contacts in their behalf. Moreover, he continued to be actively involved in the antislavery movement in defiance of his bishop's wishes.

Particularly but not exclusively for clergy, power within the community was a necessity. One, these men were competing in the task of bringing religious sustenance to the community. This competition dictated an ego that could, like John Gloucester, preach on the street corners attempting to establish a new black church in the face of already successful existing black churches. In addition, his ego had to be amenable to working within organizations that included some of the people with whom he was competing and who had more influence, larger churches, and greater real and potential resources for supplying the community's needs. Jones, Allen, and Gloucester, all representing different denominations and different manifestations of power, were able to bridge the gap and thereby avoid a debilitating series of confrontations. Thus, power could be modulated for the common good.

If we carry the illustration of modulated power further it can be demonstrated that newspapermen and other activists shared, consciously or unconsciously, a commitment to exercising power responsibly. In the often bitter rivalries among Martin R. Delany, Frederick Douglass, and Henry Highland Garnet there were also sufficient examples of grudging respect. Whatever negatives Douglass expressed about the back-to-Africa movement he understood the courage of Delany and recognized him as one of the foremost black nationalists of the time. Garnet's one-upmanship with Douglass did not obscure his perception that the *North Star* was one of the best newspapers in America. One would hardly label their competition friendly, however, and surely it was modulated at a different resonance than that among Allen, Jones, and Gloucester, but in outline it looked much the same. The three latter individuals continued to exercise their power within community-approved channels: newspapers, conventions, abolitionism, party politics, and even emigration. Like the earlier leaders Delany, Garnet, and Douglass coalesced on the issue of supporting the Union cause during the Civil War while simultaneously criticizing both Lincoln's conduct of the war and his failure to utilize black troops in the beginning.

Taken together language, religion, and power provide a cultural underpinning for black community consciousness in antebellum America. They make it clear that black awareness was not simply a reactive response to white racism. The resources and spiritual strength to confront racism were visibly reinforced by the cultural components of black survival whose existence depended more on human need than on fighting white racism. What emerged, then, was an organic community, one which possessed its own rationale, its own forms for enhancing collective life, its own structures for meeting the human needs of religious sustenance, as well as methods to address the external, often negative, power centers that had a severe and sometimes decisive impact on black life. The unfolding of the development of the organic nature of the black community is one of the contributions of the present work.

2

The Church: Spiritual Sustenance Was Not Enough

The focus in this chapter is three-dimensional. The first aim is to discuss, briefly, some distinctions between religion and church and how those differences affected black worship. A second thrust will discuss the irony and the conflicts impinging on the southern black church. The major thrust will elaborate the history of the northern independent black church movement.

Included in the discussion are several integral themes: antebellum northern black society and the black church; major themes in northern black religious thought; the multidimensional role of the church; the diminishing importance of the church as a result of the secularization of the black struggle, and consequences of institutional specialization; the contributions of the church to the building of black consciousness; and the church's importance in erecting the initial institutional framework for the black community. Finally, the chapter closes with a discussion of the historical importance of the antebellum independent black church.

I

Religion seems to be a fundamental construct of the human psyche. The northern free blacks, who are the focus of this study, found themselves in a new environment where circumstances called for drastic adjustment in order to enjoy religious pursuits. Further, as an oppressed people in a society that neither knew of nor favored their religious heritage, blacks had to seek outlets that would provide some degree of psychic relief. The traditional African environment was deeply spiritual and had few of the European distinctions between the sacred and the secular. Unable to hold to their former practices African blacks had to work to achieve a balance between religion and a practical outlet that could be expressed through the available white churches.

Although unable to affirm African religious needs, white religious practices unwittingly provided an avenue for Africans to find religious outlet. The Americans themselves took a more practical approach to their religious sustenance: they were mainly churchgoers rather than doctrine makers. This in part meant that they were not only ignorant of African religious ideals but generally ignored their own tenets in favor of a more workable system of religious practices. They were then less prone to police carefully the Africans' adherence to Christian doctrine. If Africans gave even limited compliance to the directives of the American church leaders they were thus freed to experiment with syncretizing European and African ideas.

While the lack of rigid supervision did not allow Africans to reestablish their own indigenous practices, it did allow for an approved way of sustaining their need for spiritual outlet.

By the 1770s more northern blacks were entering their second generation in the American colonies and thus were not constantly revived with African religious tenets as were blacks in the southern colonies, which continued to import slaves illegally until the late 1850s. In addition, the critical mass of blacks in the southern colonies not only created more pressing problems for the police powers of the slavocracy, but materially assisted southern blacks in retaining some autonomy over their religious and other cultural adjustments in ways that were impossible for northern blacks.[1]

Despite the long separation between northern blacks and African ideas some religious carryovers to the Christian faith were possible. Adherents to traditional African religious practices would have experienced little discomfort understanding and possibly accepting the tenets of Christianity. African traditional religions contained concepts of monotheism, methods of judging good and evil, persons functioning as leaders of the religious community, rituals and celebrations marking the indebtedness of living generations to the spirits, and guidelines on who belonged to the community of celebrants.[2] None of these ideas inherent in Christianity would have been foreign to Africans. The only structural feature of Christianity missing in African traditional religion was the existence of a written liturgy. As Africans coming from an orally oriented culture and as oppressed laborers in a foreign society, this final point was of little significance in allowing Africans to make a transition to some forms and practices of Christianity.

Moreover, white Christians themselves were more pragmatic in their approach to religion due in part to the liberalizing effect of distance from European mother churches. Even before the Great Awakening, with its stronger appeal to the emotions and which drew more blacks to

American churches, the emphasis on keeping the Sabbath rather than on creating religious doctrine in the New England colonies gave blacks the opportunity to observe and adjust to Christian norms. In those periods where the Puritans, among others, were not concerned with black assimilation, blacks had the opportunity to hold on to sometimes dimly remembered African religious practices.[3]

While the attractiveness of Christianity presented few hindrances to blacks wishing to engage in worship, African religious forms and content possessed a stunning tenacity. Two incidents, both northern in origin, attest to the staying power of African religious ideas. Newport, Rhode Island in the 1790s could boast of several African blacks who still remembered the ancestral home, longed to return to the motherland, and though participating in Christian churches still maintained knowledge of and practiced some African religious rituals.[4] In the last decade before the Civil War AME ministers were still trying to stamp out what they labeled African practices in the northern church. Thus, coming from an environment that stressed the communal, celebratory nature of religion into a society that affirmed the pragmatic side of religion, blacks chose the path of least resistance in creating a sphere for holy worship. Both black and white American clergy were driven by the need to make religion penetrable to their constituents, and did not feel the need to create philosophically challenging religious doctrines. Black clergy and thus black people came to practice an institutionally based set of beliefs (church) rather than a doctrinaire religion.

Having made the tentative adjustments to the colonial church blacks were ready to move toward greater religious independence when the opportunity presented itself. Such an opportunity presented itself during the revolutionary period and materially contributed the to thrust toward religious self-determination and black community consciousness.

Northern blacks during the colonial period were acquainted with the church almost from the beginning of their entry into the colonies. Yankee masters seemed driven by the perception that one of slavery's benefits was the introduction of blacks to Christian sensibilities. Yet masters were not sufficiently comfortable with blacks in the holy family so the conferring of church membership, even difficult at times for whites to acquire, was never consistently pursued. Moreover, blacks themselves were less interested in a religion that confirmed their earthly estate of bondage. With the reluctance operating on both sides blacks and whites attended the same worship services with different mindsets and usually separated, in keeping with local racial norms.

Although the Puritans had the greatest opportunity to recruit blacks into the church, their efforts met with scant success. Whites found it difficult to control their negative perceptions of blacks. Some argued, for example, that blacks did not possess the intellectual capacity to understand Christianity and it was therefore a waste of everyone's energy to attempt conversion. Other whites were concerned about the possibility of well-mannered Christian blacks forgetting their place. In addition, the Puritan emphasis on a rigid examination to qualify for church membership limited not only the number of black converts but the number of white members as well. Black church members and non-members alike were treated similarly within the colonial church. Confinement to Negro pews, sometimes out of the view of the white congregation, did not fire the enthusiasm of blacks for church membership. Although masters were diligent in reading the Scriptures to their slaves the Christianity served up at home and from the pulpit was a self-serving amalgam reminding slaves of their inferior status. Finally, the decorous worship services in white colonial churches did not attract large numbers of blacks.

Perhaps more than any other feature of the Great Awakening, the emotional atmosphere helped blacks look more favorably on the prospects of joining white churches. Not only was the preaching of revivalists such as George Whitefield and Jonathan Edwards more high-spirited but the message of equality before God without resort to long preparation and rigid examination was more palatable to blacks. Even before the Great Awakening the churches that fared best in gaining black converts were those such as the Baptists that were not only dissenters but also newcomers and their liturgy and ritual were more in keeping with black preferences for a religion with emotional content. Even the First Baptist Church of Boston, however, which accepted its first black member in 1665, did not offer social equality with its proffering of membership.

Similar to the Boston circumstances, in Philadelphia the staid services of the Quaker church limited black interest. The Quakers also were not free of the dilemmas of other white Christians, wondering if the conferring of Christianity on blacks would affect their civil status. It is instructive that the initial discussions of the slave question among Quakers addressed the need for masters to educate their Indian and black slaves rather than free them or bring them into the congregation.[5] The combination of the waning strength of Quakerism; the inroads of the Great Awakening; the appearance of new sects such as the Methodists; and the political debates of the revolutionary period opened new avenues for black church membership in Philadelphia.

Because of its beginning as a Dutch colony, New York City had the reputation for religious and civil tolerance and was a more cosmopolitan religious atmosphere than either colonial Boston or Philadelphia. Still, the existence of a more tolerant mindset did not translate into greater black access to church membership in the city. It was again the New Light sects or outsiders with a missionary bent that attracted more blacks. In the case of the Society for the Propagation of the Gospel in Foreign Parts (SPG), the added dimension of the personal interest of Elias Neau piqued the interest of blacks to attend SPG schools and receive religious instruction there.[6] Despite Neau's more successful recruiting techniques, black church membership ran afoul of the ambiguous attitudes of whites and of Neau himself. When the question of religious status versus civil status was broached even those whites most supportive of black religious opportunities found themselves vacillating between two polar positions: slave blacks could expect to become Christianized but would remain enslaved.

Thus, during the colonial period, while generally not accepted for church membership, blacks began to forge acceptable ways to practice their version of Christianity. Like their white counterparts blacks limited their new religious opportunities to founding black churches, sometimes autonomous within white denominations or separated from white orders, rather than to creating a new theology.

II

While the major focus here is the northern free black church it is instructive to look briefly at the southern free black church. As with northern blacks southerners used the special circumstances of the revolutionary period to begin constructing a more indigenous form of Christianity. Although the southern black church preceded its northern counterpart, its growth was stunted by the existence of slavery and its full development had to await the Reconstruction period.

The irony of the independent church movement among blacks in America beginning in the antebellum South is both obvious to and obscured by historians.[7] This contradictory set of circumstances is partly explained by the nature of slavery and southern race relations. Although the power alignments of blacks and whites remained constant the relationship itself was subject to pressures and modifications. Since Christianity was part of the apologia for slavery as well as a control mechanism there existed, to a degree, a favorable climate of white opinion toward black religious organizing. In crisis and noncrisis periods when the white political structure was in an expansive mood, religious pursuits of slaves were both a psychological safety valve and a reinforcing process. At such times, the free black southerner accepted religious outlets as concessions that hopefully could be expanded at some future date. At other times, however, the slavocracy constricted and black, free and slave, religious practices were prohibited or proscribed. Since both blacks and whites had similar reasons for manipulating religion, even during conflict periods a loose equilibrium between white tolerance and black independence was maintained. In the antebellum North the black church became the most important institution in the community while in the South, despite its earlier origins, it became an organization that was tolerated but buffeted by competing needs of blacks and whites.

As the rhetoric concerning liberty accelerated during the 1770s, all Americans were presented with contradictory choices: break with Great Britain and be considered rebels, traitors, or revolutionaries or stay within the English imperial system and suffer continued exploitation. This already complex situation was exacerbated by equating political domination with slavery. Without exception patriot agitators addressed themselves to the slavery of British oppression whether the topic under discussion was trade policy, taxation, or quartering soldiers. Such discussion not only gave pause to white patriots concerning an oppressed black minority within their midst but also forced some to question the institution of black bondage and tentatively propose elimination or amelioration.[8] Since the South was more dependent on unfree labor, southern agitators were faced with the dilemma of working actively to destroy their privileged position.

Given the ambivalence surrounding slavery and black discrimination, blacks seized the opportunity to agitate for their own self-interest. during the revolutionary era southern black interests clashed less with white needs because of the external threat of British imperialism. During this period black needs to organize became manifest and met with less resistance than usual. Churches were among the first organizing efforts of the black community. In the prerevolutionary period blacks clearly understood that organizations provided a degree of safety, impossible to obtain before that time.[9] The safety afforded by a black church is illustrated in the experiences of David George, George Liele, and Andrew Bryan. All three men were protected by indulgent loyalist masters in their efforts to bring religious training to blacks, and in some instances also to whites.[10]

David George's activities in pursuit of establishing a black church illustrate the uniqueness of the southern circumstances. George, who was born in 1742, had escaped slavery and lived for several years among the Creek and Natchez Indians. In the early 1770s Natchez Chief King Jack sold George to an Indian trader near Augusta, Georgia. There he learned to read and write, and also began to associate with a group of blacks, free and slave, who had been baptized by a white minister. Apparently George's worldly experiences and his accomplishments marked him as a leader. Within a brief time he became a song leader and began to exhort before the group. In 1778 when the British occupied Savannah, George took his family and joined His Majesty's forces.

Simultaneously two other black religionists, George Liele and Andrew Bryan, were making their presence felt in the Savannah area. In 1773

George Liele and his master arrived in Burke County, Georgia. Like David George, Liele received his first religious instruction from a white minister. As a result of his training he was licensed and spent two years exhorting slaves in the Savannah River region. Before 1778 and the British occupation George Liele had become a baptized freeman and preacher to blacks. Subsequent to the British evacuation Liele baptized Andrew Bryan, who ultimately became the most successful of the three in establishing the roots of the black church movement.[11] During the years of occupation all three worked to stabilize the religious life of blacks. In 1782, however, each man chose a different course to continue his mission.

Andrew Bryan remained in Savannah after the British evacuation. David George and George Liele, however, migrated with the departing British forces. Liele went to Jamaica, and by 1791 he had regained his liberty and established a large church in Kingston.[12] Liele had been freed before the revolutionary war but when his loyalist former master died, a number of patriots objected to his manumission and he was briefly jailed. Following his incarceration Liele became the servant of a British colonel as a means of protection. He thus left America as an indentured servant.

David George continued the peripatetic pattern of his life. He first went to Nova Scotia with hundreds of other blacks who had responded favorably to British inducements concerning land, provisions, and economic, if not civil, equality. By 1792, disillusioned with Nova Scotia and attracted by the possibilities offered in the colony of Sierra Leone, he again migrated. It is beyond the scope of this work to detail George's African experiences except to state that his restless, talented personality continued to work for black social and political causes until his death in 1812.[13]

III

In the northern experience safety was also a factor in the establishment of independent churches. Absalom Jones and Richard Allen were both confirmed in their inclinations to create a black center of worship because of rough handling they received from members of St. George Church in Philadelphia. After a series of minor confrontations concerning communion, segregated seating, and unfair worship hours, Jones, Allen, and other blacks were physically removed from the communion bar.[14] Although they vowed not to return to St. George's until there were significant reforms, both men immediately sought a location where blacks could worship unmolested. In the spring of 1787, prior to their expulsion, Jones and Allen had formed the Free African Society. Secular in nature the society, through Allen, provided a site for black worship:

an abandoned blacksmith's shop was installed at Sixth and Pine streets and served for several years as the African meeting house and sanctuary.

Not all black churches came into being in negative circumstances. The safety factor was less important in Boston where an attitude of good feeling existed between white and black members of Boston's First Baptist Church. First Baptist was one of the incubators of black religious independence in Boston. Interracial cooperation can be attributed to several factors. Probably the major reason for a lack of conflict was the existence of competent blacks and whites who endorsed the black independence moves. These leaders had not only the confidence of their constituents but also great personal respect for each other. Whatever may have been the feelings of white worshipers, their leaders the Reverend Dr. Samuel Stillman and the Rev. Dr. Thomas Baldwin personally supported Cato Gardner, Thomas Paul, and other blacks in their plans of black uplift.[15]

Even with the assistance of Stillman and Baldwin the second impetus for black religious separation originated with blacks such as Paul, Gardner, and Scipio Dalton. While cooperating with Stillman and Baldwin they continued to explore their own avenues of independence. Gardner, described as a native of Africa, had been baptized by Reverend Stillman. Both men had a vital interest in establishing a black house of worship. More important, Gardner undertook to raise a subscription for needed funds and successfully raised fifteen hundred dollars.[16] The extent to which Gardner succeeded may be measured by the respect he commanded among both blacks and whites in Boston. It may also have been reflective of below-the-surface antagonisms that neither blacks nor whites wanted to make public. The separation of blacks and whites, completed in 1805, was achieved amicably.

Yet the movement toward creating a black church was not one taken lightly by black leaders. Although they shared fellowship with whites, from 1787 on, under the leadership of Gardner and Dalton, black Baptists began meeting in private homes and schoolrooms to hold worship services. This separation meant that blacks did not have to contend with the institutionalized discrimination of the parent churches.[17] In spite of overall discrimination, a level of interracial cooperation among leaders was the norm. White church members assisted blacks in finding sites for their private meetings. Later, Thomas Paul was instrumental in keeping a viable level of cooperation going. Not only was he working toward ordination, which gave him credibililty with both groups, but also he was an indefatigable worker for both Christianity and black uplift.

In 1789, at age sixteen, Paul, after experiencing a religious conversion, was baptized in his hometown of Exeter, New Hampshire. Subsequent to his experience he moved to Boston and immediately met that group of blacks holding religious services. When he arrived the group met regularly at Faneuil Hall.[18] Almost immediately he became one of the group's exhorters—one who explained certain passages of Scripture. Nine years later, in 1798, the group moved to Master Vinal's schoolhouse.[19] Significantly, the school was in close proximity to a large segment of the black population as well as to First and Second Baptist. The new location made possible closer cooperation, especially with Reverend Stillman and Reverend Baldwin.

Coinciding with the move and the interest of the white ministers one additional factor supported Paul and black aspirations for their own church. About the year 1790 First and Second Baptist began experiencing a religious revival. This spirit of evangelism swept up blacks as well as whites, and black membership increased in both institutions. More important, although the historical record is mute, Thomas Paul must have been caught up in the new religious fervor. In 1804 before the revival spirit subsided he was "ordained" by Reverend Stillman.[20] Some confusion surrounds this act and such an ordination is missing from the original church records. If an office was given Thomas Paul it was more likely that of evangelist rather than minister. Whether a new designation was given Paul in 1804 or not one thing is clear: prior to 1805 he had attained a high profile with black and white Baptists.

Directly related to Thomas Paul's position of leadership among Boston's blacks was his actual ordination and the formal plans to separate and establish an African church. On 2 May 1805 at Nottingham, New Hampshire, Thomas Paul was ordained by the Reverend Mr. E. Nelson.[21] Following Paul's ordination two other events accelerated the creation of a black church. First, the black members of Second Baptist wrote to church leaders stating their determination to establish an African Meeting House. Scipio Dalton, a black member of First Baptist, also signed the note, received by the whites on 26 July.[22] Within thirty days Dalton and several others were dismissed from First Baptist. Dismissal did not carry the stigma of disciplinary action but simply meant blacks were free to form the First African Baptist Church of Boston.[23] The constellation of activities, Paul's ordination, the 26 July note, and the August dismissal are compelling evidence of a consistent plan by blacks to service their own religious needs.

Within a year of officially launching the church on 8 August 1805, Reverend Paul and his group had constructed the first Afro-American meeting house in Boston. Located at the corner of Belknap (Joy Street) and Smith Court the house stood on a parcel of land deeded to Daniel Wild, a white deacon of First Baptist. All of the labor on the building had been performed by blacks. On 4 December 1806, with the building completed, Reverend Thomas Paul was installed as pastor.

Significantly, by the the time the building was finished the church's membership had doubled. Beginning with an original group of twenty-two, before the end of 1806 an additional twenty-four members were baptized. The growth of membership, in the face of tremendous odds, was a tribute to the leadership and vision of Paul, Dalton, and Gardner. Although a better neighborhood than the North End the Belknap Street area had its own problems. Unemployment was rife and the focus on survival supported a religious skepticism. The task of religious recruitment seemed impossible when added to the discrimination against blacks that permeated American society. The African Baptist Church did not have exclusive recruitment rights to the area's blacks, either. They were bombarded on all sides by religious messages of every kind. Moreover, although good feelings prevailed between black and white leaders, lay blacks knew that relations within the denomination were far from harmonious.

Yet the church held out some positive tangible examples to even the most skeptical black. In the pulpit was a man like themselves—black, victimized by prejudice, but who seemed determined to overcome those impositions. His message was geared to their own circumstances and he preached a gospel of utility and equality rather than rewards in the hereafter. The significance of the social gospel was not lost on Reverend Paul's listeners, and his activities and associates marked him as much a political activist as a clergyman. And, the man could preach. Although membership grew slowly, Reverend Paul's sermons were well-attended and well-publicized. More people were being exposed to the word of God and at least two men responded positively: Paul's son Nathaniel and Eli Ball both experienced the call to preach.

From 1806 to 1814 the impact of the church can be gauged by the growth in membership and its expanding services. By the end of 1813 total membership had reached seventy-four. Although few members were added during the lean years of 1814-1817, the church's efforts were not without success. A Sunday school was established in November 1816. Only the fourth Sunday school in the city, its first fifty members were mainly children of nonmembers who were taught to read and write, and were given Bible lessons.[24] The Sunday school became an avenue of proselytizing both adults and children. Class leaders in Sunday school, male and female, improved their own education and also acquired organizational skills which helped to increase the leadership pool of black Boston. The responsibilities involved teaching, raising funds for supplies as well as the church in general, and coordinating schedules, space, and lessons. Immediately the church provided secular as well as sacred sustenance to its constituents.

External opportunities to acquire leadership training were available and eagerly sought by the church's young people. In the years 1806 through 1809 First African Baptist took an active role in local Baptist affairs. Support was given to various missionary societies including missions to

Indians and isolated frontier communities. Young men such as John Hay and the Easton brothers, James and Caleb, frequently acted as delegates to meetings. Through the pastor the African church became one of the charter members of the Boston Baptist Association.

Much of the success could be attributed to the personal example set by Thomas Paul. Not only did he work tirelessly to pursue his religious and secular duties but his relationships remained firm with Boston's white Baptists. This in turn provided his young followers with additional learning experiences and opportunities. He also was bringing new vistas, both international and black, for his constituents to examine. Paul and a fellow activist established connections with the Republic of Haiti that remained viable to Boston blacks for almost forty years.[25] Yet this boundless energy and seemingly inexhaustible supply of interracial goodwill was slowly deteriorating and created significant pressures on First African Baptist Church.

The end of the era of good feeling was signaled publicly by the resignation of the Reverend Thomas Paul. What transpired in the church leading to the break is problematic, but the disruption was an acknowledgment that future black independence was not to be channeled in the same manner. Independence would include, in addition to separation, blacks becoming more assertive and initiatory in the activities that governed their lives.[26] No longer would blacks accept the passive role or the leads offered by paternalistic whites. In fact the earlier white leadership had died: Rev. Stillman in 1807 and Rev. Baldwin in 1825. Indeed, had they survived, Stillman and Baldwin may have faced considerable difficulty maintaining the type of relationship they had with Paul. Like Paul they would have found it difficult to adapt to the new black mood.

By 1830 blacks in Boston were abandoning the relative safety of collective security for more individualized public roles. David Walker and Maria W. Stewart exemplified this trend. Born free in Wilmington, North Carolina, Walker became a Boston resident about 1823. He was a well known civic figure and businessman and operated a used clothing store on one of the city's main streets. Walker was also a member of the African Methodist Episcopal (AME) Church and a close friend of its Reverend Samuel Snowden. In some senses a rival of Thomas Paul and African Baptist Church, Boston AME never attained the status of Paul's church despite its more radical bent. Walker was deeply involoved in black affairs beyond the church and his business interests. His other activities included serving as a Boston agent for *Freedom's Journal,* the New York-based black weekly newspaper.

In 1829 Walker published an *Appeal* that stunned his readers.[26] His publication was an all-out attack on Christianity and the church for its complicity in slavery and discrimination. In addition, he castigated blacks for acquiescing in the perpetuation of slavery. He also leveled a scathing attack against the American Colonization Society. He finished by challenging white Americans to read, understand, and live up to the words of their Declaration of Independence.

Along with Walker's *Appeal* the experience of Maria W. Stewart is indicative of the growing aggressive individual voice in black Boston. Originally from Connecticut, Mrs. Stewart taught school in Boston and lost her husband in 1829. Cheated of her inheritance by her husband's unscrupulous white business associates, Mrs. Stewart began to lecture on political topics in Boston. Speaking before promiscuous audiences was as audacious an act by Mrs. Stewart as was Walker's attack on slavery. Mrs. Stewart was the first American-born female to lecture on public political topics, and Walker's tract preceded by several years both the organization of the abolition movement and the writing of abolition tracts.

Neither Walker's voice nor Mrs. Stewart's could be sustained. Walker died of mysterious causes in the same year as his publication. Mrs. Stewart suffered a backlash that drove her from the lecture circuit in 1833. Despite the short tenures of Walker and Stewart, both were significant in several ways. They were symptomatic of the leadership struggle going on in Boston. While they were beneficiaries of Thomas Paul's leadership they also were more confident about their ability to articulate black views without support from whites. This meant that they saw less reason to court white allies than the Reverend Paul. Unfortunately, in the case of Mrs. Stewart, she fell prey to race and gender prejudices. Despite the end of the era of good feeling in the 1830s, the origins of black church independence in Boston were the result of more cooperation between blacks and whites than was the case in Philadelphia and New York.

In the Philadelphia case collective security was more necessary than in Boston. Black worshipers in white churches were treated with an indifference that bordered on hostility. Segregated pews and separate communions were rigidly enforced. Even when blacks were given the pulpit they were assigned the least desirable hours, usually 5:00 a.m. Church leaders took little interest in making blacks welcome. Some cooperation was forthcoming but with the exception of Benjamin Rush, it was neither widespread nor consistent. In no instance were white Philadelphia churches headed by leaders such as Reverend Doctors Stillman and Baldwin. Hence the separation of blacks from the parent churches was rife with conflict in New York and Philadelphia and in one instance had to be settled by lengthy litigation.

As in the Boston case the catalyst for black discussion was a charismatic individual who seemed able to crystalize black discontent in a positive direction. Like Thomas Paul, Richard Allen had a religious conversion experience. Unlike Paul, however, Allen was a slave and remained in bondage several years after his conversion.

During the liberal revolutionary period Allen was allowed by his master to "preach," and did so throughout his remaining years as a slave. His devotion appeared so genuine that his master was persuaded to have himself baptized by Allen and to allow Allen to purchase his own and his brother's freedom.[27] That Allen had to purchase his freedom should not be construed as an unchristian act nor one lacking in humanity. Since Allen was allowed to pay on time and in Continental paper money, the cost of his freedom was significantly reduced. After attaining his release from bondage Allen became a Methodist circuit rider.

When riding circuit Allen supported himself by odd jobs which sometimes included butchering. It was at this time that his activities came to the attention of Francis Asbury, who later became the first bishop of the Methodist Episcopal Church. Asbury was sufficiently impressed to offer Allen a position with him, doing Christian labors in the South. The details of the appointment caused Allen to decline. Allen demurred when instructed not to intermingle with slaves and when told that his accommodations might be subject to southern veto.[28] Further, although he had been preaching for three years, and in December 1784 was one of only two blacks present at the Baltimore conference to establish Methodism in the colonies, Allen was told that the church could not support him financially. Rather than accept such a humiliating position Allen accepted a call to work at St. George's Church in Philadelphia.

By 1786 Allen succeeded in bringing an additional forty-two blacks into the church. Needing a more positive atmosphere in which to worship the blacks sought permission to conduct separate services. A site was needed but St. George's leadership was unsympathetic. Benjamin Rush and Robert Ralston empathized with the blacks and Ralston for a time became the group's treasurer. Yet the interest of Rush and Ralston, two of St. George's influential members, was not enough to deter the overall negative response. One of the elders, John McClaskey, threatened the blacks with expulsion if they did not adhere to the letter of instructions from the church's leaders. Among these were warnings that blacks could not remove their names from the church subscription list and to give up a special newsletter that was circulating among them.[29] Not yet ready to leave the church Allen's group attempted to ameliorate the negative conditions. They dropped the offending actions noted in McClaskey's letter, but simultaneously continued their separate worship and also decided to be more assertive about equal access in the church. Their assertive measures included taking seats in any part of the church and taking communion with white worshipers.

When this strategy was employed in November 1792 the reaction of the white elders was swift, physical, and proved to be the catalyst for a black exodus from the church. Interestingly, the group did not sever relations with St George's. It was optimism that St. George's would relinquish its segregation policies, not indecision, that motivated blacks to take their wait-and-see attitude. At the urging of Allen and Absalom Jones the Free African Society was used for religious meetings. Jones, an older man was the leader of St. George's blacks before Allen came to Philadelphia. He and Allen worked well together. They co-founded the Free African Society and led the organization in the period immediately following its break with St. George's. They met in an old blacksmith shop purchased by Allen. Significantly, the group refused to seek a new religious denomination. Allen, particularly, and most of his followers desired to maintain their Methodist connection.

Having arrived at this impasse neither St. George's nor the blacks seemed in the mood for compromise. On the one hand, St. George's pursued a policy of obstruction. It refused to sanction the African group or the separate meetings as part of its church. Despite requests from the blacks no white preacher was allowed to minister to their needs. Rather than initiate any positive contact, white church leaders continued treating the blacks as recalcitrant.[30] Blacks were expected to return to church on the same basis that existed before the November confrontation.

Blacks, on the other hand, had a different set of interests. While they continued to solicit support from St. George's, sentiment also was building for a more complete break from the parent church. By 1793 at least one election had been held to decide the question of affiliation with another church or denomination. Only Jones and Allen held out for continuing contact with the Methodists. The rank and file, however, indicated a preference for joining the Church of England. Allen and Jones contained the Anglican sentiment but the issue of affiliation was not resolved. Later in 1793 Allen was approached by a committee of African Society members offering him the ministry of the congregation. Allen subsequently reported that "[he] could not accept of their offer, as I was a Methodist."[31] The clear implication is that several factions existed within the group and while Allen and Jones were the group's most viable authority figures, the rank and file were not without power. A decision affecting affiliation had apparently been made in favor of an Episcopalian connection. How actively Jones orchestrated this factionalism is unclear, but a year later in 1794 Absalom Jones did lead a number of followers into St. Thomas Episcopal Church of Philadelphia.

In founding St. Thomas, Jones had achieved a degree of independence. Since the Episcopate was organized on a locally autonomous basis, blacks would not experience undue white control over their religious life. Although Jones and Allen followed different religious paths the two men remained lifelong friends and cooperated for black uplift. In the years 1793 and 1794, as the factions were working out their responses, both men represented the corporate black community.

When black honesty and service were criticized during Philadelphia's yellow fever epidemic, both men came quickly to the defense of the black community.[32]

Even after Jones' departure from the African group, its remaining members faced a considerable task. Perhaps the greatest conflict involved counteracting the new St. George's offensive. In July 1794 when the old blacksmith shop had been refurbished, Bishop Asbury officiated at its opening and the Reverend John Dickins preached. On the surface it appeared as though blacks had achieved at least one of their objectives: autonomy within St. George's. The conflict was far from resolved, though. First, St. George's trustees proposed that the African church be turned over to the Conference: the distinct governing and policy making board. This was in keeping with Methodist practices but blacks saw ulterior motives behind the suggestion.

Faced with this new stalemate St. George's trustees then suggested that the African church incorporate itself. Trustee Ezekiel Cooper drew up the papers which in reality incorporated the African church under the Conference. This duplicity was not realized until 1804 when James Smith of St. George's demanded keys to Bethel (Allen's name for the shop), its books, and forbade any meetings in the church.[33] Threats followed the announcement and Allen was forced to obtain counsel. In the tense atmosphere a vote concerning Bethel's status was submitted to the white St. George's membership. The referendum stipulated that a two-thirds majority had to support the black position to declare the incorporation papers null and void. White church members had no desire to worship in equality with blacks nor any desire to allow them their independence.

After the vote blacks were informed that they had to pay six hundred dollars per year to St.George's for services.[34] This, of course, they refused to do. The trustees then proposed a four-hundred-dollar charge which was also rejected. Blacks took the initiative and offered a compromise: Bethel be allowed to pay two hundred dollars annually directly to its assigned preacher, not to St. George's treasury.[35] In accepting this revision the elders stipulated that the preacher would be officiating only five times annually. Because his services were so infrequent blacks rescinded their original offer and proposed instead that one hundred dollars was sufficient.

When blacks refused to yield to the preacher's demands that the original fee be maintained, he discontinued servicing Bethel. For almost a year the black enclave was without a minister. At the same time St. George's issued an edict that any local preacher administering the black needs would be expelled.[36] Finally, the black participants at Bethel were disowned. Left in this spiritual cul-de-sac, blacks began supplying their own preachers.

This state of conflict continued for the next twelve years. During the period St. George's attempted periodically to assert its control of Bethel. Blacks, in the meantime, evolved a technique of passive resistance to parry St. George's authority. For example, in 1814 when Reverend Robert B. Roberts appeared at the church to preach and take spiritual control of Bethel, a black preacher was already in the pulpit. The members blocked Robert's path to the altar and his retreat out of the church and kept him surrounded until after the sermon was over. Although stung, Roberts was wise enough not to persist and again Bethel enjoyed a few years of peace.

In 1815, when Robert Burch of St. George's was rebuffed in the same manner he instituted litigation. Bethel was forced to obtain counsel. In 1816 the Pennsylvania Supreme Court rejected St. George's claim and Bethel African Methodist Episcopal Church became fully independent of white control. Struggles similar to Bethel's were repeated in other cities when blacks tried to assert themselves within the Methodist church. The successful Pennsylvania lawsuit and the shared experience of struggle in Baltimore precipitated a call to discuss the situation. What resulted was a call for a convention to form a national church body: the African Methodist Episcopal Church.

In 1816 the principal cities of AME strength were Philadelphia and Baltimore. In the Baltimore case, growth and progress had been assisted by the efforts of the Reverend Daniel Coker. Until 1816 Coker seemed to have been coequal with Richard Allen, in terms of status and charisma within the AME order. Coker's church had grown rapidly and, like Allen in Philadelphia he was widely respected by whites as well as blacks. Like Allen, Coker had been ably assisted in his religious pursuits by a group of leading men in the community. They constituted the religious and social leadership of black Baltimore. As with the Philadelphia leaders, all of the individuals in Baltimore were conceptualizing plans of social uplift in addition to their religious concerns. Among Coker's cohorts were Richard Williams, Sr., Henry Harden, Edward Williamson, Stephen Hill, and Nichols Gilliard. All attended the April 1816 convention in Baltimore.

On the first day of the gathering, in Richard Allen's absence he and Daniel Coker were elected as bishops of the African Methodist Episcopal Church.[37] Upon his arrival the second day, Allen objected that the church did not require two bishops. Coker resigned. While Allen may have attempted to create harmony within the order by eliminating a competing power center, the church lost a powerful leader.

The years between 1816 and 1820 had not helped to abate Coker's unhappiness with factionalism in the AME Church. He issued a call to emigrate to Sierra Leone. He advised potential travelers that good land was available. He also gave advice about what items to bring for trade, for provisions, and for the requisition of land: good leaf tobacco, cheap calico, pins, knives, forks, and pocketknives were needed, valuable items in the colony. Moreover, Coker counseled that all who could should sell out and come to Sierra Leone. He also suggested that conditions were more favorable in the colony: "You may do much better than you possibly do in America, and not work half so hard. I wish that thousands were here. . . ."[38] On the question of religious affiliation he was unequivocal.

> If you come as Baptists, come to establish an African Baptist church, and not to encourage division. . . .We wish to know nothing of Bethel or Sharp Street, in Africa—leave those divisions in America.[39]

Not many took up Coker's call to Africa and his loss did not slow the tide of the AME's institutional growth.

Several eastern cities had sent delegations to the 1816 convention and their progress continued. Reverend Peter Spencer represented Wilmington, Delaware. Salem, New Jersey was served by Reverend Reuben Cuff. From Attlebourough, a small Pennsylvania town came Reverend Jacob March, and two trustees, William Anderson and Edward Jackson. Mother Bethel (Allen's church), with one more delegate than the Baltimore contingent, was the most powerful. It contained, in addition to Richard Allen, Clayton Durham, Jacob Tapsico, James Champion, and Thomas Webster. These individuals all were motivated to create a national black church but their aspirations were not totally religious. Most were trustees at their respective churches and most were involved in other areas of black agitation.

Jacob Tapsico, for example, was a trustee and also served as an advisor to a women's group appropriately named the Daughters of Tapsico. This group paralleled another within Mother Bethel, the Daughters of Allen. Both groups were oriented toward community welfare pursuits and each served at least a triple function within the community. First, they were part of Allen's plan to achieve the fullest participation in pursuit of black uplift. He organized not only the sexes but also the generations into viable reform groups. For Allen and Tapsico, idle hands meant idle minds ripe for unchristian recruitment. Second, and as important as avoiding the devil's inducements, the utilization of women in leadership roles was dictated by the narrow resource base within the black community. Drawing predominantly from the black middle class meant the available pool of black males was restricted. In order not to stretch the thin resources to the breaking point, Allen and Tapsico promoted the activities of women. Although the new public roles were in socially approved categories and did not challenge male dominance, they did provide females with an opportunity to contribute to black community consciousness. Third, the cooperation between the sexes and the generations stimulated unity and was part of collective security. Indeed, the black church's position as the most viable institution within the community reinforced collective security and stimulated blacks to experiment, within the protective confines of the church, with other techniques of community organizing.

Like any human community Bethel, and by implication black Philadelphia, had need of community survival methods. Allen tried to help his community to adopt compatible standards and an authority structure to enforce general compliance.[40] To this end, he instituted a court system in the church. Complete with procedures for accepting and classifying evidence, taking testimony, cross-examination, jury selection, and rendering decisions, this legal apparatus operated from 1815 until about 1835. Although sanctioned historically by Methodism the AME court served in two unique and specific ways: it prevented blacks from having to air disputes to a white public, and it shielded blacks from the inequitable system of justice available in Pennsylvania courts.

Bethel's court system established and maintained a uniform set of values for members of the church. Philadelphia's black community was not monolithic; values and standards came from many and sometimes competing sources. For its members, however, the church court exerted a consistent and conscious moral influence. Perhaps the first level of setting standards was achieved by the site selected to hear cases and the regularity of the court. In the years 1812 to 1835 weekly court sessions were held in the home of Richard Allen or his designee. Allen's charisma and position gave the proceedings solemnity and an authority they might not have had otherwise. Holding court in Allen's home also added to the sanctity of the occasion. His home was as much a symbol of the community as Mother Bethel, but it maintained an aura of mystery and authority because it was less familiar than the church. Trustees were impaneled as jurors, and their selection on a rotating basis gave the proceedings a quality of objectivity and fairness.

The fact that no church member, including Allen, was free from complaint or legal responsibility strengthened the perception of fair play. That justice was applied to all equally reinforced the moral lessons of the church and the court. Because of the regularity, the solemnity, and the equality of the proceedings litigation, was taken seriously and decisions were adhered to rigidly.

Offenses ranged from a simple failure to keep the Sabbath, to adultery, money matters, and unbecoming conduct.[41] On 19 August 1823 the court met to hear a case against Joseph Durham whose brother Clayton was a member of Bethel's Board of Trustees. Joseph Durham was charged with immoral conduct: he was cohabitating with a woman who was not his wife. Charges were brought by the Reverend William

Cornish. Durham acknowledged the accusations and was accordingly disowned from society. During the same session Morris Dublin lost a case involving his improvident conduct. Luckier than Durham, his sentence was loss of an official position in the church and probationary status for six months. Dublin's wife brought him before the court because he sold household goods, some of which belonged to other people. He also took his clothes and marketing to one Hanna Brown. Morris's defense was that the household items were given as payment for an arrearage on the rent. He explained that he took his clothes because his wife refused to wash or mend them. Instead, she "dashed them about the floor and struck me with a brickbat."[42] The jurors, however, felt that husband and wife should settle their problems without third party interference and found against Mr. Dublin.

Apparently there was no stigma attached to being brought into court. On 15 November 1823 Abigail James was judged to be the instigator of a dispute within the Society of the Daughters of Bethel Church. The court record is mute concerning details of the disagreement. Abigail James acknowledged her culpability and was admonished by the court never to mention the subject again. The committee of the Daughters of Bethel Church was given the same advice.[43] Abigail James remained in the church and less than a month later gave testimony in another matter before the court. At the 12 December 1823 sitting David Crosby charged Mary Hinson with libel and slander. Hinson had accused Crobsy's wife of "sponging on the African Female Band Benevolent Society." Maria Crosby had received funds from the organization for an illness that some thought was feigned. Mrs. Crosby had recently lost a young child to disease and thought she might be suffering from a similar ailment. Mr. Crosby had initially engaged the services of a woman doctor but his wife refused to cooperate. She is alleged to have said that she could make the medicine herself. It was rumored about that Mrs. Crosby "was abed with the hystericks."[44] A friend warned David Crosby that the society would become suspicious and send in their own doctor. Since the society was paying Maria Crosby sick benefits and the rumors continued, a new doctor was called. He treated Mrs. Crosby's sickness, lightly stating that she was not seriously ill. Unlike the laymen he was not willing to label her discomfort hysterics. Five witnesses, among them Abigail James, all gave testimony supporting the charge that "Sister Crosby was abed with the hystericks."[45] What is interesting is that lay and medical opinion agreed that whatever was troubling Maria Crosby it was not serious enough to continue her monetary support. Abigail James' evidence was given equal weight although she had been before the bar just a month earlier.

In the cases just cited Bethel maintained its hegemony over the moral standards of its congregation. Cases were heard within the confines of the membership and one's peers stood in judgment of the merits of the case. Litigants were not forced to obtain counsel and thereby saved the community's limited resources. Judgments were generally in the nature of friendly family solutions, the harshest being dismissal from society. This decision, usually rendered in cases of sexual misconduct, serious assaults, and failure to observe church discipline had also its protective features as well. It meant that recalcitrance and promiscuity were not rewarded and that others would not be influenced by such behavior. Most important, the court was an example of blacks cooperating with other blacks in setting and maintaining a system of values apart from the discriminatory majority society.

Yet Allen was not totally successful in keeping black disputes from the notice of or intrusion of whites. As Allen feared, the culmination of one such case allowed whites to ridicule black problems and to imply that blacks had different and therefore inferior ways of settling litigation.[46] On 29 July 1812 a special meeting of the Bethel court was held to hear expulsion charges against Robert Green and William Sammons. Green, a trustee, and Sammons were charged with taking another member, Richard Howell, to court concerning an alleged debt. Contrary to the rules of the Methodist Episcopal Church regulations Green and Sammons had sought redress outside the church's arbitration system. The 29 July hearing was important enough to cause the impaneling of a select committee to hear the charges. Testimony concerning Green's and Sammons's actions was given by Wiley Quotance, Stephen Laws, and Jacob Tapsico. Richard Allen then asked the two defendants if they had any defense to make. Sammons defended his actions but Green replied in the negative. The question was then put to the committee if the men were guilty of a breach of discipline. It was unanimously agreed that both men had broken church regulations.

Subsequent to the verdict, a motion was made and seconded outlining the punishment of Robert Green. He apparently received preferential treatment because of his leadership position. It was agreed that if he acknowledged the decision his membership and trusteeship would remain in effect but he would lose his Sunday school classes. Three persons—Clayton Durham, James Green, and John Somerset—formed the committee to call on Green before 1 September to receive his answer. On 16 September Clayton Durham, reporting for the committee, stated that Green said he wanted nothing more to do with the committee or its findings and would make no acknowledgments. The committee therefore expelled him from Mother Bethel.

Robert Green was not quite finished. On 23 September 1812 at the Quarterly Conference of Bethel Church he appealed the expulsion order. William Sammons was also present to appeal his conviction. Both waived the right to have another committee appointed to hear the case and instead demanded settlement by the Quarterly Conference. The conference upheld the 29 July findings and the suspensions were upheld.

Still Green persisted and by 2 January 1815 had filed for a writ of mandamus with the Philadelphia District Court. By this action he hoped to set aside his church court conviction and return to his official role within the church. An anonymous judicial opinion on the case recommended that a writ be issued because there had been irregularities in Green's removal.[47] It was not sufficient to set out conclusions only and omit the facts on which those conclusions were based, the unknown justice stated. Green's partial victory seems not to have produced his desired results. There is no evidence that Bethel complied with the opinion or any indication that Green's case was given any further hearing by the state courts. Green's behavior, notwithstanding, Mother Bethel and other black churches in Philadelphia remained the hub of community activity.

The Bethel court system provides an interesting sidelight on gender issues within the church. Allen and his cohorts in the AME as well as other denominations were adamantly opposed to women in the pulpit. In fact, a woman could not fill the role of trustee in black churches. Given the gender bias about church leadership it is startling that women served not only as jurors but also seemingly moved with equality within the court. The court clearly stated that only trustees could be impaneled as jurors, but women frequently served in that capacity. No explanation is given by Allen or anyone else for this contradiction. Nor did there seem to be any attempt to change the eligibility requirements to sanction women or others who were not trustees to become jurors.

Allowing women to serve as jurors suggests some confidence in their ability to weigh evidence, make decisions, and render judgments. Several explanations may account for Allen's employment of women for jury duty when they were treated less equally in other areas of church administration. Allen may have reasoned that trustees were in short supply and might make impaneling a jury difficult if he adhered to the regulations. Such a set of circumstances might have created a gridlock for Bethel's court. Thus, Allen was probably motivated more by practical concerns for getting a task completed than by political ideas of empowering women. Nonetheless, the fact that women maintained some degree of equality within Bethel's court is made clear in the court records. We find neither a court system nor women's prominence in the religious life of New York or Boston blacks.

In contrast to Boston, where community life seemed tied to the African Baptist Church, black Philadelphia's religious life was more diversified. While Allen and Jones were the most noted black clergymen of their time, they were not alone in the services they rendered to the community. Several lesser-known black preachers were considered, within their own churches, to be the equals of Jones and Allen. The Reverend John Gloucester was such an individual. Little is known of Gloucester's life before he arrived in Philadelphia in 1800.[48] Born a slave in Tennessee, probably around 1772, he came to the city as the body servant of Dr. Gideon Blackburn, a Presbyterian clergyman. Almost immediately, Gloucester began preaching to small gatherings in black homes. Within a brief period the gatherings became so numerous that Gloucester went to the streets to accommodate his growing number of listeners. One of his favorite corners was at Seventh and Shippen streets. His success made him a focal point for a number of black Presbyterians who were looking to organize their own church. Gloucester was not the genesis of the black Presbyterian movement nor were his activities the impetus for discrimination by white Presbyterians. Instead, he became the organ to serve the separatist needs of some black Philadelphians who sought a church they could control and yet still maintain connection with the national church body. To assist in these plans, Rev. Blackburn tutored Gloucester to prepare him for his ordination examination.[49]

In 1807 Blackburn tried, unsuccessfully, to have Gloucester ordained. A letter of recommendation from Blackburn to the General Assembly of the Synod of Tennessee suggested that although he had not attained "all the literary qualifications. . . there is much reason to believe he might be highly useful in preaching the Gospel among his own people."[50] Unwilling to make an exception for Gloucester the General Assembly passed the request on to the Philadelphia Presbytery. On 7 July 1807 that body issued its decision "not to take the said John Gloucester."[51] Thereafter, Gloucester was accepted as a missionary by the General Assembly of Lexington, Kentucky. If he was disheartened by the Philadelphia decision the Kentucky acceptance gave him license to continue his preaching.

In 1809 Gloucester did become the prime candidate for organizing a separate church. In that year Dr. Archibald Alexander, pastor of Third Presbyterian Church and founder of the Evangelical Society, persuaded Blackburn to let Gloucester work with the society. Other society members, including Benjamin Rush, wanted to continue the efforts to coalesce the organization of black Presbyterians. By 1809 only three independent black churches existed in Philadelphia. It was clear to blacks and whites alike that there were limited opportunities available to new black worshipers. With the Evangelical Society, Gloucester was expected to continue his preaching but also, more important, to work toward establishing a black Presbyterian church.

Immediate success accompanied Gloucester's efforts. In addition to his favorite location at Seventh and Shippen streets, he also led services in a large room on Gaskill Street.The society was not lax in its support of

Gloucester. When his group began constructing a church the society initiated a solicitation for building funds. Before the end of 1809 it had purchased a lot at Seventh and Shippen.[52] In 1810 the cornerstone was laid and the church was formally dedicated on 31 May 1811.

Simultaneous with his missionary activity Gloucester continued to press for ordination by the church. His perseverance was rewarded 16 April 1810 when he was ordained at Baker's Creek, Tennessee.[53] The following April Gloucester was received as a member of the Philadelphia Presbytery. Within a month he was ready to assume the direction of the church provided by the Evangelical Society's fund-raising. For the small group of faithful worshipers the church was quite imposing. It had a capacity of 370 people downstairs and two galleries that could accommodate another 280 persons. On 16 October 1811 the church with 123 members was accepted as part of the Philadelphia Presbytery. Gloucester had established, in a few short years, the first and only African Presbyterian Church in Philadelphia and the United States.

At least one other accomplishment of Gloucester's should have made him better known to later generations of black Americans: he was the mentor of Samuel Cornish who later became the outstanding black Presbyterian clergyman of the antebellum period.[54]

Of course Gloucester's triumphs were not without problems. Although named the African Presbyterian the congregation was mixed. While this did not create overt problems it was not quite what its organizers had envisioned. Building the modest membership created another problem for Gloucester. Certainly he was a man of great personal strength and magnetism but he did not possess the public persona or the administrative skills of his contemporaries, Jones and Allen. In addition, Presbyterian proselytizing of blacks even with the efforts of the Evangelical Society, was at best lukewarm. A third problem requiring Gloucester's attention and energy was his continuing effort to redeem his family from bondage. All of these problems aggravated his already failing health. On 27 June 1820 he petitioned the Presbytery for relief because of health problems. His failing health was also mentioned prominently in a letter to the Presbytery on 18 April 1821. Gloucester recommended several candidates for the church's ministry, including his own son, Jeremiah, but the list also included Samuel Cornish and Benjamin Hughes.

On 2 May 1822 at the age of forty-six John Gloucester died.[55] His death precipitated a series of confrontations which lasted for years and from which the little church never recovered. Subsequent to Gloucester's death the board of elders met to choose another minister. After several days without resolving the conflict between competing candidates, Samuel Cornish was nominated and confirmed by a vote of seventy-eight to forty-eight.[56] This action, however, came only after there had been an attempt by the minority to postpone the meeting indefinitely. Cornish's name was to be brought before the Presbytery by a committee of Robert Douglass, Ezekial Harmond, and Quomony Clarkson. Even Clarkson, an original elder when the church was founded, could not prevent the minority's disruptions. The opposition preferred Jeremiah Gloucester, and when it failed in its attempts to have him nominated it decided to frustrate all attempts to install Cornish.

As late as 1824 the church was still without a minister. On 9 March 1824 seventy-five members presented the Presbytery with a petition to organize the Second African Presbyterian Church. When the remaining members renewed their call to Cornish he declined their summons. On 14 April 1824 Benjamin Hughes was nominated by the elders. In May he was appointed minister, but on 31 October Hughes withdrew, notifying the Presbytery that he was not receiving sufficient support from the membership. The degree to which the church had been split is obvious in the troubles of Cornish and Hughes. Both had been designated by Gloucester as competent to minister the church. Both men also had the support of significant elders. Yet each was stifled in his effort to lead the church by a small but disruptive minority.

Not until 1827 was a regular minister, the Reverend Charles Gardner, appointed to lead First African Presbyterian Church. Gardner had his own liability however: he was an ordained Methodist.[57] This did not cause problems immediately. On 12 December 1827 Gardner preached his first sermon. Two years later the controversy surrounding his appointment had not subsided and was gaining momentum. By November 1829 the opposition had gained sufficient strength to bring charges against him. A committee was impaneled to examine the case and refer its findings to the Presbytery. Perhaps seeing the handwriting on the wall, Gardner resigned on 21 April 1830.

The summer of 1830 held another trauma for the members of First African Presbyterian Church. On 2 July 1830 Quomony Clarkson died at age sixty-five.[58] He had been part of the church since its inception. He was not only an original member of the board of elders but also a friend and confidant of John Gloucester. In the eight years following Gloucester's death Clarkson had attempted to be the voice of reason in church affairs. He lacked Gloucester's charisma however, and was unable to sustain support for his two candidates, Cornish and Hughes.

Leaderless since the resignation of Gardner in 1830, the church finally persuaded Samuel Cornish to return in December 1831. But his return was not harmonious. There were conflicts over salary and Cornish's outside interests. Adding fuel to the fire were rumors about Cornish's standoffishness and his ostentatious display of wealth.[59] Cornish had no wealth to speak of; as a black minister he was paid at a lower scale than his white counterparts. As an advocate of elevating the race, however,

Cornish believed in putting his best foot forward not only when pursuing legal means to fight slavery and discrimination but also in the realm of decorum and taste.[60] Criticisms of his household furnishings, his book collection, and his wife's clothes were popular topics with his detractors. Cornish argued, but not enough to convince his critics, that he had trouble making ends meet. Finally in June 1832 Cornish resigned, left Philadelphia, and never returned to an active ministry in the city.

After Cornish's resignation no pastor was regularly in attendance at the church until Charles Gardner returned in 1836. His second tenure lasted twelve years until 1848. During his ministry the infighting disappeared and he was able to think about plans for expanding the church. By 1854 the remodeling of the church was complete.

While a claim for collective security as a motivating force for the black independence movement has been asserted there was simultaneously a great deal of ambivalence on the part of black leaders.[61] Richard Allen remained associated with St.George's through more than two decades of dirty tricks by the parent order. Black ambivalence was understandable. Despite the discrimination within the individual churches, religious idealism continued to permeate the rhetoric of the church. Blacks, perhaps unrealistically, maintained their optimism in hopes that Christian consciousness would replace rhetoric as the operative principle of white churches.

Blacks may have clung to their optimism because of their own theological preferences. Many black religious thinkers accepted the Protestant ideal of perfectionism and perceived of blacks as enduring an Egyptian or Babylonian captivity.[62] A focus on perfectionism was part of the current of American reform and the training of black clergy was not essentially different from that of their white counterparts. Blacks focused more on their plight in hopes of bringing about both Christian regeneration and divine intervention. The full acceptance of blacks by white Christians would indeed signal not only black deliverance but also America's spiritual redemption. Blacks were the chosen people and their full participation was not simply a matter of interacting with whites but also carried divine implication.

The integrationist thrust of black ministers perhaps has been overemphasized. It may be more accurate to characterize black ambivalence as part of their desire for an egalitarian society rather than a desire to assimilate with whites. The Declaration of Independence and revolutionary rhetoric, in general, were powerful inducements to blacks that their needs as citizens could be accommodated in a slowly democratizing society. At the same time the hammer blows of prejudice dictated that blacks protect themselves.

A final factor that created ambivalence for blacks seeking a religious home was the church itself. In the initial stages of black church organization there were significant whites who supported black baptism, church membership, and seemed even to understand black wishes for separate worship services. The bulk of white Baptists and Methodists tolerated a black presence on about the same basis as blacks were tolerated in American society. Fair-minded white leaders, a minority to be sure, were unable to overcome the malaise and overt racism of their membership. The competing actions of whites thus helped to create the fluctuating actions of the black churchmen, but the overwhelming strategy of black religious leaders was to pursue full acceptance and independence simultaneously.

What would have been the outcome had black leaders decided to pursue one course of action such as full acceptance? At the least, American religion would have faced its most crucial test and by implication American institutions would have had their most severe crises. Neither Philadelphia nor Boston blacks felt compelled to create that all-out challenge. Instead, like their New York brothers, they accepted more practical solutions to their problems. New York blacks had to combat not only the debilitating indifference and aggressive racism of most whites, the ambitions of Richard Allen who attempted to convert New York blacks into the AME order, but also the seeming benevolence of a few supportive whites.

IV

While there are similar elements in the development of separate black churches in Philadelphia and Boston, the New York experience has not achieved as high a historical profile. In New York City no black religious leader emerged as a national political force like Richard Allen or Thomas Paul in the period before 1840. Only Peter Williams, Jr., had obtained a status similar to Allen and Paul for a brief period. From 1807 until 1834 Williams engaged in the same political activity that captured the attention of Richard Allen. He was deeply involved with the British African Institution, a group interested in agitating against the West Atlantic Slave Trade and also in bringing black Americans to Sierra Leone. Along with Allen, Williams worked to provide a venue for Paul Cuffe to discuss his African explorations and to recruit black migrants. In 1824 Williams was a leading organizer of black emigration to Haiti. He attended conventions and meetings of black leaders along the eastern seaboard. He remained an active and frequently quoted black leader until he ran afoul of his bishop for his continued attacks on the American Colonization Society.

In the last decades before the Civil War black clergy such as Samuel Cornish, Henry Highland Garnet, and Theodore Wright were nationally known but by the 1840s the leadership cadre of the black community had grown considerably since the days of Allen and Paul. By local reputation, however, the churchmen who did lead the black independence movement were as charismatic as any who participated elsewhere. Peter Williams, Sr., his son Rev. Peter Williams, Jr., Christopher Rush, James Varick, and Joseph Jackson Clinton pioneered the movement in New York City. All contended with white churches that refused equality within the church but also refused to sanction the black independence. Within this tension-filled context black leaders pursued the dual tacks experienced in Philadelphia and Boston. As in the Philadelphia case, black New York Methodists found it difficult to leave the denomination. The senior Peter Williams is a case in point. Employed as a slave laborer for the John Street Church he maintained his connection with the Methodists until his death.

With James Varick and other blacks of John Street, Williams petitioned the Reverend Francis Asbury in 1796 to form a black Methodist group.[63] Not only did Asbury sanction this separate fellowship but he also preached to the group occasionally. Asbury was, of course, the same prelate who befriended Richard Allen at the Baltimore founding convention of the Methodist Episcopal Church. He characteristically kept himself above the fray and maintained his connections with all groups. There is no indication that he counseled blacks to accept their lot within the discriminatory churches but neither did he seem to admonish whites about their uncharitable behavior. Asbury preferred to stay out of fights and direct his efforts to the religious sustenance of the worshipers.[64] Once formed, the John Street group took a name and purchased property. Calling itself officially the African Methodist Episcopal Church, it acquired a lot on the corner of Church and Leonard streets. The first church at this location was called Zion, signifying the black refuge.

The acts of taking its own name and purchasing property signaled independence but not separation from the Methodists. Zion continued its contractual arrangements with the denomination. Although it accepted the first two acts of independence, the Methodist Episcopal order was unable to accept a third: ordination of a black preacher. In the face of this refusal the Zion blacks opened talks with other black Methodists. Their contacts, Richard Allen of Philadelphia and Peter Spencer of Wilmington, advised the Zion blacks to continue to push for ordination. Allen and Spencer suggested that once ordination was completed blacks should form their own national black church.[65] This was revolutionary advice that the Zion blacks were unwilling to pursue. Indeed, in 1813, neither Allen nor Spencer was an example of his own counsel. Allen was nearing the end of his struggle with St. George's but under the impression that he was free of its control. Between 1813 and 1820 Zion maintained its stormy relationship with the John Street Church. In the latter year a group of separatist whites at John Street ordained James Varick, Abraham Thompson, and Leven Smith. The ordination was performed by Rev. Dr. James Covel, Sylvester Hutchinson, and William M. Stillwell.[66] Having successfully made its break the African Methodist Episcopal Zion (AMEZ) began to construct its own national black church order. This brought Zion into further conflict with Richard Allen's AME Church. Zion won adherents from other black churches which were also disgruntled with Allen's strong arm tactics.[67] Among the Zion converts were members of the Philadelphia Wesley Church that had broken with Allen. Zion also established new churches in Kingston and Elmira, New York and Bridgeport, Connecticut. Once the break from John Street was complete James Varick became the first bishop of the AMEZ order. He served in the post until his death in 1828. During Varick's tenure AMEZ held its first annual conference, meeting in New York City from 18 July through 21 July 1822. Important issues were debated and resolved at the conclave including the ordination of Christopher Rush. A native North Carolinian, Rush had come to New York in 1798 and joined Zion, at age twenty-six, in 1803. His joining Zion marked an anniversary of sorts, for he had become a Christian a decade earlier in North Carolina.[68]

Rush served as the bishop of AMEZ for twenty-eight years until his loss of sight in 1852. He earned the reputation as the most able black preacher of his time. The first convention after his installation as bishop met at Wesley Church in Philadelphia in 1829. While the choice of Philadelphia may have been natural the Wesleyans were tireless workers, a degree of oneupmanship also may have been present. Wesley Church was, after all, in Richard Allen's backyard and was the scene of one of Allen's defeats in 1822. Among the attendees was Jehiel Beman who became a leading clergyman/activist in the 1840s.[69] Under the direction of Rush AMEZ stabilized and enjoyed a steady increase in membership. After the 1820s, however, with the exception of Beman in New York and Hosea Easton in Boston, AMEZ was not in the forefront of political activity in the black community. The distinction of being clergymen/activists was left to individuals who remained within white denominations such as the Episcopal and the Presbyterian churches.[70]

Unlike his father who remained loyal to his Methodist connection, Peter Williams, Jr., became an ordained Episcopal priest in 1819.[71] Williams had functioned as the spiritual leader of blacks in Trinity Parish Church. As more blacks sought a religious home in Trinity its white leadership began to support the black's call for separate services and facilities. The result of this interest and Williams's leadership was the establishment of St. Phillips Episcopal Church in 1818. Part of the support for black religious needs came from a wealthy white New Yorker named George Lorrillard. He leased St. Phillips a parcel of land for an annual rent of $270 for sixty years.[72]

Although autonomous, St. Phillips's experienced problems reflective of the conflicts facing blacks remaining within white church orders. St. Phillips' growth in its earliest years was quite impressive. Within a year after Lorrillard's gift a new church was erected at the cost of eight thousand dollars. New York dailies reported favorably on the structure and its minister.[73] But the impressive beginnings masked problems of recruiting members and limited finances. Even with the assistance of Trinity Church, which paid the $270 ground rent for the first seven years, the finances of St. Phillips were shaky. Adding to the difficulties was the fire that destroyed the original church in 1821. Although the church was quickly rebuilt Williams' money troubles did not end. He was forced to solicit funds from his major supporter, Rev. John H. Hobart. In a letter, Williams confided, "our circumstances are so poor that we are not able to meet all our other demands."[74] Williams was requesting Hobart's help on two issues. First, he wanted Hobart's assistance in making a new application for Trinity to continue paying the annual ground rent. Second, he wanted Hobart's advice on approaching the bishop with the request. Williams sounds almost abject in his pleas.

The financial troubles and the need to seek extra monetary support were not even the most restrictive pressures for Williams. His political activism was the ultimate affront to his white superiors. Williams was forced to choose between representing the black community and maintaining his denominational appointment. Over the years Williams' activities encompassed temperance, antislavery, moral reform, and protection of black community interests. He was involved, for example, in calling the Philadelphia convention to respond to the plight of the victims of Cincinnati's riot in 1829.[75] The issue that caused Williams the most trouble, however, was his relentless attack on the American Colonization Society (ACS). The society, organized in 1816, had been quickly and clearly perceived by most black American leaders as a menace to their existence.[76] Most whites, on the other hand, were convinced that ACS was a positive organization. They accepted the ACS call to repatriate blacks to Africa as a lesser evil than slavery or its concomitant, the threat of slave revolts.

Many leaders and the rank and file of the Episcopal church supported ACS and chafed under Williams's continuing criticism. Finally, in 1834, Williams was warned by Bishop Onderdonk that in order to maintain his direction of St. Phillips, he would have to curtail his criticism of ACS.[77] Williams did not find it possible to renounce the church, instead he curbed his political activism. Most of his contemporaries were vocal in their disagreement with Williams' choice.

Unlike Williams, Samuel Cornish, Theodore Wright, Henry Highland Garnet, and J. Sella Martin, although faced with the racism of the Presbyterian church, continued their political work. It would be safe to say that the four Presbyterians were better known for their political activism than for their active religious life, but that activism was, in at least one sense, substantially different from the work of black clergymen in Richard Allen's generation. Unlike Allen, Jones, Rush, and Williams the later black ministers did not found independent black churches. Instead they sought to achieve political liberties for the community. They assumed their right to political participation and its responsibilities and tried working within white denominations to force those institutions to accommodate black aspirations. To Cornish, Wright, Garnet, and Martin the black church was an established entity and none of them felt compelled to continue the process of separation.

More important, the general cessation of hostilities within the separated church aided the stability of the community and signaled change for the church and the community. By the 1830s the older charismatic and versatile leaders such as Allen and Thomas Paul had passed away, but they left national institutions. By engaging themselves in so many secular matters they laid the ground-work for the change in status of the independent black church. They had also provided many opportunities for its membership to gain leadership skills which were utilized in secular activities. Whether the individuals formed political, social, or business organizations the process had at least two effects on the church. One, having more leaders to choose among caused a relative decline in the church's importance; it was no longer the only institution in the black community. Faced with problems of discrimination and/or survival black individuals could choose more specialized means to combat their disabilities: women's clubs, debating societies, reading rooms, mechanics societies, and political associations. Two, although the new organizations contributed to a decline in church power they also provided support for the sacred institution. The more specialized groups relieved some of the pressure on church resources. They also provided structural supports for the church by creating a more diversified institutional structure for the community. While the church suffered a decline in power and influence it still retained its status as the most important single institution within the black community. Any secular pursuit depended on a level of cooperation from, or participation by, the church. The church building stood as a visible reminder of community consciousness, history, and power.

Perhaps the best and most extreme example of the simultaneous decline and continuing influence of the church was the abortive Denmark Vesey revolt in Charleston, South Carolina in 1822. When the authorities discovered that Vesey, a trustee of Bethel AME, had used the church in planning his revolt the church was immediately closed.[78] The Vesey affair is not without relevance for the northern free black community. Morris Brown, the popular pastor of the Charleston church, was forced to flee for his life. He was given refuge by Richard Allen in Philadelphia. Although keeping a low profile Brown became, after the death of Allen, the second bishop of the AME Church. Despite his lack of civic agitation he possessed administrative skills, preaching ability, and a commitment to community growth and cohesion.

Brown's lack of civic political activity notwithstanding, the church continued its monopoly of producing educated leaders for the community. Certainly a high percentage of the education of black clergymen took place in white institutions or was sponsored by white denominations. Even within the separate black church, which had no outstanding educational institution until the late antebellum period, education was prized. Especially in large urban areas black clergy received some formal training. Those who did not usually spent a period of apprenticeship with recognized ministers before they moved out on their own. At least two important factors helped to keep education a premium commodity for black clergy. The church offered the greatest professional opportunities for black males. More options were available for those trained as preachers than those trained as educators. It was sometimes possible for black clergy to pastor white congregations but seldom did white boards of education hire black teachers for white children.

The religious cohesiveness of the northern free black community maintained the stimulus for an educated clergy. Blacks at this time were generally associated with the Baptists, Methodists, and Episcopalians, all of whom possessed a national leadership with some formal education. This in turn provided a standard for the black clergy. The northward movement of freedmen with their formalized "invisible institution," bringing with them the storefront churches and emotional services, is a post-Civil War phenomenon. When leaders confronted what they considered less than decorous practices they tried with some success to stamp them out or redirect those energies within the church.[79] Storefront churches in antebellum Philadelphia or Boston were usually temporary expedients reflecting either the beginning stage of church organization or the collective migration of ambitious blacks from the upper South. At any rate, their leaders' focus on liturgy and ritual did not differ substantially from the behavior of the surrounding black and white churches.

While the church declined the black clergy maintained prominence in the councils of the black community. Every activity in the community between 1830 and 1865 had participation by black preachers. In all three cities black ministers continued to be in the forefront of political activism. School boycotts, political agitation, reform activities, and social actions benefited from the role of the black preacher. Black preachers even began to experiment with writing church history. They tried not only to chronicle the church's experiences but also to set a charter for the community. In 1857 the Reverend William Catto published his special sermons as a history of black Presbyterianism in Philadelphia. Although Rev. Catto's primary interest was the first sixty years of First and Second African Presbyterian churches he also included brief mention of all the other black antebellum churches. Catto's work is perhaps the clearest statement of black independence within a white denomination. He makes it clear that, once established, the national church did little to interfere in the internal workings of the black churches. Even in disputes the local Presbytery never tried to impose solutions on its black member churches. While blacks were free to run their own churches without interference, no blacks were included at the highest levels of church leadership.

Within the AME Church its first historian was also a ranking member of the church. Bishop Daniel Alexander Payne, an educated man but not a trained historian, painstakingly reconstructed the early years of the AME Church. Unlike Rev. Catto, Bishop Payne spent a considerably brief period in Philadelphia, the year from 1842 to 1843. Like Rev. Catto, however, he made a considerable impression on black Philadelphia. During that year Payne became a member of the Philadelphia Vigilance Committee. In that capacity he planned and assisted in the protection and survival of fugitives passing through the city. The interdependent nature of the community is demonstrated by the Vigilance Committee membership. In the 1840s the committee included, in addition to the AME bishop, a number of Presbyterians.

Certainly the clergy were valued members of political action committees but, unlike the earlier periods, clergy in the 1840s were not assured of leadership. Among the leaders of the Vigilance Committees in all three cities were a number of laymen. William Still of Philadelphia was one of the most readily identified participants in vigilance activities. Equally important in Philadelphia were Octavius V. Catto, son of the Reverend Catto, and Jacob C. White, Sr. and Jr. Although not a clergyman, the senior White was an influential trustee of First African Presbyterian Church.

In New York the cooperative, interdependent spirit dated to the early antebellum period and continued through the opening of the Civil War. Until his activities were curtailed by his bishop, Rev. Peter Williams was associated with a number of black laymen in political pursuits. Although their association could best be described as cooperation with conflict, the Reverend Samuel Cornish and David Ruggles were the impetus for Vigilance Committee action in New York City. Thus it was not by religious sustenance alone that black clergymen and the black church met their obligations to the black community. Their activities were as multilayered as the organizational infrastructure that was beginning to emerge in the three cities.

Despite the church's major contribution to black community consciousness by, 1835, in all three cities, it was no longer a leading player in the community's thrust for political empowerment. Instead its main role was to provide religious sustenance for black members. This role was more in keeping with earlier American church norms: providing a place where services and other things religious could be carried on. In the three cities the church was no longer making policy on the nature, direction, or targets of political agitation. Since it had never indulged in the making of religious doctrine it more closely resembled the early Protestant churches that had denied access to blacks before the revolutionary period. While similar to the white institution it was also distinctly different in style and in substance, if we accept the continuing relevance of Africanisms that plagued black church leadership in the North into the 1860s. The apparent dichotomy between leaders and followers was a healthy tension within the community and supports the assertion that blacks were trying to create a community based as much on internal need as acculturation would allow.

Finally the uneven development of the church as a leading voice in political dissent and the tension between leaders and followers does not invalidate the community consciousness model. The black churches of Boston, Philadelphia, and New York had established an unchallenged reputation for community leadership during the rough-and-tumble days of revolutionary America and through the early national period. It was the church, more than any other organization, that led the way through private discussions of the community's need for religious worship unfettered by racism. It was the black church in all three locales that supplied the leadership through the periods of limited interracial cooperation that characterized the final thrust toward black church independence during the period 1787 through 1835.

After 1835 outside our three cities the black church continued to play the role fashioned during the earlier period with one significant difference. After 1835 when black communities began forming independent churches, they were no longer dependent on supportive whites to endorse their liberation from discriminatory white churches, nor was it necessary to turn to white clergy for ordination any longer. There were now black churches that not only legitimized the new aspirants' struggles, but also provided officials for ordination, and an ongoing religious infrastructure through which new black churches could participate more fully in religious life. Thus, even given its shortened lifespan as the major community voice, the church remained a vital element in newly emerging local consciousness activities. The church's curtailment of political activism did not cause a leadership power vacuum because of the simultaneously developing secular institutional structure in Boston, New York, and Philadelphia that continued even after 1835.

Notes

1. Peter H. Wood, *Black Majority: Negroes in Colonial South Carolina from 1670 Through the Stono Rebellion* (New York: W. W. Norton and Company, 1974), 131-95; Gerald W. Mullin, *Flight and Rebellion: Slave Resistance in Eighteenth Century Virginia* (New York: Oxford University Press, 1972), 140-65; Ira Berlin, "Time, Space, and the Evolution of Afro-American Society on British Mainland North America" *The American Historical Review* 85 (1 February 1980), 44-78; Lawrence Levine, *Black Culture, Black Consciousness* (New York: Oxford University Press, 1972), passim, and Sterling Stuckey, *Slave Culture: Nationalist Theory and the Foundations of Black America* (New York: Oxford University Press, 1987), 3-96.

2. John M. Mbiti, *African Religions and Philosophy* (New York: Praeger Publishers, 1969); John M. Mbiti, *Concepts of God in Africa* (New York: Frederick A. Praeger, 1970); Geoffrey Parrinder, *Religion in Africa* (Baltimore: Penguin Books, 1969); Bill Cole, *Coltrane: A Biography* (New York: Da Capo Press, 1976), passim. Janheinz Jahn, *Muntu: The New African Culture* (New York: Grove Press, 1961).

3. William D. Pierson, *Black Yankees: The Development of an Afro-American Subculture in Eighteenth-Century New England* (Amherst: The University of Massachusetts Press, 1988), 48-61.

4. Ibid., 58.

5. Herbert Aptheker, "The Quakers and Negro Slavery" *The Journal of Negro History* 25, no. 3, (July 1940): 331-33.

6. Faith Vibert, "The Society for the Propagation of the Gospel in Foreign Parts: Its Work for the Negroes of North America before 1783" *The Journal of Negro History* 18, no. 2, (April 1933): 171-212.

7. Most historians recognize the existence of independent black Baptist churches in Virginia, South Carolina, and Georgia during the American Revolution. Some controversy surrounds the viability of the early southern institutions. See Gayraud S. Wilmore, *Black Religion and Black Radicalism: An Interpretation of the Religious History of Afro-American People* (Maryknoll, New York: Orbis Books, 1983); Carter G. Woodson, *The History of the Negro Church* (Washington: Associated Publishers, 1921); W.E.B. DuBois, *The Negro Church* (Atlanta: Atlanta University Press, 1903); and Joseph R. Washington, *Black Religion* (Boston: Beacon Press, 1964), for the older view which questions the authenticity of early southern churches. James Melvin Washington, *Frustrated Fellowship: The Black Baptist Quest for Social Power* (Macon: Mercer University Press, 1986), accepts the Virginia, South Carolina, and Georgia black churches as legitimate christian organizations. See also Charles H. Long, "Assessment and New Departures for a Study of Black Religion in the United States of America," in ed. Charles Shelby Rooks, *Black Religious Scholarship, Reflection and Promise: Addresses at the Tenth Annual Meeting of the Society for the Study of Black Religion* (Maryknoll, New York: Orbis Books, 1979), Albert J. Raboteau, *Slave Religion: The Invisible Institution in the Antebellum South* (New York: Oxford University Press, 1978); Walter H. Brooks, "The Priority of the Silver Bluff Church and its Promoters," *Journal of Negro History* 7, no. 2 (April 1922); and Milton H. Sernett, *Black Religion and American Evangelicalism: White Protestants, Plantation Missions, and*

the Flowering of Negro Christianity, 1787-1865 (Metchuchen, New Jersey: The Scarecrow Press, Inc., 1975).

8. David Brion Davis, *The Problem of Slavery in Western Culture* (Ithaca: Cornell University Press, 1966), 134-35; Ira Berlin, *Slaves Without Masters: The Free Negro in the Antebellum South* (New York: Vintage Books, 1974), 11-21; Arthur Zilversmit, *The First Emancipation: The Abolition of Slavery in the North* (Chicago: University of Chicago Press, 1967), 315-74; Benjamin Quarles, *The Negro in the American Revolution* (Chapel Hill, North Carolina: University of North Carolina Press, 1961), 111; and William H. Freehling, "The Founding Fathers and Slavery," in Allen Weinstein and Frank Otto Gatell, eds., *American Negro Slavery: A Modern Reader* (New York: Oxford University Press, 1973), 209.

9. Albert D. Shipley and David O. Shipley, *The History of the Black Baptists in Missouri* (Kansas City: National Baptist Convention, USA, Inc., 1976), 19-20; Washington *Frustrated Fellowship* 10-11; Luther P. Jackson, "Religious Development of the Negro in Virginia from 1790 to 1860," *Journal of Negro History* 16 (April 1931): 168-239; and James Melvin Washington, "The Origins of Black Evangelicalism and the Ethical Function of Evangelical Cosmology," *Union Theological Seminary Quarterly Review* 32, no. 2 (Winter 1977): 104-10.

10. Ellen Gibson Wilson, *The Loyal Blacks* (New York: G. P. Putnam's Sons, 1976), 6-16, 29-35; James W. St G. Walker, *The Black Loyalists: The Search for a Promised Land in Nova Scotia and Sierra Leone, 1783-1870* (New York: Holmes and Meier, 1976); Washington, 8-11; Brooks,"Silver Bluff Church"; and Kenneth K. Bailey, "Protestantism and Afro-Americans in the Old South: Another Look," *Journal of Southern History* 41 (November 1975): 451-72.

11. Wilson, *The Loyal Blacks* 12, 29; Brooks, "Silver Bluff Church"; Washington, *Frustrated Fellowship,* 10-11.

12. Wilson, *Loyal Blacks*; James M. Simms, *The First Colored Baptist Church in North America* (New York: Negro Universities Press, 1969); John Hope Franklin, *From Slavery to Freedom: A History of Negro Americans* (New York: Alfred A. Knopf, 1988), 93; and John W. Davis, "George Liele and Andrew Bryan, Pioneer Negro Baptist Preachers," *Journal of Negro History* 2, no. 2, (1918): 120.

13. Wilson, *Loyal Blacks,* 340-54; Walker, *The Black Loyalists,* 301

14. Richard Allen, *The Life Experience and Gospel Labors of the Rt. Rev. Richard Allen to which is annexed the Rise and Progress of the African Methodist Episcopal Church in the United States* (Nashville: A.M.E. School Union, n.d.), 7-20; Charles H. Wesley, *Richard Allen: Apostle of Freedom* (Washington: Associated Publishers, 1935); Carol George, *Segregated Sabbaths: Richard Allen and the Emergence of Independent Black Churches, 1760-1840* (New York: Oxford University Press, 1973), are the standard biographies of Allen and the AME church. The above volumes date the black split with St. George's Methodist Church as November 1787. Milton H. Sernett, *Black Religion and Afro-American Evangelicalism 1787-1865* (Metuchen, New Jersey: The Scarecrow Press, Inc., 1975), 117, revised the Allen chronology and claims November 1792 as the date of the break. Clarence E. Walker, *A Rock in a Weary Land: The African Methodist*

Episcopal Church During the Civil War and Reconstruction (Baton Rouge: Louisana State University Press, 1982), 4-5, employs the 1792 date.

15. Nathan Wood, *The History of First Baptist Church of Boston (1665-1899)* (Philadelphia: American Baptist Publication Society, 1899), 297; Charles L. Coleman, "A History of the Negro Baptists in Boston 1800-1875" Master's thesis, Andover Newton Theological School, Newton Center, MA, 1956, 27-29, 32-33; John Daniels, *In Freedom's Birthplace: A Study of the Boston Negroes* (New York: Houghton Mifflin Co., 1914), 22; George A. Levesque, "Black Boston: Negro Life in Garrison's Boston, 1800-1860" (State University of New York, Binghampton, 1976, Ph.d. dissertation), 268-70; James Oliver Horton and Lois E. Horton, *Black Bostonians: Family Life and Community Struggle in the Antebellum North* (New York: Holmes and Meier Publishers, Inc., 1979), 40; Ms. Records, First Baptist Church, vol. 2, 1800-1831, 25 July 1805, Newton Center, Ma.

16. Levesque,"Black Boston," 270; Coleman "History of Negro Baptists," 42; Wood,"History of First Baptist Church," 287; William Cooper Nell, *The Colored Patriots of the American Revolution* (Boston: R.F. Wallcut, 1855).

17. Nell, *Colored Patriots*, 33-35; Coleman, "History of Negro Baptists," 42; Carter G. Woodson, *The History of the Negro Church* (Washington: Associated Publishers, 1921), 121; and Daniels, *Freedom's Birthplace*, tend to downplay discriminatory acts against blacks and focus on the public reasons for blacks leaving the church. George Levesque, "Inherent Reformers-Inherited Orthodoxy: Black Baptists in Boston, 1800-1873," *Journal of Negro History* 60, no.4 (October 1975): 495-98, provides the most balanced account of the feelings and issues leading to the separation.

18. Coleman, "History of Negro Baptists," 27-29, 34; J. Marcus Mitchell, "The Paul Family," *Old Time New England* 63, no.3 (Winter 1973).

19. Levesque, "Black Boston," 270; Coleman, "History of Negro Baptists," 28, 31, 35; Daniels, *Freedom's Bithplace,* 22; unidentified Boston newspaper 1905.

20. Wood, *History of First Baptist Church*, 297.

21. Coleman, "History of Negro Baptists," 37; "Obituary Rev. Thomas Paul;" *The American Baptist Magazine* 11, no. 7 (July 1831).

22. Levesque, "Black Boston," 269-70; Wood, *History of First Baptist Church*, 297; Ms. Records, Second Baptist Church, 1788-1809, 26 July 1805.

23. Coleman, "History of Negro Baptists;" Wood, *History of First Baptist Church.*

24. Horton and Horton, *Black Bostonians*, 41-42.

25. Coleman, "History of Negro Baptists," 29; James Oliver Horton, "Generations of Protest: Black Families and Social Reform in Ante-Bellum Boston," *The New England Quarterly* 69, no. 2 (June, 1976): 246.

26. David Walker, *An Appeal in Four Articles Together with a Preamble to the Colored Citizens of the World But in Particular and very Expressly to those of the United States of America* (Boston: The Author, 1829).

27. Allen, *The Life Experiences* 17, 22; George, *Segregated Sabbaths,* 28, 32; Wesley, *Richard Allen*, 15-17.

28. Ibid., 27, 30; George, *Segregated Sabbaths,* 64.

29. Ibid., 28.

30. Ibid., 30; George, *Segregated Sabbaths*, 57-58.

31. Ibid., 31.

32. Richard Allen and Absalom Jones, *A Narrative of the Proceedings of the Black People during the late Awful Calamity in Philadelphia*, 2d ed. (New York: Abington Press, 1960); George, *Segregated Sabbaths*, 130-40.
33. Allen, *The Life Experiences,* 32.
34. Ibid., 33
35. Ibid., 34.
36. Ibid., 35; George, Segregated Sabbaths, 81-84; Daniel Alexander Payne, *History of the African Methodist Episcopal Church* (New York: Johnson Reprint Corporation, 1968), 6-9.
37. Since no minutes were kept of this significant event several versions of what transpired there are in existence. See Wesley, *Richard Allen*, 152-53; George, *Segregated Sabbaths*, 87-89; Josephus R. Coan, "Daniel Coker: 19th Century Black Church Organizer, Educator, and Missionary," *The Journal of the Interdenominational Theological Center* 3, no. 1, (Fall 1975): 23-24; and Lewis V. Baldwin, *"Invisible" Strands in African Methodist: A History of the African union Methodist Protestant and Union American Methodist Episcopal Churches, 1805-1980* (Metuchen: The Scarecrow Press, Inc.,1983), 55.
38. Daniel Coker, *Journal of the Rev. Daniel Coker* (Baltimore: Edward J. Coale, 1820), 42-43.
39. Ibid., 44.
40. George, *Segregated Sabbaths*, 92-93; Richard Allen and Jacob Tapsico, *Doctrines and Disciplines of the AME Church* (Philadelphia: Cunningham, 1817); Leonard P. Curry, *Blacks in Urban America: The Promise of the Dream, 1800-1865* (Chicago: University of Chicago Press, 1982,); Phillip Staudenraus, *The African Colonization Movement* (New York: Columbia University Press, 1961), 190.
41. *Minutes and Trial Book, 1822-1835,* microfilm 8, held at Historical Society of Pennsylvania, (Philadelphia). 1973
42. Ibid., 19 August 1823.
43. Ibid., 15 November 1823.
44. Ibid., 12 December 1823.
45. Ibid.
46. Joseph L. Inglis (Secretary, the Supreme Court of Pennsylvania), *First African Methodist Episcopal Church, Philadelphia: Documents Concerning the Court Case Involving the Legality of the Expulsion of One of Their Members, Robert Green* (Yeates Papers, miscellaneous papers, 1815, [box, ifi.]) Historical Society of Pennsylvania. The Green case was originally heard in July 1809. Green's actions resulted in the expulsion order of July 1812.
    The committee ruling on Green's expulsion included: Richard Allen, deacon, chairman; Stephen Laws, trustee; Jacob Tapisco, deacon; James Champion, deacon; Prince Prudence, trustee, class leader; James Grey, class leader; Clayton Durham, trustee; Joseph Johnson; John Somerset, class leader; Adam Clincher, preacher;
47. *Opinion Robert Green Case,* Supreme Court of Pennsylvania, 16 January 1815, (Yeates Papers, miscellaneous legal papers, f1), Historical Society of Pennsylvania.
48. William T. Catto, *A Semi-Centenary Discourse, delivered in the First African Presbyterian Church, Philadelphia, May 1857* (Philadelphia: Joseph M. Wilson, 1857), 21; George, *Segregated Sabbaths*, 151.

49. Ibid., 25; George, *Segregated Sabbaths*.
50. Ibid., 25-26; George, *Segregated Sabbaths*.
51. Ibid., 22; George, *Segregated Sabbaths*.
52. Ibid., 54.
53. Ibid., 23.
54. David E. Swift, "Black Presbyterian Attacks on Racism: Samuel Cornish, Theodore Wright and Their Contemporaries," *Journal of Presbyterian History* 51, no. 4, (Winter 1973): 435. Gloucestor also worked closely with Richard Allen in protests against the American Colonization Society, see George, *Segregated Sabbaths*.
55. Catto, *A Semi-Cetenary Discourse*, 41.
56. Ibid., 69, 79-82.
57. Ibid., 84-88.
58. Ibid., 86.
59. Ibid., 69-71.
60. Swift, "Black Presbyterian Attacks."
61. Monroe Fordham, *Major Themes in Northern Black Religious Thought, 1800-1860* (Hicksville, New York: Exposition Press, 1975), 27-28; Wesley, *Richard Allen,* 109; Harry V. Richardson, *Dark Salvation: The Story of Methodistism as It Developed Among Blacks in America* (Garden City, New York: Anchor-Press/Doubleday, 1976), 77.
62. Fordham, *Black Religious Thought,* 14-16; Hosea Easton, *A Treatise on the Intellectual Character, and Civil and Political Condition of the Colored People of the United States* (Boston: Isaac Knapp, 1837); Maria W. Stewart, *Religion and the Pure Principles of Morality, the Sure Foundation on Which We Must Build* (Boston: Isaac Knapp, 1831); Richard Allen, *Life Experiences* 67-70; and Vincent Harding, "Religion and Resistance Among Antebellum Negroes," in *The Making of Black America* (New York: Athenaeum, 1969), 185.
63. Bishop James Walker Hood, *One Hundred Years of the African Methodist Episcopal Zion Church; of the Centennial of African Methodism* (New York: AME Zion Book Concern, 1895); John M. Burgess, *Black Gospel/White Church* (New York: Seabury Press, 1982), (reports establishment of black separatism at John Street in 1799.)
64. Marcia M. Mathews, *Richard Allen* (Baltimore: Helicon, 1963), 84.
65. Ibid.
66. Hood, *One Hundred Years*.
67. *Minutes and Trial Book, 1822-1835,* 11 August 1822 is a detailed description of Allen's struggle with the African Wesley Church which resisted Allen's attempts at incorporation. Wesley, *Richard Allen,* 164; George *Segregated Sabbaths*; and Hood, *One Hundred Years*.
68. Hood, *One Hundred Years*.
69. Ibid., 136. In addition to Rush other important personages attending the first conference included James Smith, James Anderson, William Coleman, Edward Johnson, and Tilmon Cornish.
70. Stuckey, *Slave Culture*, 172-74. Stuckey presents an enlightened discussion of the odd phenomenon of the shared nationalist and integrationist characteristics of several nineteenth century black political spokesmen.

71. Burgess, *Black Gospel/White Church*, 9; George F. Bragg, *History of the Afro-American Group of the Episcopal Church* (Baltimore: Church Advocate Press, 1922), 82.

72. Bragg, *Afro-American Group*, Bragg uses $250 as the rental fee. See *Letter*, Peter Williams to John H. Hobart, 14 August 1826, Papers of John H. Hobart, New York Historical Society, microfilm H 31:31.

73. *The Commercial Advertiser,* 21 October 1819, .

74. *Letter,* Williams to Hobart, 14 August 1826.

75. George, *Segregated Sabbaths*, 156; Wesley, *Richard Allen*, 235; and Louis R Mehlinger, "Attitudes of the Free Negro Toward African Colonization" *Journal of Negro History* 1, no. 1 (1916).

76. Mehlinger, *"Attitudes of the Free Negro,"* 145; Roi Ottley and William J. Weatherby, *The Negro in New York: An Informal History* (Dobbs Ferry, New York: Oceana Publishers, Inc.), 95.

77. George, *Segregated Sabbaths*, 183.

78. Robert S. Starobin, ed., *Denmark Vesey: The Slave Conspiracy of 1822* (Englewood Cliffs, New Jersey: Prentice-Hall, Inc.), passim; Wesley, *Richard Allen*, 186-87; Julie Winch, *Philadelphia's Black Elite, Activism, Accomodation, and the Struggle for Autonomy* (Phildelphia: Temple University Press, 1988), 14, 57.

79. Daniel Alexander Payne, *Reflections of Seventy Years* (New York: Arno Press, 1968), 253-54, Stuckey, *Slave Culture,* 92-93.

3

Organizations: The Role of Self-Help, Fraternal, Women's, and Miscellaneous Groups in Creating a Community Infrastructure

Concurrent with the church other elements of community organizing and community consciousness began to emerge in the antebellum North. It is clear that this consciousness was made up of many interrelated factors. Paramount among these was a rich variety of organizations to serve the ever-shifting needs of the people within the community.

Certainly, as members of the community began to create organizations, they did so in ways which were tentative, seemingly misguided, and sometimes too individualized. Although organizations in this period of awakening may have had brief, uneventful life cycles, all the efforts were part of the learning process of leadership which is useful, perhaps necessary, in gauging the strength of commitment to change which the community's adherents advocated. These efforts, too, were part of the important developments in the community building process.

Experimentation sometimes led to reorganizing and redirecting the thrust of particular organizations. Seeking a venue to speak to community needs helped move the organizational structures through distinct phases of growth. In the early experimental stage many organizations tentatively sought to bring relief only to their membership. As they and the community gained some confidence in their ability to deliver services to their constiuents the process moved into a period of maturation.

Usually occurring in the mid-1830s, the maturation of organizations helped leaders to establish national networks among churches, vigilance societies, debating and reading room groups, women's clubs, and other self-help groups. For the black rank and file the maturation of the organizational structure allowed them to move to new locales and still be able to locate groups to help them meet individual and collective needs.

Even false starts produced the possibility of real progress. Need, effort, and even marginal success became reinforcing entities which verified that trial and error was a valid learning process. To nineteenth-century black community organizers, creating and directing change rather than achieving equilibrium was the more important goal.[1]

In pursuit of change the organizational efforts depicted here conform to a five-phase pattern.spanning the years 1770 to 1865. In the first phase black organizers received assistance from outsiders, as in the case of petitions during the earliest stages of the revolutionary period. In the second phase, when the outside assistance was neither successful nor long-lasting, black individuals and fledgling organizations began to experiment with their own public voice. Once entered on the stage of public expression, the third phase featured an accelerated movement which increased the number of black organizations. This movement reflected the widespread needs of the community to control their resources and the direction of change. In the fourth phase recognition, sometimes begrudgingly given, came from the white community. Even this development could not assure black equality. Although the first four phases helped the community to mold a voice, to control its resources, and to meet many of its own needs, the search for power was not completed. This fifth phase could only be completed when particular organizations shaped their activities to conform to a vision of black political empowerment.

Organized activities of the newspapers and the convention movement pursue one form of empowerment: inclusion in the American body politic. Only when the focus turned to presenting an alternative vision to the American political economy did the black community become whole, organic, and best able to express its own ethos. The black ethos or final stage of black organizational development required the simultaneous blending of visibilty and voice. Combining visibility and voice allowed black organizations to seek rational alternatives to the discriminatory associational activity of white America. Visibilty and voice did not result in equality with white organizations but it did provide the opportunity for black groups to provide for most of their own needs.

Beyond simply indicting America, the organized attempts to create liberation philosophies such as emigrationism demonstrate the black belief in their ability to govern themselves and simultaneously reveal that final stage of black empowerment. The experience of the emigrationists is a prime example of the need to acquire visibility and voice. For a brief period in the early 1850s the emigration factions had neither visibility nor voice, even within the black community. Only when specific conventions were held and organizations devoted to their cause were founded in 1853 and 1854 did the emigrationists combine visibility and voice. Even so, emigrationism remained an important but minority philosophy within the community.

It is not useful for our purposes to engage in the chicken-and-egg discussion of which came first: organizations/ institutions or the community? The data suggest that in antebellum Philadelphia, Boston, and New York a community of opinion existed which stimulated the creation of organizations. This in turn fostered the origins of an infrastructure which demonstrated to adherents and opponents that a black institutional structure was emerging. Many community studies display an overreliance on majority group norms that do not adequately encompass the black historical experience.[2] In addition racism, as the sole generator of black community consciousness, seems to permeate historical and sociological literature. This is especially true of works by black scholars.[3] Racism cannot be ignored but this writer will give emphasis to an interpretive dimension largely missing in the existing record. Black responses to life in America were triggered by a complex of human needs and not simply conditioned by reactions to racism.

Significantly, each attempt to create a structured community became part of the shared, collective, internalized experience of the group. Organizers hoped that the competence gained by individuals in the founding and the maintenance of organizations would lead to sophistication and differentiation about how best to complete the assigned tasks; to set and accomplish objectives; conduct fund-raising and membership drives; to train future leaders; to influence and sometimes lead public opinion; to shepherd the growth of organizations; and finally, to combine with existing entities to form an infrastructure catering to and protecting the community's interests and existence.

I

In the period 1770 to 1865 black American activists worked steadily to transform their lives through the establishment of groups, associations, and societies. Initially such organizations served as focal points for private black religious worship or as a secular umbrella to consider many specific needs of black enclaves. Such efforts generally antedated by a few years the establishment of formal churches among northern blacks. Once the church attained status it then became the incubator giving birth to and protecting the growth of the fledgling organizations. By the 1830s a secularizing trend assisted black associations to move from the confines of the church. In this period diversity and differentiation characterized black efforts. Yet the secularization of black organizing did not diminish the church's position as the predominant institution. Quite the contrary, the secular pursuits reinforced the church by leaving it free to provide specifically religious services. Simultaneously, the church provided a successful role model for new organizations to emulate and a refuge should the new efforts fail. Groups focused on all the needs of the black populace. Educational and intellectual societies, vigilance committees, women's groups, and welfare agencies blossomed. While there was some duplication of effort the overall effect was institutional specialization. By 1860 the northern black community had established an institutional infrastructure which attempted to service the needs and aspirations of its constituency.

The organizational pursuits of black northerners between 1770 and 1865 show several distinct patterns. In the initial stage of organizational growth black efforts were sometimes given a boost by outsiders. Once the group of individuals creating the association had finalized their internal structure they began immediately to experiment with a public voice. This public voice was meant to inform blacks as well as whites concerning the mission of the organization. Another pattern in nineteenth century black American life illustrates the uneven development of organizational growth and differentiation. Differentiation involved not only specialization but also a secularization of black organizing efforts. In New York the two processes were taking place as early as 1812. After 1817 black Philadelphians accelerated the secularizing process of their institutional growth. Although Boston started to form black organizations earlier, it did not begin to experience institutional maturity until the period 1826-1830. As stated earlier institutional maturity came when an infrastructure was in place that allowed leaders and followers to move from one locale to another and find needed services similar to those left behind in their native communities.

Two other patterns can be clearly discerned; these sometimes occurred simultaneous with and sometimes after organizations were completing the secularization and differentiation phases.. Usually some recognition of black organizations began to emerge in the white community. This recognition could be negative, as in the case of riots against black firefighters or black abolitionists, or positive, as in the call for volunteers to build city defenses or to act as paramedical personnel in times of trouble. Both forms of recognition attest to the relevance of black organizing efforts. Finally, the organizations serviced the internal needs of the community while exhibiting a degree of black power in their ability to speak to and for the black community.

Just as the revolutionary period ushered in individual efforts to redress black grievances, so it also marked the slow beginning of black organizational activities. Whatever motivated British Army officers to give their qualified permission for a small group of blacks to meet as a masonic lodge was of little import to blacks; they took seriously the responsibility implicit in becoming the first public black organization in Boston.[4] The British regiment may have been manipulating the black desire for respectability in order to tweak the patriots' racial sensitivities or they simply may have desired to secure supporters among Boston's black citizenry.

For their own purposes blacks could neither accept fully nor reject totally British racial attitudes or the political opportunities that arose from them. At the time the British officers gave permission for black independent organizing they also continued to respect black bondage. Indeed, the men who formed the lodge were acting as servants to the English officers. Blacks found themselves in an ambiguous situation which dictated that they make the most of any opportunity to gain status. While still a legally recognized category, slavery had ceased to exist as an economic reality for most of the region. Yet the patriots' insistence on equating their political relationship with Britain as slavery did not make them any more lenient toward black aspirations. War conditions broke the former equilibrium that had generally existed between blacks and whites. As bonds directing their estate began to shift and loosen blacks were able to take advantage of the small interface between slavery and freedom.

February 1773 was such an occasion for a black individual to push wider the parameters of action afforded to blacks. In that month the Massachusetts General Court received but ignored a petition focusing on the end of slavery. "How could America," the petitioner asked, "seek release from English tyranny and not seek the same for disadvantaged Africans in her midst?"[5] Not content to allow the court's inaction to deprive them of their rights, blacks repetitioned the court. Just as Prince Hall had depended on the aid of British officers to form the first black masonic lodge, the first detailed black petition needed the assistance of an outsider to gain a hearing. Through the offices of the representative of the town of Thompson, four male slaves found a platform to address their grievances but also to speak for and to the collective slave community.

On 20 April 1773 the Massachusetts General Court considered briefly but refused to act on the new petition. The black position was more than a restatement of the earlier petition. At least one new option providing for a release from slavery was clearly stated.

> We are willing to submit to such regulations and laws as may be made relative to us, until we leave the province, which we determine to do as soon as we can from our joint labors procure money to transport ourselves to some part of Africa where we propose a settlement.[6]

The petitioners explained that the idea to labor for themselves came from the Spanish "who have not those sublime ideas of freedom that Englishmen have."[7] Spaniards were conscious of certain rights of slaves to a portion of their labor. Africans were allowed to work one day a week to earn money toward their purchase price. It was further explained to the representative of the town of Thompson, to whom the petition was addressed, that an appraisal of the African's services was equivalent to a purchase price.

In theory, what the four slaves stated was true. Under the Spanish slave code, the Siete Partidas, the Catholic church had the responsibility, if not always the authority, to bring together a master and his slave who sought manumission. An equitable price would be arranged and a payment plan agreed upon. Peter Bestes and his companions used the Spanish example masterfully.

Although slaves trying to achieve their freedom, the four men cast their hopes on two factors: the American stand against the designs of their fellowmen politically to enslave them and on their own resonable plan of manumission.

> The efforts made by the legislative of this province in their last sessions to free themselves from slavery, gave us, who are in that deplorable state, a high degree of satisfaction. We expect great things from men who have made such a noble stand against the design of their fellow-men to enslave them. We cannot but wish and hope Sir, that you will have the same grand object, we mean civil and religious liberty, in view in your next session. The divine spirit of freedom, seems to fire every humane breast on this continent, except such as are bribed to assist in executing the execrable plan.[8]

Significantly, Bestes, Sambo Freeman, Chester Joie, and Felix Holbrook underlined their approval of the Patriots' stand. Yet they also quickly demonstrated that they were reasonable and appreciative of the financial burdens resulting from an abrupt end to bondage. "We are very sensible that it would be highly detrimental to our present masters, if we were allowed to demand all that of right belongs to us for past services; this we disclaim."[9] No motive of revenge for past grievances activated their request. The four were quick to point out that as men they naturally sought liberty. Morevover, liberty was their natural right.

> But since the wise and righteous governor of the universe has permitted our fellow men to make us slaves, we bow in submission to him, and determine to behave in such a manner, as that we may have reason to expect the divine approbation of, and assistance in, our peaceable and lawful attempts to gain our freedom.[10]

Even in the heat of revolutionary rhetoric the reasoned approach undertaken by the four blacks did not prevail: quietly the court tabled the measure. The blacks were alerted, however, to the possibilities for collective action in their own behalf by the conflict between the colonies and the mother country.

We have no direct evidence that the general slave population knew of the petition's existence, but even in the absence of such evidence there are ample actions by blacks strongly suggesting that the war period offered new and sometimes conflicting opportunities. The social world was changing rapidly, introducing shifting standards of behavior along with challenges to constituted authority. Under the stress of war the Americans and their British opponents frequently acted toward blacks in ways that were simultaneously restrictive and expansive.

In the context of this flux, six weeks after Lexington and Concord, on 6 March 1775, Prince Hall and fourteen other blacks became members of an army lodge of Free and Accepted Masons. The British regiment gave the small number of blacks its qualified blessings to meet as a lodge. When the British left Boston, Hall and his companions tried unsuccessfully to gain acceptance from the American masons. Although rebuffed, the black lodge continued meeting throughout the war. Finally, in March 1784, Hall wrote the London office requesting a charter for his group.

Not until the spring of 1787, however, was sanction received from London for the black Bostonians. What had been identified as African Lodge No. 1 was officially designated Lodge 459. Having acquired an official ranking with the international order but still ignored by the American organization, Hall set forth to establish black lodges up and down the eastern seaboard. His efforts represent the first attempts to establish a national organizational structure within black America. Within months Hall had succeeded in opening lodges as far south as Baltimore. Although secular in its thrust, the black masonic group combined with its fraternal role a religious message supporting enlightened Christianity, citizenship, and racial upfilt.

Before receiving official acceptance of his group Hall was plagued by the new republic's failure to grant full citizenship rights to blacks and briefly flirted with the back-to-Africa solution suggested by Bestes, Joie, Freeman, and Holbrook. On 4 January 1787, the date of Hall's petition to the new Massachusetts Congress, blacks were no longer in bondage.[11] Slavery had ended in the state in 1780, the result of judicial decisions in the Quock Walker cases. Yet, as Hall well knew, blacks had not experienced an appreciable gain in status or new opportunities as the result of the Walker interpretations. His document was a cry of frustration rather than a carefully considered nationalist assertion. After the brief flirtation with emigration Hall returned to more orthodox pursuits.

Disdaining the return-to-Africa solution did not signal any lessening of zeal in Hall's agitation on behalf of black equality. Instead, his focus became the elimination of the two major restrictions on black life: discrimination and slavery. By ending those two Hall hoped to achieve full black citizenship. Understanding clearly that the elimination of the two crippling aspects of black American life required a broad-based attack, he fought discrimination in education and protested successfully against kidnapping and the slave trade.

In October 1787, a time when Boston possessed no black school and whites seemingly lacked the interest to take seriously black educational aspiration, Hall resorted to a petition drive against the discriminatory treatment given black youth. The collective nature of black social agitation is clearly discernible in Hall's educational plans. Other individuals within Boston's black population were keenly aware of the educational shortcomings of the blacks. Like Hall, they protested against the indifference shown by the Boston Common School Committee. Yet at the same time they recognized that petitioning was at best part of an evolutionary process, so they moved to combat the contemporary educational disabilities. Primus Hall, Prince Hall's son, opened the first Boston school for blacks in his own home in the year of his father's petition. The younger Hall's actions were not critical of his father's efforts. Their different approaches represented a joint effort to attack a present danger and to avoid future discrimination in education. Yet the coordinated program produced little positive response from the Boston School Committee.

Not discouraged by the meager results of the school agitation, Hall continued to act as a guardian of black society. Beginning on 27 February 1788 he organized and led another petition drive against the slave trade. In addition to the petition Hall organized a continuous protest campaign to secure the freedom of three black Bostonians who had been kidnapped and sold as slaves.[12] Since the recovery of free men wrongfully kidnapped was more appealing to white New Englanders than the potential race mixing in integrated schools, powerful whites began to offer assistance, but the day-to-day energy of the campaign was still provided basically by blacks. Continuing for five months, the plan involved newspaper propaganda, publicity, and political administrations, until by July all three young men had been returned.

After 1788, having experienced the necessity of organizing to achieve political and social objectives, Hall accelerated his efforts to establish a nationwide black masonic order. Toward this end he worked to acquire a high profile for the masons. The lodge became the site of annual messages to the black community which not only extolled the truimphs of blacks surviving in America but also suggested prospects and designs for elevating the whole race. For all purposes the lodge became the arbiter of religious orthodoxy and standards for the black community. In Boston particularly, where blacks had not worked out their independent religious orientations, the lodge served as the community's institutional focal point.

This responsibility is clearly affirmed in the dual role in which the lodge functioned. It was simultaneously an organ for reflecting community aspirations and concerns and also a platform from which white benefactors and black activists attempted to guide the blacks. Although the bulk of speakers delivering the annual orations were black, they shared to a surprising degree some similar perceptions about black uplift with their white counterparts. All stressed hard work, thrift, religious observance, and a Protestant sense of community welfare.

While they promulgated the same themes, black and white speakers using the public rostrum differed in one fundamental way. White speakers without exception added a caution which gave their message a paternalistic thrust.[13] It would appear that blacks listened courteously but took such advice with a considerable portion of salt. Black speakers, on the other hand, even when acknowledging the prevailing racial ideologies, put forth an unambiguous message. They asserted in part that an Old Testament God of revenge would ultimately act on behalf of the disadvantaged and oppressed Africans.[14] Here was a charge that a secular organization could oversee for its black constituency. The message was at once accommodating and hopeful: it acknowledged the inferior status of Afro-Americans but prodded white Americans to get their house in order before it was too late. Such doomsday utterances were tempered with proposals for black racial uplift.

An inescapable conclusion concerning the annual lodge speech is that it was meant for general black consumption. Each annual message was quickly printed and distributed or sold. The fact that they were published in runs larger than lodge membership attests not only to their general appeal but also to the acceptance by blacks that the oration was projecting a black viewpoint. It also demonstrates literacy in black America. An aim to achieve wide black support can also gauged by the didactic nature of most of the offerings. Usually incorporated in the annual messages would be lessons of African and New World black history. Such inclusions had of course the dual purpose of informing blacks and whites but also functioning as mechanisms for instilling black pride. Thus the lodge served as part of an informal educational process for the black masses. In the absence of a strong institutional infrastructure, the masonic lodge serviced the black community's needs beyond their own fraternal mission. Typical of consciousness raising was the tone and content of Hall's 1797 *Charge*.

> . . .Patience I say, for were we not possessed of a great measure of it you could not bear up under daily insults you meet with in the streets of Boston; much more on public days of recreation how you are shamefully abused, and that at such a degree, that you may truely be said to carry your lives in your hands: and arrows of death are flying

about your heads; helpless old women have their clothes torn off their backs, even to exposing of their nakedness. My brethren, let us not be cast down under these and many other abuses we at present labour under. My brethren, let us remember what a dark day it was with our African brethren six years ago in the French West Indies. . . .[15]

The narrow concern of speaking only to his membership was a luxury Prince Hall could ill afford. Coincident with his activities were other groups of blacks groping toward organizational clarity. So long as religious study groups met for worship and the discussion of affiliation, it was left to the masonic lodge to manifest a public image of a black organization. Thus the order was able to use its annual charge to expand the consciousness of the community. Significantly, while much emphasis had to be placed upon being a good mason, the language used to set the standard was ambiguous enough for non-masons to identify with positively. "The duty of a Mason . . . is that he believes in one supreme being," Hall wrote.[16]

Continuing, Hall illuminated those powers of the Supreme Being which all save atheists could accept. Hall asserted that He governed all things here below and kept a watchful eye over all our works. Hall argued that as good subjects blacks must obey the law of the land and give honor to lawful governers and magistrates. Further, he counseled that blacks should not be involved in plots, conspiracies, or rebellion. The devastation and bloodshed which accompanied such activities were too high a price for present and future generations to pay. He concluded the opening paragraph with a call to practice universal love for our brother fellow man.

Beyond the obvious generalities Hall's message is obscure. Why use the description "subjects"? Was it Hall's attempt to reach back into the revolutionary era and reiterate the patriots' criticism of Parliament but their support of the king? Surely the thrust seemed to be that blacks can agitate lawfully for their rights without being subversive. Rather than sustain the political focus, however, Hall's beginning degenerates into a call for love and fellow feeling. Using the Scriptures Hall continued to instruct his audience in how to be good masons. Lest anyone accuse him of uplifting only masons "because some men will catch at anything," Hall chided his listeners that not all who did good deeds in the Bible were Christians and his world surely needed love and fellow feeling because it was conspicuously absent.[17]

Another need was to establish black-oriented standards and assert to blacks and whites alike an attitude of black unity. Hall proposed to accomplish those ends by making the black masons a national body, although he fell short of his national goals. Masonic lodges were established even in southern locales but they never achieved the same public prominence as their contemporary, the African Society in Philadelphia. Nevertheless, Hall succeeded in demonstrating the potential for black community development. Hall stressed themes of unity, education, uplifting the race, Christianity, political agitation, self-criticism, working with whites when it was possible and practical, and creating associations that were national in structure. While he enjoyed only limited success in any of his goals, Hall brought out certain themes that later would become more fully developed. Although examples of the fits and starts of early community building, Hall's activities also are characteristic of the evolutionary path of community development. He embodied the movement through being assisted by outsiders, by creating his own public format and to refining his own particular association all in the name of bringing the group together as a conscious collective.

Even as Hall worked at the masonic organization other blacks in Boston and elsewhere struggled to establish groups with similar ideas. That these were not competing efforts can be illustrated on a number of relevant levels. First, the membership was not exclusive, but cut across institutional lines. When black males in Boston formed the African Society in 1796, many of them were also masons.[18] The organization represented a broader range of community participation and therefore a wider basis of attack on discrimination, disfranchisement, and slavery. The African Society also spoke to specific black needs beyond racism.

Men not attracted by the secret nature of the masonic order could become part of the leadership within the African Society. Their role was not only more public but their image was more egalitarian. While their role was primarily political, the society also began to address the social needs of Boston's blacks.

Second, the consciously shared impulse of black organizational ties can be seen when one reflects that the African Society itself grew out of the informal religious discussion groups in Boston. Thus in the beginning stage of consolidation the black Boston movement had at least three distinctly separate yet unified thrusts. Two of these encompassed secular pursuits: the narrower fraternal direction of the masonic order complemented the communal appeal of the African Society. Religious aspirations were of course the province of the informal but intensely active discussion groups.

Moreover, in addition to sharing a collective mind about black unification the African Society explicitly made operative its plans for a physical black community. During the period 1796 to 1804 when African Society members discussed how best to formalize a religious consensus among Boston's black populace they also sought a device that would geographically consolidate black Bostonians. It seemed natural that a meeting house or some edifice would draw blacks around it. If chosen with care the site would afford blacks a more congenial neighborhood than the lower-working-class-environment of the north Boston docks where most blacks resided.[19] Although a certain class and ethnic snobbery tainted the perceptions of African Society members, they acted out of benevolent motives for their black contemporaries.

Safety was a prime factor motivating the leadership's desire to relocate. Blacks and Irish not only competed for employment on the docks but also contested each other for scarce resources such as living space. The resulting clashes, given white indifference, were extremely distruptive for blacks. Scipio Dalton, Cato Gardner, and others argued that blacks who continued to reside with their white employers might be induced to buy property around the proposed African meeting house. They further argued that in a clearly designated area blacks would feel themselves more permanent and secure members of Boston society, thereby allowing for the development of manners, morality, and community.

Selecting a site behind Beacon Hill afforded additional advantages. Blacks would be near their principal places of employment, the rich homes of Boston's leading families, and they would also be in close proximity to that class of white who possessed the most favorable attitude toward them. Yet the achievement of Gardner and his coworkers should not be interpreted only in the narrow view. More than trying to gain approval and acceptance from whites, Boston's blacks were organizing for survival and enrichment. Remarkably, consensus of purpose and outlook characterized the endeavors of Boston's black leaders until the late 1820s.

During the era of good feelings Gardner, Hall, Paul, and Dalton supported each other in missionary, educational, and political pursuits. To be sure the consensus was in part maintained because of conservative political ambitions. Yet between 1787 and 1829 the institutional structure created by blacks sustained them through the crisis years when black agitation accelerated and white attitudes hardened. Although David Walker's *Appeal* was the most public manifestation of the loss of consensus, his oration was not solely responsible for the adjustments in black community consciousness after 1830. Walker's *Appeal* did not destroy the conservative consensus in black Boston but it did deeply rend black organizing activity. Locally the *Appeal,* like the formation of the Massachusetts General Colored Association, signaled some dissatisfaction with the conservative agenda.[20] Blacks were moving from working with small coalitions of fair-minded whites to demanding rights and privileges as part of the human family. They seemed less tolerant of white sensitivities and more openly condemned the lack of changed attitudes even during the era of good feelings. At the national level Walker crystallized the more militant concerns of an emerging young leadership group. Richard Allen and Thomas Paul had been content to make small incremental gains while fighting with local churches, but without condemning the church as an institution. Walker condemned the church as an institution for its failure to pursue humane treatment of blacks.

Clearly his publication crystallized the burgeoning militance within the black enclave. As early as 1826 a more radical group, the Massachusetts General Colored Association, emerged in Boston. Ironically the new group included sons of black leaders who had presided over the initial efforts and the ensuing era of good feeling. Their radicalism was characterized more by impatience at white intransigence than a desire for structural change of the American political process. Nevertheless the new leadership helped to direct black development successfully through its phase of institutional differentiation.

Equally important as the accelerated black militance was the diminishing of the ranks of the older leaders. Blacks and whites who had emerged in the postrevolutionary generation were by 1830 either deceased or too old for effective leadership. With their demise came the loss of mutual respect, bringing in its wake fewer close contacts between black and white. Now black leaders possessed no sense of loyalty to earlier established contacts with white benefactors. Their focus and capability for generating change came from their own assessment of discrimination and black needs. Black institutional growth resulted from a combination of factors. One was the movement away from interracial cooperation which characterized the Paul-Stillman generation. The other was the lessening of postrevolutionary interracial cooperation that forced blacks back on their own resources. Blacks were forced to rely on the new organizations because, ironically, the African Baptist Church was the most damaged institution.

Following the resignation of Thomas Paul the African Baptist Church suffered loss of membership, frequently changed ministers and lost its position of community leadership. Not until 1840 did the church return to its pre-1829 position, but then it had to compete with other black institutions. The new organizations had emerged during the period of the church's decline. Yet the new circumstances were more beneficial to the enlarged black populace. In the leadership vacuum resulting from the decline of the church, the community had grown more decentralized, more secular, and slightly less class-conscious. More diverse opinion was represented in Boston and a more complete institutional infrastructure was available to black agitators.

Yet institutional differentiation in Boston also constituted a double edged-sword. While greater participation had been achieved, and blacks in new areas could feel secure in knowing that organizations existed to protect their self-interest, consensus was more difficult to guarantee. Formerly institutional specialization and the diversity of black opinions were seen as examples of black disunity. More correctly interpreted, the specialization is clearly reflective of a modernizing trend within the black American conscious. Although Boston blacks did not lose sight of the overall emphasis against slavery and discrimination, different options and perceptions meant that not all blacks expressed the same level of commitment to every disability confronting their existence. Consensus was not absent, but it was harder to achieve than in the years prior to 1829. After 1829 consensus consisted of coalitions of individuals and organizations around specific issues.

II

Institutional specialization, consensus, and identity followed a different path in Philadelphia's black community. Perhaps a primary reason for the difference from the Boston case had to do with the origins of Philadelphia's organizational structure. In the spring of 1787 the black members of St. George's Episcopal Church formed the Free African Society. Blacks had been meeting informally since 1784 to discuss topics of mutual interest. Among the items discussed was fairer treatment within St. George's. Unlike their Boston counterparts the Philadelphia blacks did not seek white counsel. While they were concerned about religious tolerance they also discussed topics of support and protection. Unlike the masons, Boston's initial black association, the Free African Society was less exclusive in its membership. Nor did the society have a paramilitary, semi-secret character as did the masons. Moreover St. George's blacks were united in the concerns of the special circumstances within the discriminatory white denomination. Yet their interests were not purely religious. The Free African Society was to assist blacks in social areas quite outside the church. It was possible, then, from the beginning to identify a multitude of interests and directions for black activity. It was this initial umbrella organization that made it unnecessary for blacks in Philadelphia to rely too heavily on white benefactors and, once independent churches had grown out of the Free African Society, they were not traumatized by discordance as was the Boston African Baptist Church.

Dissension was present, of course, in the Free African Society but the years of close cooperation protected the growth of community consciousness. Between April 1787 and November 1792 the society maintained a consensus of purpose and direction. It was concerned about the inappropriateness of the regularly scheduled black worship services. Moreover, it objected to, and made representations to St. George's leadership to change, segregated seating and communion. Black cooperation allowed the group to act with unity when St. George's expelled the group. In November 1792 following the reassignment of blacks to seating in the gallery, Allen and Jones mistakenly assumed they were to take the front seats. At the communion bar the white reaction was immediate and decisive: blacks were pulled from their position of prayer and escorted to the door.

After the expulsion from St. George's the Free African Society members debated the issues of continuing religious sustenance and continued affiliation with St. George's. All were not of like mind about their circumstances yet they remained united until 1794. While the tensions mounted, which ultimately resulted in Richard Allen's expulsion from the society, the consensus remained. To the degree that Allen refrained from denouncing the society for its discipline and, more important, that he continued to maintain intimacy with Absalom Jones even after Jones had elected to form St. Thomas Episcopal Church, speaks to an expanded capacity for identifying common interests among Philadelphia blacks. Allen singlemindedly continued to adhere to his Methodism when other blacks decided to seek more compatible religious affiliations. Moreover, Allen continued to cooperate with Jones on a series of reform issues of importance to the black community. Specific religious choices did not in this case become a barrier to community progress.

When civic service was requested from the black community, white politicians sought out Allen and Jones. They in turn solicited support from Philadelphia's black inhabitants and seldom was such a request denied. In 1793, as the city was being ravaged by a yellow fever epidemic, several leading whites who believed blacks were immune to the disease asked Allen and Jones to form a black nursing corps and burial squadron.[21] Although Richard Allen had not believed that blacks were immune to the sickness, he assented to the city's request. This volunteering for dangerous service was motivated by more than Allen's sense of Christian charity. He was particularly aware of the potential for raising the esteem of the black community by serving the city in this crisis.[22]

Having served the city in its hour of need Allen and Jones further cooperated in defense of the community's integrity. Subsequent to the crisis there appeared in the spring a pamphlet describing the epidemic. Matthew Carey, its author, singled out Allen's and Jones's commendatory service. But he condemned those blacks who allegedly took advantage.[23] Although personally free of any misconduct or charges, both men felt compelled to refute Carey's assertions. To this end they collaborated on the pamphlet, *A Narrative of the Proceedings of the Black People During the Awful Calamity in Philadelphia in the Year 1793; and a refutation of some Censures thrown upon them in some of the late publications.*[24] They admitted that there may have been a few who were dishonest in their dealings with the sick and dying but, they asserted, the majority carried out its commission with honor, compassion, and dispatch. Some whites were guilty of the charges of which Carey accused blacks, but Allen and Jones quickly pointed out that the minority behavior was not the basis for condemning all whites.

Simultaneously, Jones and Allen demonstrated that blacks had not received some of the fees that had been authorized for their services. These losses, although considerable, were absorbed by black individuals. The losses were due to the necessities of burying several hundred poor people and strangers, and for this activity the blacks asked no compensation. Other losses resulted from the cost of coffins and the hiring of five men to do the burials.

More important, Jones and Allen illustrated that popular medical beliefs to which Carey subscribed were not true. Their critic had charged that since blacks were less susceptible to yellow fever they should have served more willingly and more widely. Jones and Allen countered with case histories of blacks who succumbed to the disease, suggesting perhaps that black sacrifices were more heroic than Carey and most whites were willing to admit. Equally damaging to Carey's case was the fact that he had fled the city and much of his pamphlet was based on hearsay and rumor. Later the Jones and Allen rebuttal was instrumental in vindicating the conduct of the black community.

Not all whites had shared Carey's earliest view and those closest to the black activities commended their efforts. As early as 23 January 1794 Mayor Matthew Clarkson registered his approval of black assistance. He observed that his daily contacts not only with Allen and Jones but also the people they hired allowed him to declare their conduct and deportment as filling him with much satisfaction. Benjamin Rush, an old Jones/Allen confidant, also cited their work approvingly.[25] He also corroborated their assertions about hiring extra personnel. Moreover, according to Rush the blacks had not initially charged for their services and even when forced to ask for fees, they accepted what their patients could afford. After instructions by Rush, Jones and Allen had printed instructions for bleeding and giving mercurial purges. They reportedly saved several hundred persons by this method. A further commendation of black conduct written anonymously appeared in the *Massachusetts Magazine.*

Neither Jones nor Allen was a one-dimensional activist and their pamphlet included an address to slaveholders. Thus they attacked the two most debilitating features of black life: the negative assessment of free blacks and the institution of slavery. Although their religious views were becoming more divergent, their activities in the area of elevating the race, building organizations, and attacking slavery crystallized early black community consciousness in Philadelphia. Equally important, Jones and Allen continued to press for and to utilize every opportunity to strengthen black identity, even after each had selected separate religious paths, by providing an institutional framework for black activities.

When Prince Hall approved the attempt by Philadelphia blacks to establish the Second African Lodge, No. 459, on 20 September 1798, it was the culmination of the correspondence between the principal members of the Free African Society. Joined by James Forten, a wealthy black sailmaker, Jones and Allen petitioned Hall for permission to organize a Philadelphia lodge. On 24 June 1797 after receiving a favorable response from Hall, the Philadelphia group elected Absalom Jones, Worshipful Master, and Richard Allen, Treasurer.[26] Although by this time Allen was trying to clarify his status within the Methodist Episcopal Church, he continued his efforts on behalf of the fraternal organization. Later while engaged in litigation which ultimately gave his African Methodist Episcopal Church independence, Allen pursued his lodge efforts so well that in 1815 the four Pennsylvania lodges were designated a Grand lodge. Finally, on 25 February 1818 the Grand Lodge assembled at Mother Bethel for the funeral services of Rev. Absalom Jones.

This unhappy occasion accentuated the growing strength of the black community. The nexus of church and fraternal pursuits emphasized the underlying unity of black energy. For more than thirty years Jones and Allen reflected the diversity and continuity of the black mind in confronting civil disabilities, organizing for survival, and meeting their human needs. What seems to have been more important than religious homogeneity to Allen and Jones was a fundamental conviction of the necessity of black unity and a commitment to change black status not only within religion but also within the city at large and in the nation. On at least three levels their continuing friendship embodied that dedication. First they demonstrated to their contemporaries, both black and white, that doctrinal differences could be overcome in pursuit of a greater cause: black community development. Second they attempted in countless ways to build a broad based institutional structure to enhance the quality of black life. Finally, their efforts crystallized the interrelatedness of activities that heretofore were thought to have been ad hoc and separate black responses to the negative conditions of their existence. With their black contemporaries Jones and Allen transformed the tensions of American existence into an opportunity for black organizing and change.

Further, the solid foundation provided by the Jones and Allen collaboration provided Philadelphia blacks with a foundation on which it was possible to initiate other organizing attempts. Within each of their churches, subordinates took the lead in organizing to meet the multiplicity of challenges blacks faced. Before 1815 the outburst of black energy had created within Mother Bethel an interlocking network of social, educational, and secular societies. Clearly, the security of the church made it possible for Bethel's trustees to test their own organizing abilities. Moreover, Allen's catholic perceptions concerning black uplift was a further positive stimulant to organizational growth. The result was a proliferation of agencies within Bethel, most of which eventually became fundamental to the sense of black pride and protection in Philadelphia.

Not all blacks, of course, had the leisure or the means to take advantage of or participate in the events at Bethel. In the rough-and-tumble society of nineteenth-century American urban life most blacks in Philadelphia and elsewhere went about the business of survival and had little time or energy for other pursuits. Yet the activities of representative men such as Allen were not lost on or foreign to the experiences of his less fortunate black contemporaries. In several ways the efforts of representative persons touched intimately the lives of everyone in Philadelphia's black enclave. Even representative men had to work: Allen, for example, worked for years at the shoemaking trade. Although self-employed, his employment kept him in daily contact with the masses. Unlike some of his black contemporaries Allen's successful economic pursuits did not isolate him, nor were proceeds from his business achievements used to acquire an estate or build buffers against urban contact. Much of what Allen acquired through his business pursuits was rechanneled into the community as poor relief, personal gifts, loans and other charitable outlets.

With Allen providing a successful role model, Bethel attracted an unusually large number of nonaffluent blacks. Several trustees of Mother Bethel epitomized working-class participation in the process of black community organizational growth. Outstanding among such representatives was Jacob Tapsico. Tapsico could not write and numerous documents include an X and a crudely written signature attesting to his presence at church councils.[27] Even given his educational disabilities it appears that he was a powerful member of the church hierarchy. As a trustee he was privy to the inner councils of church organization and after Richard Allen he was one of the most visible symbols of the church to members and nonmembers alike. His organizational activities, perhaps more than Allen's, more consciously and consistently touched Philadelphia's black masses.

Particularly in the Sunday school activities were the benefits of Tapsico's organizing felt by the black populace. Competing for memberships in Sunday school classes was not restricted to church members. The benefits of participating were immediate: an essential part of Sunday school activity was learning to read and write, skills to which the average unskilled worker had no other access. Sunday school classes were also used in competitive fund-raising and other competitions. Although unable to write himself, Tapsico never disdained education. That his own deficiencies were no barrier to organizing can be discerned in the three tier-process Tapsico instituted in the church. First, women in the church organized themselves and sought out Tapsico's sponsorship. Thus, in 1805, the Daughters of Tapsico appeared as a group but with a social welfare rather than a strictly religious orientation. Second, educated women among the daughters conducted Sunday school classes.

They also sometimes induced educated nonmembers of Bethel to lead classes. Third, the classes functioned as recruitment devices for increasing church membership. Astoundingly, an educational process was assisted by a man who was functionally illiterate. Moreover, he engaged, in modern community organization jargon, a system of community outreach.

Clearly, Quomony Clarkson availed himself of the supportive structure of the church and its embrace of secular pursuits when he became the organizer of the Committee for the Education of Colored Youth. Assisted by Richard Allen, Clarkson began agitating for formal recognition and support for black education. He constantly memorialized the Philadelphia Board of Education to endorse a plan encompassing regular and specific allocation of money, locations of schools, and a commitment to employing black educators. Like most of his black contemporaries Clarkson was not initially motivated toward integrated education. In their minds separate education could be quality education if certain conditions were recognized and accepted. They insisted, among other demands, on equal funding for schools serving black youth; for ease of access to schools located in black areas; and on teachers who, if white, could empathize with black aspirations and abilities. With the full backing of Allen, Clarkson pursued the program they thought could best meet black educational needs.

Simultaneously, Clarkson was attempting to establish himself as a teacher. To this end he wrote educators and administrators whenever openings appeared in Philadelphia schools. Few of his inquiries seem to have elicited serious consideration or courteous response. In an age dominated by black spokesmen seeking to elevate the race, personal rebuffs were another of many expected obstacles to be overcome. Clarkson persisted in his dual educational odyssey, and his personal goals did not interfere with his mission on behalf of his black constituents. To secure a teaching position would in his and his comtemporaries' eyes, not be an individual/personal truimph but an example of the race's success. Like most of his coworkers Clarkson combined great reserves of energy: in addition to being both a practicing and aspiring teacher, he was a church trustee, class leader, social organizer, and leader of various associations. Like reformers throughout American history Clarkson sought to expand his perceptions to include as many ways of changing society as one man possibly could.

III

For the Philadelphia black community, energy such as that demonstrated by Tapsico and Clarkson was infectious. Not only did men get into the act but women too began to forge new social roles. Cautiously at first and conservatively always black, females in Philadelphia contributed to the burgeoning institutional infrastructure. Caution, of course, had to be the guiding principle since eighteenth- and nineteeth-century males were not keen on women taking public roles that might possibly lead to political participation. The conservatism of the initial efforts by females must also be viewed in light of prevailing sexual mores. Though desperately short of manpower, black males believed, implicitly, that the woman's place was in the home. Thus early female efforts came in areas where males had given first their approval and their paternalistic supervision. Within the church sisters were allowed to compete as class leaders or to form female social welfare/educational/religious auxiliaries so long as they took an appropriate male trustee's name for their organization.[28] The wives, sisters, and daughters of the black social elite took the lead in organizing Philadelphia's black females.

Although confined by male prerogatives black women learned much that would later be valuable for the entire community. Within their limited sphere females began to acquire the skills of their male counterparts. The bolder ones began to exhort at church functions. Those who remained cautious learned the intricacies of fund-raising for church socials, picnics, building funds, and class competition. Others began an apprenticeship in record keeping, addressing audiences, speech writing, and propaganda. By their energies they forced black males to readjust, however slightly, their previous perceptions about the weaker sex.

Certainly by the 1830s there existed in Boston and Philadelphia a cadre of black females who came to the forefront in the formation of female antislavery societies. At the outset they were invited to attend and to participate in those activities which characterized the early period of American reform. From an initial interest strictly in local issues, Susan Paul by 1835 had gained a national platform. Likewise the mother-and-daughter team of Margaretta and Harriet Forten broadened its public role within the Philadelphia and national female antislavery societies.

Beyond the organizational experiences individual black women found new voices and talents to confront what had been formerly a male prerogative: some began an articulate attack on institutional racism in the North. In 1838 Sarah Mapps Douglass spoke to and published articles condemning discrimination within Quaker churches.[29] The resulting criticism of Ms. Douglass did not cause her to recoil from being a spokesperson as it had a number of women activists.

Few black or white women had the exceptional abilities and personality of Sarah Mapps Douglass and most preferred the collective security of anonymity. Yet within the confines of organizations these black women made tremendous contributions both to the antislavery cause and to black institution-building. From 1831 to 1837 the Pan-Afric Female Intelligence Society (PAFIS) of Boston participated in most reform activities in that city. Its existence was favorably reported on in newspapers as far away as Tennessee.[30] Even a superficial perusal of the *Liberator* would show the frequency of the society's promotion of abolitionist debates, dramatic readings, fund-raising, establishing reading rooms, and other community welfare projects. Yet the members of the group were not subjected to the treatment of their contemporary, Maria W. Stewart.

When Mrs. Stewart became the first American born woman to attempt to support herself by public lecturing in 1832, the response was negative. She was reminded that her place was in the home and that it was unfeminine to be associated with the public arena.[31] Initially, Mrs. Stewart addressed the issues of discrimination, education, and Christianity, but the negative reaction forced her into a feminist defense. In 1833 her last speech drove home the point of her talent, dedication and energy for liberation by inquiring, "What if I am a woman?" Moreover, Mrs. Stewart was genuinely unhappy with the lack of support from the black community. She asserted, bitterly, that "our race does not appreciate those who go among them. . ."[32] She understood quite clearly that her reception was not that given to all black activists but reserved for females only. The sisters of the Pan-Afric Female Intelligence Society were more cautious about prevailing social mores and chose collective security over individual expression.

Several other important factors may underscore the different reactions. Mrs. Stewart was a widow seeking an economic option in public speaking. The Pan-Afric women were apparently married or economically self-sufficient or both. As a widow Mrs. Stewart was free from dominating male restraint. On the other hand, married women in the society would have risked private as well as public censure. If the women were married to prominent black leaders, as was often the case, individual public political activity would have been embarrassing to their mates. In short, black females shared to an astonishing degree American society's perception of the limited female role.

Another important factor which dictated the Pan-Afric strategy involves the complexity of elevating the race. Black males had been characterized as unwilling and unable to defend the country in times of war, even though, of course, the reverse was true. On the domestic front black males felt it necessary to protect and control their family. The American ideal was based on the male authority figure and the elevation of the race depended, in part, on how closely one could approximate the ideal. Upper-class black women affirmed American standards and supported their husbands, fathers, and sons by protecting those interests.

In the Boston case the name they chose at once affirmed their commitment to the prevailing mores, gave them some operating room, and did not create resentment. Female Intelligence Society connoted that the women were pursuing a perfectly logical path allowing men to take the lead in politics. To be sure, PAFIS women were welcomed into the abolition forums, which they may have organized, but as observers, not participants. The knowledge they gained could not then be used in the public arena by the women themselves. Women of the Pan-Afric society accepted these male restrictions. Further, by acting behind the scenes and advocating educational uplift the women were operating in a manner that was sanctioned by men.

Perhaps most important in shaping the positive response to the Pan-Afric group were two related factors. One is that the society sponsored and promoted but did not itself participate in public debates or lectures. Two, the breadth of members' interests was so wide they could not be attacked on a narrow anti-female basis. Moreover, the society's charter indicated the social welfare nature of their concerns, and all that it did could be subsumed under the rubric of the Protestant ethic and a concern for the welfare of the community.

Finally, its anonymity was protected by the collusion of male activists, both black and white. For example, the group rented halls and sponsored lectures by William Lloyd Garrison. He reported extensively on the activities for several years, but never was any individual mentioned by name in the numerous accounts.[33] It may be more than incidental that the activities of the Pan-Afric group ceased soon after the establishment of national female antislavery conferences.

Even with all the qualification surrounding its existence, the Pan-Afric Female Intelligence Society made important contributions to the institutional fabric of the black community. Its activities continued the precedent of black women assisting the cause of liberation. More important, by downplaying their individuality, members pioneered a method for women to increase the sphere of their actions without arousing the suspicions or resentment of males.

Clearly, by the end of the 1830s women had taken a place alongside black males in the struggle to achieve organizational diversity in the community. Although operating on a basis of more equality than had previously existed, most of the shared action remained in male-approved areas. In 1838 considerable emphasis was placed on the inclusion of women in several educational societies.

Certainly the societies were open only to the black elite Philadelphia and their perceptions of the masses included a good portion of paternalism. Yet this separation of mind could be taken too far because there was little physical separation between black haves and have-nots, and all blacks were presumed by whites, if not to be slaves, at least to be some lesser species which an indifferent white society could ignore at will. Thus blacks in the upper classes could not ignore their less fortunate brothers and sisters. Perhaps, more important, the elite blacks which could form educational societies saw themselves both as arbiters of taste and standards and role models for the less privileged masses. Accordingly, their pursuits were not entirely for personal enrichment. Much energy and many resources were devoted especially to the establishment of reading rooms. These were envisioned as centers where members of the black community could borrow books, attend lectures, hold discussions, and encounter new opportunities for enriching their lives. By 1846 several Philadelphia societies supported reading rooms with hundreds of circulating volumes.[34]

IV

Unlike the Philadelphia case Boston's black educational organizations maintained a definite protest profile. In both cities the issue was quality/integrated education. The black Bostonians, however, were more adamant about interracial education and pushed for integrated schools. Their desires can not be dismissed as simply those of blacks wishing to emulate white society. By the 1830s the inadequacy of the Boston Common School Committee conceptualization of black educational needs was apparent. The committee, which had the authority to accredit schools and allocate tax funds, seemed not to be committed seriously to black education. Annual appropriations had to be negotiated each year and seldom totaled more than two hundred dollars, which was usually earmarked for teacher salaries. Seldom were funds given for supplies and services, maintenance, equipment, or scholarships.

Moreover, blacks were moving beyond the confines of the African School located behind Beacon Hill. Greater opportunities for acquiring real estate were opening in the western section of the city. Blacks began migrating especially to Roxbury. Yet the number of schools did not increase to meet this black geographic expansion. On the other hand, whites were opposed to accommodating blacks in already existing schools. These two factors added a transportation difficulty to the problems of black students.

Simultaneously, a division of opinion within the black community concerning educational goals allowed the Common School Committee to continue its unresponsive policy. Some blacks wished to stem the flow of migration from Beacon Hill. They argued that migrants were destroying the community which visionary blacks had established in the 1790s. They also feared a recurrence of the economic and social confrontations that had marked the pre 1790 existence on Boston's northside. Probably, too, a number of community leaders feared for their own loss of status should the community become decentralized. Those who wished to stem the tide of out-migration were not totally opposed to integrated education. Their energies were directed more toward providing an attractive educational environment for blacks in the old locale.

Another group of blacks, fundamentally opposed to allowing white paternalism to direct black life, directed its energies toward creating greater educational opportunities for black students.[35] This group correctly pointed out the inadequacy of the African School's physical plant, the proximity of the school to smaller and smaller numbers of black students, and the insufficiency of both money and the procedures by which it was obtained. Their rational arguments, however, did not carry against white opposition to integrated schools or black acceptance of separate facilities. Thus the Common School Committee was free to choose which black faction to support. Under the circumstances it chose to support the status quo.

In pursuit of this policy, in 1835, the committee accepted a bequest from Abdiel Smith to build a new school for blacks in the Beacon Hill area. Instead of satisfying the various factions the Smith School intensified their differences. Added to the opposing faction's list of grievances was that black tax money still was not spent for black education because the Smith legacy had provided that the interest on the bequeath would cover annual operating costs. Moreover, the appointed white adminstrator soon insulted even those blacks who supported the school. He insisted on a larger salary than was intended and employed his wife at the school, but most damaging were his negative public statements about black potential. It added fuel to the controversy when he was supported in his position by white Boston educators including Horace Mann.

Soon even the facilities of the Smith School were overburdened. Again the call for decentralized integrated education was sounded. Frequent appeals were made to the Common School Committee concerning distance and length of time black students had to travel in order to reach Smith School. In their travels many black youth had passed white schools that could have accommodated them. Even when a favorable ruling on integrated education was rendered by Judge Fletcher in Salem it provided no relief for Boston blacks.[36] Instead of affirming every child's right to an equal education the judge's opinion provided a loophole for cities such as Boston by stating that it was economically unrealistic to provide a separate system for so small a number of students, as in Salem's system.

Increasingly, the behavior of Abner Forbes, the white teacher/administer hired by the Boston Common School Committee, disturbed the black community. No matter how white officialdom tried to blunt his remarks, blacks were not happy. Yet when he was replaced by a black administrator the furor hardly diminished. For example, the opposition seemed to be uninterested that not only was Nathaniel Paul an able individual but that his father Thomas had been one of the leading black spokesmen of his day.[37] The school, and not its administrator was the target. The opposition claimed Smith School was inadequate, too much a symbol of second class status. Thus they pressed for new options.

For more than a decade the opposition sustained its drive against the Common School Committee. The campaign for better schools demonstrated that blacks had achieved a degree of organizational maturity not previously seen in the community. Naturally, there were periods when no activity took place, but the basic strategy remained constant even if the membership of the opposition fluctuated. Some leaders, despairing of a positive resolution in the Boston case, began enrolling their children in schools of surrounding cities. Yet, as in the case of Benjamin Roberts, they could be tapped on for their expertise when needed. Although sending his child to school in Cambridge, Roberts remained active in other black causes in Boston.

V

New Yorkers seemed to be slower in forming community organizations than either black Philadelphians or black Bostonians. Once established, however, organizations founded by blacks in New York after 1830 became some of the most militant of the time. Militance was a double-edged sword. It may have accounted for the relatively late start of black organizing in New York. Although relatively small in number, blacks in prerevolutionary New York had a more explosive history of black/white conflicts than either Boston or Philadelphia. Such actions possibly prohibited blacks in New York from making even the mimimal contact with white benefactors that had occurred in the other two cities. During the revolutionary war as many as three thousand slaves joined the British forces and were evacuated in 1783. That number was larger than the free black population of New York in 1790, which numbered only 1,011 people.[38] Thus militance had cost blacks white allies and also deprived the postrevolutionary community of a great deal of elan.

Those blacks remaining in New York City after the revolutionary war initially were rewarded by the early federalists. Such rewards were short-lived because the waning of federalist power in the early national period brought in its wake a counterattack on the minimal black gains. Militance among black clergy was frowned on by their white supporters. The silencing of the Reverend Peter Williams successfully signaled to black activist clergy the limits of their autonomy.

Two additional brakes on black New Yorker's organizing efforts were the reliance on black pioneers from Philadelphia and Boston and the fact that no black in postrevolutionary New York had the charisma or the visions of Richard Allen or Thomas Paul. Peter Vogelsang, Peter

Williams, Sr., William Faunces, Rev. Peter Williams, Jr., Christopher Rush, and others, while dedicated to black uplift, were disposed to slower, more conservative methods, especially prior to the late 1820s.

A major reason for slow black organizational growth was the very small number of free blacks in New York. After the revolutionary war the black population grew slowly. At the same time blacks in Boston and Philadelphia were already experimenting with their first organizations. The early New York efforts were limited in vision. For example, once Zion Church became independent of the Methodist Episcopal Church its leaders seemed content to lend support to agitation but not to sponsor new organizations. This was particularly true of Christopher Rush and James Varick, who were more concerned about the community's religious sustenance than about political agitation.[39] Varick was a participant in attacks on the American Colonization Society and in suffrage drives but mostly as a member of a group and as a signer of declarations but not as an individual spokesperson.

The same narrow vision seemed to characterize the Abysinian Baptist Church founded in 1809. Seldom was this church represented in the rough and tumble debates forming in the community. A partial explanation of Abysinian's lack of civic aggressiveness may be attributed to the political style of its founder, Thomas Paul. He was, within Boston, the black leader most willing to work with white benefactors and to work on projects unlikely to alienate whites. Moreover, once he had helped to found Abysinian, Paul seems not to have been a major factor in its development. Paul was certainly a leader in developing the contacts between Haiti and American blacks, but he emphasized the missionary element of the connection and ignored Haiti's potential as an alternative to the designs of the American Colonization Society.

Ironically, it was black New York City clergymen with the least autonomy who provided the greatest challenge to the status quo. Operating within white denominations that, by their silence, had given tacit consent to slavery and discrimination, put these men at risk. What was true for clergymen was equally true for black businessmen, particularly those catering to a white clientele. Prior to 1830 most whites supported the ACS, and so blacks seeking licenses, certifications, and good standing could be jeopardized by black agitation. Despite the real and imagined threat, black leaders persisted. When one of their number was circumscribed by white organizations, black leaders found alternatives. Although the Reverend Peter Williams was censured for his agitation against ACS, others persisted.[40] Theodore Wright and Samuel Cornish continued until the end of their lives to work against the ACS.

Before his forced resignation from a number of black reform groups Peter Williams, Jr., had been in the vanguard of black leadership. One of his earliest organizational activities involved the founding of the

Haytian Emigration Society of Coloured People in 1824.[41] He took a leading role in this association whose purpose was to help blacks relocate to the island. Williams was assisted in the task by a board of managers that included other prominent black agitators.[42] Like most blacks, Williams abhorred white forced colonization but he understood some blacks' desires to leave America. Without accepting the negative characterization of blacks circulated by ACS, Williams did act as an agent for black inspired colonization. He even visited Haiti in 1824 to ascertain, first hand, the conditions for black emigrants. One of the more interesting members of Williams's association was the Reverend Samuel Cornish. This stint in the Haytian Emigration Society of Coloured People appears to have been his only affiliation with supporting colonization, black or white. By 1827 Cornish was a confirmed anti-emigrationist and ultimately became the most outspoken foe of all forms of emigration.

The New Yorkers' militance from the mid-1820s on can be seen in their responses to two acute pressures on antebellum New York. First, much of their organizational thrust and competence was channeled into the suffrage fight. In 1821 blacks in the city and state, as the result of the new constitution, were faced with new restrictions barring access to the franchise. While the black vote was not eliminated the new property and residence requirements severely reduced the number of eligible black voters. From 1821 through 1865 blacks in the state organized petition drives, political lobbying, interviews with governors, and political education to restore their right to vote. Although unsuccessful in restoring the franchise to its pre-1821 accessibilty, the campaigns demonstrated the black ability not only to organize but also to sustain a political campaign.

Second, the continued activity of ACS conspired to test black organizing abilities. But until the 1850s this fight did not result in the creation of new organizations. Samuel Cornish and Theodore Wright directed their agitation toward the holding of conventions and the publishing of newspapers and magazines rather than specific organizations. Yet we must consider their efforts in the 1830s and 1840s as part of the maturation of black organizational skills. Given the difficulty of travel, the limited resources, the hostility of whites toward blacks objecting to colonization, the well-publicized successes of ACS, and the fact that black leaders never had the luxury of one-issue fights, the energy and dedication of Wright and Cornish were amazing. They were able to hold meetings in almost every northern locale where colonization was discussed. They were adept at finding disgruntled blacks who had returned from Africa and were willing to tell the story of their disillusionment.[43]

In the 1850s, following the enactment of the New Fugitive Slave Law, New Yorkers re-entered the emigration discussions. In 1850 Haiti commanded less of the New Yorkers' attention than it had in the 1820s, probably because for all its longevity the Haitian-black American connection had not made the island republic very attractive. Instead, New Yorkers turned their focus to Liberia, which produced a number of organizations. The African Civilization Society founded in 1858 was the most powerful and the most controversial.[44] Rev. Henry Highland Garnet, the founder, provided much of the strength for the new organization. Simultaneously, his charisma and some shadowy features about the society drew criticism. Much of the critical thrust came from the suspicion that the Civilization Society was a front for the old nemisis of blacks—the ACS. Although not as publicized as the Civilization Society, two other organizations had preceded its existence.

Immediately following passage of the new slave act blacks Louis Putnam, acting as a one-man organization founded the United African Republic Emigration Society. By 1853, after having experienced two name changes in its brief life, the organization was defunct. In the three years of its existence, however, Putnam's New York and Liberian Emigration and Agricultural Association had expended much energy. In 1852 Putnam succeeded in sending fifteen hundred dollars worth of goods to Liberia. These items were supposedly for the one hundred farmers who the organization hoped would follow. As part of the flurry of activity Putnam requested that Congress provide $25,000 for the purchase of land, outfitting, and preparing emigrants to go to Liberia. While no funds came from the United States government the Liberian government did provide six hundred acres for the projected emigrants. Putnam's organization was unable to take advantage of the Liberian government's offer.

In opposition to leaving the United States, the Committee of Thirteen made up of blacks from professional and business backgrounds was more successful than Putnam and his various groups.[45] As an immediate response to the Fugitive Slave Law, John T. Zuille called a meeting which resulted in the committee's formation. The committee included T. J. White and Phillip A. Bell as secretaries. Dr. James McCune Smith served as treasurer. Other members were the father-and-son combination of Thomas and George Downing, Junius Morel, J. T. Raymond, and William J. Wilson. These men were powerful black business and civic leaders. Their Philadelphia counterparts were leaders such as Octavius V. Catto, William White, Jr., and William Whipper. In Boston the new middle class leadership was represented by Benjamin Roberts, John Hilton, James G. Barbadoes, and others.

New York's Governor Hunt provided a cause and a major triumph for the Committee of Thirteen. In his annual message to the legislature, in 1850, Hunt requested funds to support the ACS. Subsequent to that speech John Zuille and James McCune Smith, acting for the committee,

called for a convention in Albany to confront the governor. The committee prepared and circulated a long address to blacks in New York state.
They then met with the governor and roundly criticized his plan. As a
result of the meeting no bill was ever introduced that incorporated funding for ACS. By 1853 the Committee of Thirteen had disbanded but several of its members were to figure prominently in the reactions to the
African Civilization Society.

Robert Hamilton, one of the Committee of Thirteen, had apparently
changed his mind by 1858 and supported Garnet and the African
Civilization Society. James McCune Smith, a boyhood friend of Garnet's,
nevertheless voiced strong opposition to the group.[46] George Downing,
another of the Committee of Thirteen, also opposed Garnet. The ensuing conflicts were played out in newspapers and conventions until the
beginning of the Civil War. Both black and white newspapers termed
the 1850s fight over colonization a low point in black leadership.
Although the African Civilization Society was defunct by the outbreak of
the Civil War, the battle between Garnet and McCune Smith continued.
By 1861 Garnet had switched his allegience to James Redpath's Haitian
Exposition. Garnet's choices were, to a degree, unfortunate: the
Civilization Society was tainted by Garnet's autocratic behavior and its
alleged connection with ACS; and although James Redpath was the official agent of the Haitian government, he held some negative perceptions
about blacks.[47]

. Many antiblack white officials applauded the black conflict. Many
blacks were embarrassed. Neither group was accurate in its assessments.
Prejudiced whites generalized about all black activities from the one conflict over colonization. Blacks lamented the loss of unity and vitality that
they thought the fight symbolized. Actually, there was both unity and
vitality in antebellum New York's black community. It was this same
period that also witnessed the evolution of black literary societies.
Despite the militance and pugnaciousness of the New Yorkers on colonization, the development of many literary societies proceeded peacefully as it had in Philadelphia and Boston during the same period.

VI

Long years of sustained agitation on a variety of issues with shifting
emphasis and changing personnel had inculcated in blacks the desirability of not only diversified organizational activity but also the necessity to
organize around specific issues. During the violently antiblack 1850s,
blacks in Boston demonstrated their grasp of organizational techniques
and the linkages between various issues and organizations. Little if any
stress was encountered as blacks moved from fraternal, social welfare, or
educational societies to viligance committees and an open defiance of

the dreaded New Fugitive Slave Law of 1850. From 1790 to 1850 organizational growth and experimentation had been evolutionary and generally characterized by an emphasis on legality. In the emotion-packed 1850s, however, changes became epidemic and organizational activity and growth accelerated accordingly.

Seemingly, black agitators such as William Cooper Nell and Benjamin Roberts moved without pause from abolitionist meetings to petition gatherings; to interracial opposition to the Fugitive Slave Law; to considering and sometimes rejecting membership in newly formed political parties; to writing newspaper columns, pamphlets, histories, opinions at law and organizational broadsides; and to functioning as parents, husbands, and advisors. Most, if not all, of these activities were accompanied by an appropriate organizational structure. Such activity cannot be characterized as ad hoc responses but rather as part of the commitment to changing American society, which was felt by all reformers, black or white, in the antebellum period.

Similarly, the pace of Philadelphia's black organizational activity quickened in the two decades before the Civil War. Much of the Philadelphia activity continued to be characterized by middle and upper-class leadership. For some as yet unexplained reason fugitives never attained the leadership prominence in Philadelphia that they did elsewhere. It is interesting to speculate why this may have been. First, its location so close to Maryland and Delaware may have caused uneasiness in a number of fugitives. Thus they hurried on to more northern locales. This may have been the case for a number of precocious slaves who, like Frederick Douglass, had escaped from Maryland. The families of Henry Highland Garnet and Samuel Ringgold Ward, all Maryland fugitives, also skirted Philadelphia.

Second, by the 1840s prominent black Philadelphia families had for several decades served as the social and political arbiters for the community. This upper echelon had seemingly indoctrinated its youth into a sense of leadership. Son followed father in directing both the family business and the community's political life. Such was the case particularly with the Jacob C. White family. Perhaps more than in any other black communities, women of prominent families in Philadelphia were more accepted in public roles. Certainly, Philadelphia had its male chauvinist traditions and enclaves. Why else would it have been necessary in the 1840s for the Gilbert Lyceum to continually refer to its status as the city's only educational society that accepted males and females on an equal basis? Thus in Philadelphia there existed perhaps as early as the time of Richard Allen a leadership class whose membership was based on attainments, wealth, family position, and acquired status. Even the least perceptive fugitive would quickly have understood his or her limited options in Philadelphia.

For the most part the elite black leadership seemed little interested in integrating fugitives into leadership cadres. After the war, in 1867, an interesting confrontation between William Still and Jacob C. White, Jr., revealed some of the class antagonisms, which had gone on even earlier, after Still received a dun letter for back dues to the Pythian Baseball Club. He wrote White a letter excoriating the club's interest in the frivolity of baseball while "our people daily starve at the South."[48] Yet Still had been roundly, although privately, criticized for his arrogance and paternalism toward fugitives. During the war Still helped publicize the exciting escapes of Henry "Box" Brown and William and Ellen Craft, but none of them was invited to remain in Philadelphia and take part in directing the "underground." It seems the only fugitive whom Still got close to personally was Harriet Tubman, but her restless, peripetetic personality precluded her from being a threat to Still's position. White reformers, too, commented unfavorably on Still's dictatorial and haughty ways. Thus class status and personality limited the opportunities for new leadership to develop independently in black Philadelphia.

Moreover, by the 1840s the institutional infrastructure of Philadelphia's black community was set. This is not to suggest that organizational growth became stagnant. New organizations after 1840 differed in degree not in kind. For example lyceums and debating societies proliferated but no new informal educational formats were introduced. Those organizations founded after 1840 fit into an already existing pattern, and the organizational network of black Philadelphia expanded horizontally rather than vertically. Because the upper and middle classes were substantial, new avenues of leadership were still limited for fugitives.

Even those subtle changes in outlook, structure, and mission that were occurring in black organizations did not incorporate fugitive slaves. In antebellum Philadelphia fraternal organizations, for example, began moving slowly toward incorporating themselves into business enterprises. After all they had started in part to give financial counsel and security to their membership. By the 1830s that role had enlarged to include employment agencies, advocating vocational training, counseling thrift, and economic tips to the whole community. By the 1850s expanding economic opportunity, the failure of several family businesses, and the continued lack of interest by white financial institutions contributed to the transformation of social/political societies into business groups. Membership in business as in social clubs was still based on recommendation, approval, and probation and was principally limited to an already existing social clique.

While access to membership in new business ventures limited the role of fugitive slaves it probably intensified the process of institutional specialization more quickly in black Philadelphia than elsewhere. At the beginning of the war and lasting until the 1890s several black businesses were organized on a joint stock company basis. Among these were a lumber and coal company, a shipbuilding enterprise, and several small insurance companies. Although the White family's real estate and mercantile holdings were increasing, they survived as a family business partly by bringing more generations into the activity. Family businesses and financial organizations built on prior social fraternal bases did not provide ready access to all levels of black society. Thus the leadership profile of antebellum Philadelphia was top heavy with representatives of the middle and upper classes.

It is nonsensical to argue that black capitalist enterprises should have been any more democratic than capitalist organizations were generally. What is clear is that by 1840 black Philadelphia reflected the structure of most American communities. At the level of community consciousness they were also strikingly similar, indicating that the lower or unrepresented black masses either accepted or were indifferent to the recognized leadership cadre. Therefore, there were no direct challenges to this privileged leadership class. Lack of opposition to the upper-class leadership cannot be deemed complacency in the working class. Rather it speaks more accurately to the fact that the leadership had identified, spoken to, and attempted to resolve those problems blacks shared regardless of their class status.

Equally important, the leadership class itself was not monolithic and much healthy in-fighting went on concerning tactics, emphasis, and use of energy. Philadelphia blacks disagreed over such issues as a national newspaper, emigration, legal or extralegal fugitive slave activity, the extent and choice of political participation, and countless other issues. Corresponding factions grew up around each issue. Since the practice of founding organizations permeated American society during the period of reform, societies, clubs, and associations profliferated in the black community. Thus lower-class Philadelphia blacks had a multitude of choices through which to express their political preferences.

Nor was the working class totally without organizations of its own. Several working-class societies took the initiative in attempting to organize for workmen's rights. In 1829 the Humane Mechanics Society began with a membership of sixty-five, and collected $195 annually in dues. As part of its mission the society attempted to provide survivor and sick benefits to its members. Thus the working class duplicated the structure and mission of the privileged class when forming its own societies. It must be noted that lower-class organizing efforts were mostly in the economic sphere. As the most pressing issues of their lives were related to supporting themselves, less energy was given to purely social or political causes. A degree of leisure seems to have been a necessary accompaniment to a wide ranging organizational focus.

In contrast to the Humane Mechanics Society the Agricultural and Mechanics Association pursued a more expanded agenda. In part this was possible because its list of subscribers and supporters included members of the upper classes. As we have seen with Jacob C. White, wealth was not based on his labor in agriculture or mechanics, yet he was enrolled as a member. It is difficult to determine his actual involvement with the association but some interesting facts about the organization have survived. Again, in contrast to the Humane Mechanics whose membership list was private, this association published frequently a partial membership list. Included were a number of White's peers such as Charles Bustill, John Douglass, and James McCrummell. By 1839 the list of subscribers also included a few females, Elizabeth Ann Bias, Ruth Harding, and Edith Miller.

More than workingmen's rights and survivor benefits were involved in the Agricultural and Mechanics Association. The inclusion of middle-class leaders meant that the group sponsored and participated in a range of reform acitivtes. In addition, the Association's format provided for upper-and working-class interaction. In short the black elite could not and did not choose only issues that supported its own self-interest. While promoting race elevation and consciousness it was also necessary to stay aware of class interests and divisions within black Philadelphia. Although inherently conservative in its social/political perceptions the privileged class had to maintain a degree of the common touch.[49]

In antebellum America no national political party espoused a full-scale recruitment of blacks. Thus no separate group of "representative men" emerged in the three cities who were more closely related to national politics than to black grassroots needs. For that matter, no national party or party bloc supported the call for women's suffrage which emanated from the Seneca Falls Convention in 1848. Middle-class black leaders seemed to follow a national norm in not counting on the interest and support of elements outside their own socioeconomic class. In this they were neither more radical nor more conservative than their white male counterparts. Thus, racial and gender politics along with class ideologies conspired to keep the black working class aware of and at least loosely attached to the positions and pronouncements of the black elite leadership group.

While racial and class politics acted as a brake on independent working-class activities, some pressures also operated to keep middle-class leaders from becoming overly tied to white leaders. Although some interracial cooperation was promoted by the 1830s there existed simultaneously a system of criticism which attempted to control the degree to which cooperation became co-optation. In Boston and Philadelphia several blacks were singled out for adhering too closely to white paternal direction. William Cooper Nell was criticized frequently for seeming too much under the control of William Lloyd Garrison. Philadelphia blacks also frequently reminded William Still how he seemed to be following a course separate from the majority of his black contemporaries.

Black class interests were to a degree blurred by the differences in perception between black reformers and their white counterparts. White reformers seemed one-dimensional in their focus on slavery. While slavery greatly shaped the northern black's quality of life, discrimination was a more present danger. It was left to the black elite leadership to attack the twin evils of slavery and discrimination, and the black masses more closely identified with this black elite and emulated them when possible. Appropriate focusing on discrimination was more important than exclusion from upper-class social/political organizations. Despite the chasm between white leaders and the bulk of the black community, among the leadership cooperation and simultaneous conflict seemed to be the norm.

Beyond the interaction of black and white abolitionists a high level of cultural interaction was characteristic among black and white activists and their white benefactors. This interaction can be glimpsed not only in the late eighteenth-century connection between Richard Allen and Benjamin Rush but also in the experiences of the eighteenth-century white members of New York's Phoenix Society. There also seemed a substantial cross-fertilization of ideas between white and black activists. For example, America during the antebellum period might be termed a society of joiners. White reformers who envisioned a method for changing American society for the better, even when they retarded certain developments, quickly arranged an organizational framework. So, too, did black activists. As with whites, black activists quickly formed local, regional, and national associations to publicize their particular actions.

Further evidence of the cultural interactions between black and white can be noted in the secularization of reform activities. While churchmen such as Theodore Wright, Samuel Cornish, and Samuel Ringgold Ward continued their agitation, most black leaders emerging in the three cities after 1830 were not dependent on the church for either their livelihood or for a following. This change toward secular leadership and a worldly ideology was mirrored by similar changes in American reform. Conservative Protestant evangelicalism in white American reform also gave way to the more worldly concerns of John Humphrey Noyes, William Lloyd Garrison, the Grimke sisters, and others more focused on practical ways to achieve perfection.[50]

One must avoid the easy generalization that one group copied the other's lead. It is more accurate to see black and white reform as responses to the same historical forces of change, modernization, territorial expansion, the extension of slavery, and economic and political change.[51] Given the similarity of resources to react to these changes black and white reformers generally responded in like fashion. What they shared was the ability to, without the necessity of large initial capital outlays, found associations committed to promulgating their ideas. Not all reformers, black or white, were committed to the whole spectrum of reform; most had one central interest and several auxiliaries. Thus blacks tended to focus primarily but not exclusively on combating slavery and discrimination. Those two causes, however, did not encompass the whole of black concerns. We must reject the idea that the black community's concerns never got beyond the two causes.[52] A third pressure compelling black community organizing can be simply stated as human need. This incorporated the necessity for providing and obtaining human services; the requirement of distributing goods and information; the responsibility of articulating who black people were; and the mission of effectively creating leadership.

While not following a smoothly banked progression, organizational growth in the three cities presents some clearly discerned patterns. As with the growth of the church, there are examples of uneven development. None of the cities experienced all of the phases of institutional growth at the same time. In some instances there were stronger emphases on certain phases. For example Boston clearly reflects the developments of assistance from outsiders, the achievement of finding public voices, and a concentration on internal refinements and the founding of new specialized organizations. Boston, on the other hand, is less associated with the phase of white recognition of the legitimacy and impact of black organizations. Too often when blacks and whites addressed the same or similar causes it was the white spokespeople and organizations that caught the public's attention. Abolition is a good case in point: While William Lloyd Garrison worked closely with Boston's blacks and was less critical of them than of Frederick Douglass, his observations and utterances were those that were circulated in the abolitionist as well as the oppositionist press. In Boston the last phase—the search for and manipulation of power—came later than in the other two cities. Still, Boston blacks seemed more prone to accept white allies throughout the community-building process than were blacks elsewhere. Blacks working for relocation in Boston continued to interact with whites when the same whites, had been basically ignored by blacks in New York and Philadelphia.

Finally, whether working with whites or strictly with other blacks, the black impulse toward organizing provided an atmosphere, an infrastructure, and several methodologies that satisfied local needs. Successful organizing at the local level became the bedrock in the birth of visibility and voice at the national level. The chief results of local organizing efforts were the national manifestations of visibility and voice promoting the birth of black newspapers, the convention movement, and the development of black ideologies.

Notes

1. James E. Blackwell, *The Black Community: Diversity and Unity* (New York: Dodd, Mead and Company, 1975), 15. Blackwell is critical of the emphasis on homeostasis and equalibrium pioneered by Parsons, see Talcott Parsons, *The Social System* (New York: The Free Press, 1951); and Walter Buckley, *Sociology and Modern Systems Theory* (Englewood Cliffs, N.J.: Prentice-Hall, 1967).

2. Ibid., 4. See also Robert K. Merton, "Insiders and Outsiders: A Chapter in the Sociology of Knowledge," *American Journal of Sociology* 78, no.1 (July 1972): 9-47; Robert Blauner, "Internal Colonialism and Ghetto Revolt," Social Problems 16, no. 4 (Spring 1969): 393-408; W.E.B. DuBois, *The Philadelphia Negro: A Social Study* (New York: Schocken Books, 1967).

3. Blackwell, *The Black Community*; W.E.B. Dubois, "The Negro and Social Reconstruction" in *Against Racism: Unpublished Essays, Papers, Addresses, 1887-1961,* Herbert Aptheker, ed. (Amherst: The University of Massachusetts Press, 1985), 104-113; E. Franklin Frazier, *The Negro Family in the United States* (Chicago: University of Chicago Press, 1948), 15, passim; Robert Staples, *Introduction to Black Sociology* (New York: McGraw-Hill, 1976), 3, 89, passim; and Robert L. Allen, *Reluctant Reformers: Racism and Social Reform in the United States* (Washington, D.C.: Howard University Press, 1974), 11-48.

4. Prince Hall, *A Charge Delivered to the Brethen of the African Lodge 6 June 1792.* (Boston: The Bible and Heart, 1792).

5. Petition to Governor Hutchinson and The Massachusetts General Court, Boston, 6 January 1773, Massachusetts State Archives. See also Sidney Kaplan, *The Black Presence in the Era of the American Revolution, 1770-1800* (Washington, D.C.: Smithsonian Institution,1973), 11, and Dorothy Porter, ed. *Early Negro Writing, 1760-1837* (Boston: Beacon Press, 1971), 254-55.

6. Porter, *Early Negro Writing*, 255.

7. Ibid.

8. Ibid.

9. Ibid.

10. Ibid.; Donald M. Jacobs, *A History of the Boston Negro from the Revolution to the Civil War* (Ph.d. dissertation, Boston University,1968), 31-35.

11. Petition to the Massachusetts General Court, 4 January 1787, Massachusetts State Archives; Kaplan, *Black Presence,* 186; Lorenzo J. Greene, "Prince Hall: Massachusetts Leader in Crisis" *Freedomways* 1, no. 3 (Fall 1961): 238-40.

12. Kaplan, *Black Presence*, 189.

13. Jedidiah Morse, *A Discourse Delivered at the African-Meeting House in Boston, July 14, 1808, in Grateful Celebration of the Abolition of the African Slave-Trade By the Governments of the United States, Great Britain and Denmark* (Boston: Lincoln and Edmands, 1808), 13-18; William Minot, *Address Delevered at the Dedication of the Smith School House in Belknap Street, 3 March 1835,* (Boston: Webster and Southard, 1835), 3-5; Abner Forbes, *A Few Friendly Suggestions to the Colored People of Boston*

(Boston: Webster and Southard, 1835); and John S.J. Gardiner, *A Sermon Preached Before the African Society on the 14th of July 1810, the Anniversary of the Abolition of the Slave Trade* (Boston: Munroe and Francis, 1810).

14. Prince Hall, *A Charge Delivered to the African Lodge 24 June 1797* (Boston: Menotomy Lodge, 1797), 2-5; Hosea Easton, *A Treatise on the Intellectual Character and Civil and Political Condition of the Colored People of the United States and the Prejudice Exercised Toward Them* (Boston: Isaac Knapp, 1837), 5; William Grimshaw, *Official History of Freemasonry Among the Colored People in North America* (New York: n.p., 1903), 64-87.

15. Hall, *A Charge, 1797*; William A. Muraskin, *Middle-class Blacks in a White Society: Prince Hall Freemasonry in America* (Berkeley: University of California Press, 1975), 22-23.

16. Hall, *A Charge 1792,* 2.

17. Ibid., 5.

18. Muraskin, *Middle-Class,*162; Jacobs, *Boston Negro,* 42; John Daniels, *In Freedom's Birthplace: A Study of the Boston Negroes* (Boston: Houghton Mifflin, 1914), 21-26.

19. Daniels, *In Freedom's Birthplace;* Jacobs, *Boston Negro,* 42-44.

20. Henry Highland Garnet, *Walker's Appeal, with a Brief Sketch of His Life* (New York: J.H. Tobitt, 1848); James Oliver Horton and Lois E. Horton, *Black Bostonians: Family Life and Community Struggle in the Antebellum North* (New York: Holmes and Meier Publishers, Inc., 1979,) 57, 81, 101; Charles M. Wiltse, ed., *David Walker's Appeal* (New York: Hill and Wang, 1965), 7, 9, 11; Herbert Aptheker, *"One Continual Cry" David Walker's Appeal to the Colored Citizens of the World (1829-1830) Its Setting and Its Meaning* (New York: Humanities Press, 1965), 45-53; Sterling Stuckey, *Slave Culture: Nationalist Theory and the Foundations of Black America* (New York: Oxford University Press, 1987), 98-137.

21. Benjamin Rush, *An Account of the Bilious Remitting Yellow Fever, as it Appeared in the City of Philadelphia, in the Year 1793,* 2d ed. (Philadelphia: Thomas Dobson, 1794); *Proceedings of the Committee Appointed on the 14th of September, 1793, by the Citizens of Philadelphia, the Northen Liberties, and the District of Southwark, to Attend to and Alleviate the Sufferings of Those Afflicted with Malignant Fever, Prevalent in the City and Its Vicinity* (Philadelphia: Select and Common Councils of the City of Philadelphia, 1848); Carol V.R. George, *Segregated Sabbaths: Richard Allen and the Emergence of Independent Black Churches, 1760-1840* (New York: Oxford University Press, 1973), 123; Charles H. Wesley, *Richard Allen: Apostle of Freedom* (Washington, D.C.: The Associated Publishers, Inc., 1935), Julie Winch, *Philadelphia's Black Elite, Activism, Accomodation, and the Struggle for Autonomy, 1787-1848* (Philadelphia: Temple University Press, 1988), 10, 15-17.

22. Winch, *Philadelphia's Black Elite,* 15-18; George, *Segregated Sabbaths*; Walker, *Rock in a Weary Land: The African Methodist Episcopal Church During the Civil War and Reconstruction* (Baton Rouge: Louisiana State University Press, 1978), 5-8, 16-19; Gary B. Nash, *Forging Freedom: The Formation of Philadelphia's Black Community, 1720-1840* (Cambridge, Mass.: Harvard University Press, 1988), 123.

23. Matthew Carey, *A Short Account of the Malignant Fever, Lately Prevelant in Philadelphia: With a Statement of the Proceedings That Took Place on the Subject in Different Parts of the United States* (Philadelphia. The Author, 1793).

24 Richard Allen and Absalom Jones, *A Narrative of the Proceedings of the Black People, during the late Awful Calamity in Philadelphia, in the year 1793 and the refutation of some Censures Thrown Upon Them in some late Publications* (Philadelphia: William W. Woodward, 1794).

25. Wesley, *Richard Allen,* 102; Unpublished letter of Benjamin Rush, 29 December 1793 in *Magazine of American History,* January-June 1892, 27.

26. Wesley, *Richard Allen,* 95.

27. Ibid., 150, 160, passim.; *Minute book of the United Daughters of Tapsico 1823-1849* Papers of Mother Bethel, Historical Society of Pennsylvania, microfilm 8, and Tapsico X

28. *Minute Book.*

29. Winch, Philadelphia's Black Elite, 192, 193; Gerda Lerner, ed., *Black Women in America: A Documentary History* (New York: Oxford University Press, 1974), 362-64; Maria W. Stewart, *Productions of Mrs Maria W. Stewart* (Boston: Friends of Freedom and Virtue, 1835), 15-17.

30. Lerner, *Black Women,* 83-85; *Genius of Universal Emancipation* (March 1832): 162-63; *Liberator,* 7 January 1832; Bert James Loewenberg and Ruth Bogin, eds., *Black Women in Nineteenth Century American Life: Their Words, Their Thoughts, Their Feelings* (University Park: Pennsylvania State University Press, 1976), 21, 183.

31. Lerner, *Black Women,* 83-85; Loewenberg and Bogin, *Black Women in Nineteenth Century,* 21, 23, 184; Marilyn Richardson, *Maria W. Stewart: America's First Black Woman Political Writer: Essays and Speeches* (Bloomington: Indiana University Press, 1987), 21-22; Paula Giddings, *When and Where I Enter: The Impact of Black Women on Race and Sex in America* (New York: William Morrow, 1984), 49-51; Porter, *Early Negro Writing,* 129-40.

32. Richardson, *Maria W. Stewart,* 70-73; *Liberator,* 28 September 1833.

33. See the *Liberator,* 1832-1835 for numerous references to PAFIS without identifying any individual; Lerner, *Black Women,* 437-39.

34. Joseph Wilson, *Sketchs of the Higher Classes of Colored Society in Philadelphia* (Philadelphia: Merrihew and Thompson, 1841), 96-109 lists the following: The Phildelphia Library Company of Colored Persons (1833), The Rush Library Company and Debating Society (1836), Demosthenian Institute (1839), Minerva Literary Society (1834), Gilbert Lyceum (1841).

35. Carleton Mabee, "A Negro Boycott to Integrate Boston Schools," *The New England Quarterly* 41, no. 3, (1968): 341-61; *Boston Public School for Colored Children Scrapbook* Manuscripts, Boston Public Library; *Report of the Annual Examination of the Public Schools, Boston, 1948* Documents, Massachusetts Historical Society, 5, 29b; James Oliver Horton, "Generations of Protest: Black Families and Social Reform in Ante-Bellum Boston," *The New England Quarterly* 49, no. 2 (1976): 250.

36. Hon. Richard Fletcher, "Opinion on the Rights of Colored Children in Common Schools," *The Commom School Journal* no. 20 (1844): 326-28; William B. Fowle, *Letter to Hon. Horace Mann,* 11 July 1844,

Massachusetts Historical Society; Arthur O. White, "Salem's Antebellum Black Community: Seedbed of the School Integration Movement," *Essex Institute Historical Collections* 108, no. 2 (April 1972): 114.

37. *Boston Atlas,* 28 June 1844, 6; William H. Pease and Jane H. Pease, *They Who Would Be Free: Blacks' Search for Freedom, 1830-1861* (New York: Atheneum, 1974), 26, 153-55;

38. Rhoda Golden Freeman, *The Free Negro in New York City in the Era Before the Civil War* (Ph.d. diss., Columbia University, 1966), 16.

39. Bishop James Walker Hood, *One Hundred Years of the African Methodist Episcopal Zion Church, or The Centennial of African Methodism* (New York: AMEZ Book Concern, 1895); William J. Walls, *The African Methodist Episcopa; Church: Reality of the Black Church* (Charlotte, North Carolina: AMEZ Publishing House, 1974); Aaron Hamlet Payne, "The Negro in New York Prior to 1860," *The Howard Review* 1, no.1 (June 1923): 60.

40. Peter Williams, "To the Citizens of New York," *New York Spectator,* 15 July 1834, Bishop Benjamin T. Onderdonk's letter of 12 July 1834 requesting Williams' resignation following critical remarks about the American Colonization Society and an attack on Williams' church during rioting in New York City earlier in the month. The Onderdonk letter and Williams' resignation are contained in several anthologies. See Milton W. Sernett, ed., *Afro-American Religious History: A Documentary Witness* (Durham, North Carolina: Duke University Press, 1985), 196-202.

41. Williams, *New York Spectator,* 197-98; Freeman, *The Free Negro,* 28-29; Robert A. Bennett, "Black Episcopalians: A History From the Colonial Period to the Present," *Historical Magazine of the Protestant Episcopal Church* 43, no. 3 (September 1974): 237.

42. Freeman, *The Free Negro,* 28-29 lists the following members: Rev. Samuel E. Cornish, James Varick, Thomas L. Jennings (also Jinnings), Samuel Ennalls, Peter Vogelsang, Thomas Sipkins, Boston Crummel

43. Samuel E. Cornish and Theodore S. Wright, *The Colonization Scheme Considered* (Newark: A. Guest, 1840); David E. Swift, "Black Presbyterian Attacks on Racism: Samuel Cornish, Theodore Wright and Their Contemporaries," *Journal of Presbyterian History* 51, no. 4 (Winter 1973): 433, passim.; *Freedom's Journal* and *The Rights of All* contained some of Cornish's most compelling writing against colonization.

44. Freeman, *The Free Negro,* 49-63; Robert C. Dick, *Black Protest, Issues and Tactics* (Westport, Conn;. Greenwood Press, 1974), 12-22; Pease and Pease, *They Who Would Be Free*; and Frederick Douglass, *Douglass' Monthly* (February 1859): 3.

45. Freeman , *The Free Negro,* 46-50.

46. Ibid.

47. Michael Meyer, "Thoreau and Black Emigration," *American Literature* 53, no.3, (November 1981): 386-87; David M. Dean, *Defender of the Race: James Theodore Holly, Black Nationalist Bishop* (Boston: Lambeth Press, 1979), 33-34, 37.

48. *Letters* between Jacob C. White, Jr. and William Still in March 1869 are in the Pythian Baseball Club file, Leon C. Gardiner Collection, Historical Society of Pennsylvania.

49. Winch, *Philadelphia's Black Elite.*

50. Raymond G. Walters, *American Reformers, 1815-1860* (New York: Hill and Wang, 1978), 61-75.
51. Ibid.
52. George A. Levesque, "Inherent Reformers, Inherited Orthodoxy: Black Baptists in Boston, 1800-1873" *Journal of Negro History* 60, no. 4 (October 1975): 491-92.

4

Black Newspapers: Defenders of the Community Establishing and Maintaining a Public Voice

By the first quarter of the nineteenth century blacks in New York, Boston, and Philadelphia could choose among a number of activities to help meet their human needs. They could, for example, seek out a number of black social welfare organizations to assist them in times of trouble. Equally important, the church movement had expanded, and blacks could worship in their own congregations and lead their own houses of worship. Moreover, the church had squarely placed itself in the forefront of defending the community. It had been, after all, part of the instigating force that had called the 1817 convention in response to the American Colonization Society. The 1817 convention would later serve as the model for national leadership conclaves.

Even with this burgeoning institutional structure the black community was without representation in the print media. No city with a black population boasted a black newspaper. If organizations and churches had newsletters their distribution was severely restricted. Few big-city newspapers devoted much space to activities in the black community. When news of the community did reach print it was usually derogatory in nature. Quite apart from racist attacks, the community suffered in other ways because of the absence of its own newspaper. Only a few black businesses were able to advertise in white papers, and that privilege was usually restricted to black businesses that catered to a white clientele. Absence of an advertising venue constituted a double jeopardy for blacks. Black entrepreneurs were denied one of the basic avenues to advertising their products and maximizing their profits. Black consumers, on the other hand, were limited in their knowledge of and access to black merchants.

I

In keeping with the focus of the work we will concern ourselves with the development of black newspapers in the cities of New York, Boston, and Philadelphia. Newspapers performed several important functions that complemented the move toward black awareness.[1] This chapter will discuss the growth and importance of black newspapers and how papers reflected the community, or a significant segment of the community, and how they felt about issues confronting them. Some attention will be given to the fact of uneven development in black newspapers. Of the three cities, only New York developed viable black newspapers before the Civil War, but Philadelphia and Boston played vital roles in the dissemination of news to blacks around the country, and to supporting black newspapers and white organs devoted to issues of black interest.

Although the restrictions on economic opportunities and political news were important, lack of their own newspaper exacerbated other debilitating features of American life for black people. In certain ways a newspaper speaks to the idealization that a community holds of itself. Blacks had little hope of projecting that ideal self-image to the wider world or for informing themselves and shaping their own identity. They lost, therefore, an opportunity to penetrate the racism, the indifference, and the ignorance of the majority populations' stereotypes. Moreover, without a newspaper it was difficult, but not impossible, for blacks to form and shape a consistent public image. Part of a newspaper's mission was to inform a people and others about its life, its activities, and its aspirations; it was equally important for a newspaper to interpret the life of a community. This constellation of functions—shaping a public self-image, informing blacks about their own activities, and interpreting black life through a black controlled media—were all missing in black America before 1827.

In the years between the founding of *Freedom's Journal* in 1827 and the end of the Civil War, the black press made a valiant effort to represent the community. Not only did the papers defend the race but they also catered to its need to know itself, and to chronicle its existence and activities. Undoubtedly, political news and the defense of blacks were the most important functions of black journalism, but matters social, educational, cultural, and historical were not omitted. Political debate, social reform, economic ideas, and development of a consensus on important issues constituted the important focus of black news in antebellum America. To see only the crusading political modality of the black newspapers is to miss much of its essence.

Phillis Wheatley's problems in getting a volume of poetry published offer an interesting cultural look at the jeopardy of the community not having a print media voice. Even after she had acquired an international reputation, Phillis Wheatley's talents were questioned and denigrated in the white Boston dailies.

The attack on Wheatley was so vehement that no publisher could be persuaded to publish her volume of poems in 1773. Although she had obtained subscriptions and attestations proclaiming her authenticity as a poet, the negative mood prevailed. Apparently occasional offerings from Wheatley were acceptable but a volume of poems was beyond the pale. In Wheatley's Boston there were no black institutions or newspapers available to defend her talent or to lobby for publication. It was her mistress, Mrs. Susana Wheatley, who had the power and resources to arrange publication of the volume. This was completed in England rather than in Boston. Once successfully published in England, Boston printers were less reluctant to be involved. As Wheatley's private correspondence indicates, publication of her book did not still the criticism.[2] Without a black newspaper or a black church, and Boston in 1773 had neither, Phillis Wheatley lacked public institutional means to respond to her critics.

Most black Americans between 1773 and 1827 pursued more mundane tasks than Phillis Wheatley. Yet they were similarly affected by the lack of their own newspapers. Not only did blacks face restrictions on gathering race news, but the simple expedient of writing a letter to the editor was generally unavailable. In the years before 1827, most white dailies would charge a black letter writer for the privilege of having his or her letter appear in print.

City editors possessed several methods for determining the race of the letter writer. None of the devices was foolproof but taken together they could produce fairly accurate results. First, an editor could check the correspondent's address. Black housing in nineteenth-century urban America was pretty restrictive. Even when blacks physically occupied the same neighborhood as whites, usually they were confined to residing in alleys and courts of the district.[3] Restricted living quarters generally affected the middle class and working class alike. Second, the letter's contents might serve to identify its writer. If the letter was a defense of the black community it could generally be assumed that the writer was black. White defenders of black causes, while not absent, were few in number and easily identifiable because their novel social actions were generally known in the community. This was particularly true in the postrevolutionary war period. In New York federalists such as John Jay and Alexander Hamilton were identified as supporters of black rights. Philadelphia had Benjamin Franklin, Benjamin Rush, some Quakers, and a few others who were liberal on questions of the race's right to legal protection. In Boston clergymen, some individuals of means, and especially Baptist churchmen such as the Reverend Dr. Samuel Stillman and the Reverend Dr. Thomas Baldwin, could be found defending black civil rights. Most whites in Boston and elsewhere preferred to remain silent.

If the first two methods failed to identify the race of the individual, the techniques had not been exhausted. Editors could always resort to dispatching a worker to seek out the letter writer to make an assessment of race based on physical appearance. Sometimes editors simply billed the correspondent with a notation that as soon as payment was received in full the item would appear. If no response was forthcoming or if an indignant letter followed, judgments could be made accordingly. Money was no guarantee that the item in question would appear. The editor could return the money stating that the sentiments of the writer were of no interest to the readership. In some cases editors simply kept the funds, did not run the letter, and sent no letter of explanation. In short most, if not all, of the black community was severely restricted in the exercise of freedom of the press and freedom of speech through the news media.

II

Undeniably there was sentiment in the black community for its own papers. Even after the demise of the first black newspaper, *Freedom's Journal,* and its predecessor, *The Rights of All,* there continued to be discussion concerning the efficacy of black newspapers.[4] Significantly, the discussion ensued even when there were circulating black newspaper and the discussions covered the pros and cons of a black paper: not all were convinced of the wisdom of a separate enterprise.

An influential black leader, William Whipper, believed that it was not wise to foster a separate paper. Whipper had not based his beliefs on any lack of faith in black capacity to run a newspaper. Instead he argued that the greater goal was to be an American, to break down and eliminate the barriers to equality. Too often superficial historical analyses asserts that individuals such as Whipper represented the integrationist tendency in the history of the black community. Such analyses are not only too simplistic, but also ahistoric, and perhaps mask a latent racism among historians. Whipper and others were clear about their reasons for rejecting separate institutions. It was never grounded in a desire to be white, or to surrender their race, or the race's genius to white ideals, goals, or perceptions. Their speeches make clear two specifics. One, they had no desire to let white society off the hook, or allow it to escape its responsibility of living up to Christian, democratic principles. Such men felt that separate institutions could later become a barrier to black equality by letting whites push blacks further from the mainstream of American life. If blacks operated in their own little sphere developing their own institutions, whites would still control the power and relegate black aspirations to white-approved channels. Second, Whipper was not blind to the stigma of black failure. He thought individual black failure would be interpreted by whites as the failure of the race. Whipper saw the unfairness of white's perceptions, but also knew its realities.

Later in the 1830s and 1840s, courageous black men argued against founding and funding a national black newspaper.[5] Hotly debated during the last decades before the Civil War, the argument against a newspaper failed for reasons more complex than the desire to be integrated into white society. There were successful black newspapers in the 1830s and 1840s. Although most lasted less than two years, they lasted long enough to have settled, in most black minds at least, several questions. Paramount among these was the question of whether blacks could run a competent newspaper. Would blacks support their own paper? Could a paper attract a white following? Would the failure to acquire white readers automatically mean the paper was not successful? How would a black paper influence public opinion and political decisions? Could a black paper prove solvent over the years?

Keeping a newspaper solvent was a desperately hard business. Advertising revenues were small, almost nonexistent. Blacks who possessed enough discretionary income to act as angels to black publications were equally scarce. While black newspapers were of necessity crusading journals, they were also expected to produce a profit. The profits could only be produced by unceasing effort, yet most black editors also had to pursue other means of support. It must also be noted that the entrepreneurial skills in the black community for running a large-scale, profit-making venture were limited. No blacks had been apprenticed to American businesses or companies to learn finance, bookkeeping, investment, and inventory. Still black individuals continued to try to make a success of newspapers.

Despite the difficulty of founding and sustaining a black paper, there were techniques that allowed black editors to minimize the economic risks. Among the stabilizing devices was the use of the joint-stock company model. Thus risks could be apportioned among a number of individuals by lowering the indebtedness of each investor. On the joint-stock model, finances to a large extent were separated from day to day publishing chores. Unfortunately, no financial records of the first black newspapers have come to light. We can, however, infer certain ideas about the papers' operations. Apparently stockholders were willing to absorb low or minus returns on investment but would not countenance a soft editorial policy on the critics of the race.

Important factors about the origins of *Freedom's Journal* are still shrouded. For example, we do not know who the principal investors were. Nor do we know how much money they put up to launch the paper. Boston Crummell and Peter Williams, Jr., were involved in the financial operations of the paper but their specific investments, if any, are unknown.[6] It would be difficult to conceive of the paper as a one-man effort and Peter Williams' finances could not have been ample enough to support the venture. He was constantly in the limelight, working with various individuals and organizations, but these activities did not result in personal gain. His small church, St. Phillips, was struggling to meet its annual mortgage at the time *Freedom's Journal* was founded.

Williams does, however, hold a key to some speculations about the paper's financial backing. Earlier, in 1816, Williams had been asked by a member of the New York Manumission Society to supply the names of blacks in the city who could meet the state's rigid voter regulations. Unlike whites, black voters had to meet both residence and property qualifications in order to vote. After some initial inquiries Williams responded that there were about forty-five blacks in the city qualified to vote.[7] They could meet residence requirements but more important they could also meet the $250 property qualification. He further commented that he knew most of the individuals on the list he provided the organization. It is probably a good speculation that some of the men on the list were involved in financing the *Journal.*

Boston Crummell's role in the rise and demise of the paper was significant. His home was the site of the planning meeting to found the paper.[8] Later he was extremely disturbed by the paper's change in policy toward ACS. Unable to continue supporting John Brown Russworm's equivocations about colonization, Crummell was one of the major voices calling for suspension of the *Journal.* Before Crummell's call, however, the first black newspaper had made its presence felt.

On 16 March 1827 the first issue of *Freedom's Journal* appeared. Although not recognized by its white contemporaries, the paper represented a major turning point not only in black community life, but also in American reform. For its patrons, the first editorial announced: "We wish to plead our own case. Too long have others spoken for us."[9] The paper was asserting its intentions to defend the races interests, and to protect members and benefactors. Coming two years before David Walker's *Appeal,* and four years before William Lloyd Garrison's *Liberator,* the paper was the opening salvo in a new offensive against slavery. More important, the *Journal* was leading the way in the assertion of black civil rights. No white journal, not even Benjamin Lundy's *Genius of Universal Emancipation,* had forthrightly attacked black civil disabilities. Those like the *Genius* that raised the issue of discrimination sought solutions which separated blacks from the United States. The *Journal,* however, coupled its defense of the black community with a call for the exercise of the vote, and an independent posture in politics.

> The civil rights of a people being, of the greatest value, it shall ever be our duty to vindicate our brethren, when oppressed;and to lay the case before the publick. We shall urge upon our brethren, |who are qualified

by the laws of the different states] the expediency of using their elective franchise; and making an independent use of the same. We wish them not to become the tools of party.[10]

This was a heady brew. With the exception of the postrevolutionary war federalists in New York and briefly in 1820s Rhode Island, no political parties had befriended the black franchise or counted black votes. While short of a nationalist declaration, the *Journal* was the most militant and dramatic signal the free black community could send white society.[11] As such, the *Journal* combined the functions of protest, social conformity, and crusading journalism. Like all black public assertions, the *Journal* and later newspapers reflected the basic nature of blacks' reactions to slavery and discrimination. Of the twin evils, slavery was more easily dealt with. Black speakers advocated its elimination from American life. Discrimination, on the other hand, was a more difficult adversary. For northern free blacks, discrimination constituted a clear and present danger. Yet avenues to its elimination or amelioration were not as clear as the choices available for confronting slavery. Elimination and amelioration went hand in hand when confronting prejudice. Some black leaders, including the *Journal* editor, thought prejudice could be significantly reduced if blacks could exhibit and whites could accept the elevation of the race. The twin black disabilities called for different, and sometimes, changing methodologies. Unless Cornish and Russwurm were prepared to ignore or insult white allies, they could not call for a blanket elimination of prejudice. Since owners sinned by keeping blacks in bondage they were fair and safe game to attack. Uninformed whites practiced discrimination, but Cornish, Russwurm, and probably most blacks felt that given better information and better examples of black achievement, most whites would adjust their negative perceptions of blacks. Unfortunately, the optimism of Cornish and Russworm was not justified.

Still the paper performed a needed service during the formative years of the American reform movement. It set in motion discussions leading to the 1830s call for immediate emancipation.[12] Although the opening editorial is lukewarm about slavery, the indictment and direction are clear. The editors, who were free blacks, attached themselves to slaves as brethren. In subsequent issues the question of emancipation gained more prominence, and the editors availed themselves of the opportunity to discuss how emancipation might be achieved.[13] More articles appeared noting emancipation celebrations than direct calls for immediate relief from bondage. The articles themselves, however, provided an outlet to question gradual emancipation plans, and the fact that the South had not ever taken this mild, but progressive stance. Following the demise of the *Journal,* in its brief existence *The*

Rights of All discussed slavery and emancipation. The tones were hardly ringing nationalist declarations, but they were considerably beyond anything in contemporary newspapers. No American newspaper except *The Rights of All* criticized the conflicts between the Declaration of Independence and the existence of black bondage.[14]

Even in the midst of the trials of *Freedom's Journal*, the inquiry of whether or not a black newspaper could survive had been answered positively. Given the economic restraints, the community may have been expected to forgo having its own newspaper. That seems not to have been the case. David Walker, an adamant foe of the American Colonization Society, was willing to accept an editorial policy favorable to ACS rather than see the paper's demise. He argued eloquently, if not successfully, that the paper's service to the community far outweighed single policy issues. Walker, a militant spokesperson for black self-reliance and defending the race, seemed more willing to accept the diversity of political views within the community. On the other hand, his contemporary and former editor of the *Journal,* Samuel Cornish, was willing to let the paper die, but he was not concerned about the absence of a black weekly. He sought consensus of black opinion and was willing, even eager, to see one paper fail in hopes of creating another more in line with his political philosophy. Coming at the problem of the papers from different vantage points, both leaders affirmed their belief in the need for a community journal

The question of blacks supporting their own newspapers is not entirely positive. Certainly, pioneering newspapermen kept trying to produce a quality black newspaper, but the problems of gaining subscribers and getting other revenues were always uppermost in black editors' minds. In the maiden issue of *Freedom's Journal* Cornish and Russworm approached, in a low key, the question of support. The editors pointed out ". . .that there are five hundred thousand free persons of colour, one half of whom might subscribe, and the whole be benefitted by the publication of the journal."[15] No black editor of the antebellum period had the luxury of ignoring the support question. Agents in the field were ever vigilant in drumming up financial support for the papers under their care. In Boston David Walker enlisted the aid of Rev. Thomas Paul and John Hilton to stimulate interest and sales in the *Journal.*[16] He successfully engaged Thomas Paul to serve as an agent. Walker himself remained as a Boston agent until the paper's demise. He not only publicized the *Journal,* but also advertised his clothing store in its pages. Charles B. Ray, in an attempt to generate subscriptions for *The Colored American,* resorted to collective guilt. Borrowing from the first editorial in *Freedom's Journals* he stated that: "If among the few hundred thousand free colored peoples in the country,—to say nothing of the white population from whom it ought to receive a strong support, a living patronage for the paper cannot be obtained, it will be greatly to their reproach."[17] Walker's techniques were more subtle.

Walker and Ray were indefatigable in their activity for the papers, and the editors reciprocated. Walker's speeches for black solidarity before various black organizations were duly reported in the *Journal*. He also used the sheet to publicize a scheme to raise money to sell George Moses Horton's volume of poetry.[18] The proceeds from the sale were earmarked to purchase Horton's freedom. Although Walker contributed to the fund, and other attempts were made in Philadelphia and New York, the needed amount was never raised. Despite the Horton setback, Walker's energies and support for a black press never flagged. When *The Rights of All* emerged Walker quickly volunteered his service as agent and advertiser.

In the 1830s and 1840s several blacks matched David Walker's earlier exertions to create and sustain a black press. Along with Cornish, who stayed involved with black papers until the 1840s, were New Yorkers Phillip A. Bell, Charles B. Ray, and Theodore S. Wright. In January 1837 Phillip A. Bell's first newspaper venture was *Weekly Advocate*. He remained active in New York papers and appeared as the proprietor and editorial writer for *The Colored American*. Before the end of the antebellum period Bell ranged far and wide founding and running black papers. Among his creations were the *Pacific Appeal* and *The Elevator*. Both papers were run by Bell during the 1860s in San Francisco.[19]

When on the East Coast, Charles B. Ray was associated with *The Colored American*. If David Walker's activities for *Freedom's Journal* were worthy of the editors' attentions, the same was true for Ray's activities as agent for *The Colored American*. Almost every issue reported not only his travels, but also his success at raising subscriptions. From New England, Buffalo, Syracuse, Chester, Pennsylvania, and other points, he sent weekly progress reports for the readership. He reported sums ranging from thirty-five to seventy dollars from new subscribers.[20] It was energy like Ray's that kept *The Colored American* afloat as the longest existing New York City antebellum black newspaper.

III

Despite the energies of editors and agents duch as Charles B. Ray, support was not guaranteed, and sometimes strong editors produced a backlash. A crusading and political newspaper could hardly avoid the internal warfare of the American reform period. Each reform activity attracted strong personalities and this result could sometimes be explosive. Black newspapers were most closely tied to the abolitionist movement and to black calls for moral reform. Not surprisingly, black abolitionists in Boston and black moral reformers in Philadelphia found themselves arrayed against the journalistic New Yorkers'. Naturally such confrontations over means and ends were fought among editors and in the pages of the papers.

Closely tied to William Lloyd Garrison, Boston blacks interpreted the New Yorkers' middle-of-the road stance on some issues as unwarranted criticism of Garrison. Both Samuel Cornish and Charles Ray, working on *The Colored American,* traded barbs over the questions of politics, women's rights, and attacks on religion. The fallout from all these issues forced blacks to take sides. Black Bostonians such as William Cooper Nell and John Hilton defended Garrison's tactical changes and attacked Cornish and *The Colored American* for its failure to follow their lead.[21] Actually, the *American* was counseling blacks to avoid schismatic behavior because such arguments were disruptive of abolition and detrimental to blacks. In 1838, a year after Cornish's first bout with the Bostonians, Charles Ray was engaged in a similar confrontation. Ray had to balance his rhetoric of an open paper against the support of one abolitionist faction against another. His admonition that blacks would suffer if they continued in this way was lost on the Bostonians.[22] Although the struggles continued, *The Colored American* survived the Boston conflicts.

Simultaneous with its Boston battles *The Colored American* also fought with the American Moral Reform Society (AMRS) of Philadelphia. As early as 1834, interest in the society had been generated by Robert Purvis and William Whipper. The two Philadelphians were hoping to harness the energy of black and white abolitionists who had been involved in the early black convention movements. They wanted to institutionalize interracial cooperation for two basic purposes. One, they were opposed to "complexional" organizations. Two, in the wake of the decreasing fervor for convention projects, the AMRS proposed a broad-based attack on the moral laxity of the black community. Like some middle-class leaders throughout history, antebellum black leaders placed great emphasis on social deportment. Although the group formed in 1834, it did not meet nationally until 1837. Samuel Cornish, then editor of *The Colored American,* and a staunch social deportment man, attended the first convention. Initially, favorably impressed by the membership and the agenda of AMRS, Cornish quickly became disillusioned. Within the pages of the newspaper he took the organization to task for its lack of action. His criticism led to exchanges and a debate with William Whipper over the organization's merit.[23]

Later in August 1838 the conflict became even sharper. When plans for the AMRS's *National Reformer* were circulated, the pages of *The Colored American* continued as a battleground. It was charged that the AMRS did not represent the views of the black community. Moreover, critics suggested that the organization's views and directions were mis-conceived. While Whipper's *National Reformer* lasted only a year it was an affirmation that community leaders perceived newspapers as part of the apparatus of a viable community. Lack of success had not diminished the community's need for newspapers. A decade before the battles between *The Colored American* and the *National Reformer, Freedom's Journal* had served the community's needs in an exemplary fashion. Certainly its major thrust was waging political battle in defense of the race on all fronts. Not only did it fight against the invidious ACS, but also it aspired to teach its readership. Conducting a scientific study of race and researching Africa's glorious past were two chores the editors pursued.[24] Both items were political but their impact was educational as well. Informing a black and white readership of subjects neglected in for-mal education curricula was a task of some critical significance. No other newspaper of the times attempted to verify the unity of the human fam-ily. Even later abolitionist organs were so busy confronting the issue of slavery that they seldom had time to explore race. Moreover, it was a huge undertaking. Educated and uneducated whites possessed a store-house of unscientific knowledge about race, Africa, skin color ,and human development.

Educated whites, heirs of classical and enlightenment learning, could and did cite authorities in their negative assessments of color, race, and black history. Thomas Jefferson's observations on race in *Notes on the State of Virginia* were part of a continuum reaching all the way back to the ancient Greeks.[25] Sacred and intellectual authorities had done little to refute the attacks on black humanity. When scholars entered the dis-cussion of black capacities they added to the already existing store of race mythmaking. The enormity of the task the *Journal* was undertaking becomes evident when one considers that this single black weekly was fighting against the entrenched intellectual and emotional foundations of Western civilization.

Simultaneously, blacks needed to be made aware of the scientific grounds for their inclusion in the family of man. Buffeted by slavery, dis-crimination, and a lack of educational opportunities, few blacks had the intellectual or emotional resources to combat directly their negative image. Not willing to allow the degrading stereotypes to be internalized by their black readers, the *Journal* editors proclaimed publicly the unity of mankind.

Such assertions not only attacked the stereotype and its basis of sup-port, but also attempted to assist black Americans to forge a new ethnic charter and a new persona. Richard Allen, bishop of the African Methodist Episcopal Church and an elder statesman among black activists, used the pages of the *Journal* to circulate ideas of race, class, and the oneness of humanity. Although few whites saw *Freedom's*

Journal, Allen was not simply preaching to the already converted. As he had done decades before the paper's existence, Allen sought to shore up the Afro-American psyche. He continued to spell out the black birthright and its convergence with defending the young nation in all its crises.[26] Allen informed his readers that blacks could take pride in their support of the government. While these items were not lost on the American public, the revolutionary war fervor and liberalism had waned considerably. More and more he asserted that it was necessary to quietly and confidently project a sense of manhood, accomplishment, and readiness for equality.

Allen's ethnic charter supported the views of the paper's senior and junior editors. Samuel Cornish and John Brown Russworm had designed both a format and an editorial direction to inform, elevate, and invite the participation of its black readers. All three men thought practical matters such as confronting the ACS could be combined with the establishment of the charter and the need to involve the community at a basic level in the success of the paper. Toward this end, the paper solicited agents to collect subscriptions and to distribute the weekly. The agents were numerous and represented a cross section of the black community. In large communities such as New York, Philadelphia, and Boston the large force of agents ensured that most readers would have access to the paper. It was also hoped that inclusion in the enterprise would help dispel in black and white minds any lingering doubts about black capacities. Moreover, the consistency of the undertaking would have a positive impact on its black readers. Far from bemoaning the oppressive quality of their existence, the two editors balanced a fighting stance with steady revelations of black abilities, especially to survive in the face of oppression.

IV

A united black persona was important to the editors and no aspect of the community's population was ignored. Columns were directed to informing and uplifting women and children. While the content of the women's column and occasionally a women's page was usually traditional and sometimes sexist, a wide range of opinions was exhibited. Black women could, and did, avail themselves of the chance to chide their males about sexism. In an early issue Matilda left no doubt about her perceptions of black female capabilities.[27]

It is peculiar, but understandable, that no black female writer equated black men's attitudes toward women with the slave masters' attitudes toward slaves. That kind of sentiment would have put black females at risk. In the unlikely case that Matilda's letter would have contained such sentiments and met the approval of the editors it would have been sure to stir up controversy. While generally open-handed, the editors tended also to steer clear of intraracial conflicts. Different points of view were certainly featured. Differences usually amounted to discussions of means, not a conflict over ends: the eradication of slavery in the South and the elimination of discrimination in the North. Black women were under a double requirement to keep their protests in check. Societal norms certainly did not appear receptive to female rebellion. Yet a major thrust of female dissatisfaction was that black males were overlooking valuable allies by neglecting the female view. The harbingers of a black feminism, although faint, can clearly be discerned in the pages of America's first black newspaper.

Although not fully developed feminism, there was something new in black female assertions. Black women who had the ego-strength to write letters to the editors on public issues were seldom apologetic about their assertions. The disarming disclaimers that characterized much white female public prouncements are absent in black women's letters that appear in *Freedom's Journal*. During the revolutionary war Mercy Otis Warren characteristically opened her essays with a statement such as, "being a woman, I probably don't understand the topic currently being discussed, nevertheless. . . ."[28] She then proceeded to give a cogent analysis of the situation. Black women seemed to go to the heart of the matter without preparatory niceties. Matilda was direct, but her opinions were in the minority. Despite her pioneering voice the majority opinion appearing in the *Journal* warned black women not to be too modern and to work to appeal to masculine sensibilities.

Not until black women became editors could they begin to circulate a more aggressive position in the print media. The advent of black female newspaperwomen did not occur until the 1850s. The first black female to publish her own paper did so in Canada, in a particular set of circumstances. Although this paper was not founded in New York, Boston, or Philadelphia a discussion of her effort is relevant. The editor/owner of the journal was the daughter of Abraham D. Shadd, a self-proclaimed radical abolitionist and an agent for the *Liberator* in the slave state of Delaware. More important, he operated within the Philadelphia orbit, attending conventions, corresponding with Richard Allen and others, and generally identified with that group of leaders.

His daughter was also well known to the East Coast elite leadership. Through an early publication, she had expressed herself ably on subjects of relevance to the black struggle. A convergence of several historical events stimulated Mary Ann Shadd Cary to publish *The Provincial Freeman* in 1853.[29] In 1851 the twenty-eight-year-old Ms. Shadd (she married in 1853) appeared quite attractive to black leaders in Canada West and was invited there by Henry Bibb publisher, of *The Voice of the Fugitive*. Early in life she supported herself as a teacher. By 1851 she had gained teaching experience in New Jersey, Delaware, and Pennsylvania. At the same time she was gaining a reputation as an able political thinker. Noted newspapermen such as Frederick Douglass and Martin Delany responded favorably to her ideas. In 1849 they welcomed her publication, *Hints to the Colored People of the North.* This pamphlet, directed at the free black population, stressed self-sufficiency and elevating the race.[30] Intellectually and politically, her work did not break new ground, but it set another standard. She became the first black female to gain approval for her public political opinions. Her favorable impression notwithstanding, Ms. Shadd was less successful disseminating her views when they ran counter to the views of the powerful black male leaders.

Almost immediately after arriving in Canada she became embroiled in a fight with her host, Henry Bibb. Initially, Bibb and his wife had been staunch supporters of Ms. Shadd, residing in Canada West, but shortly after arriving they quarreled over differences about opening a school. Shadd saw the need for an interracial school supported by fees and donations from abolition and missionary societies. The Bibbs already had support from American missionary societies and had no wish to jeopardize their sources of support. In any case, their support was specifically for educating the children of fugitive slaves. Shadd struggled with minimum support to keep her interracial school. Bibb was able to use his connections as well as *Voice of the Fugitive* to isolate Ms. Shadd. At the same time as the school conflict, Ms. Shadd uncovered the misappropriation of funds by Henry Bibb. As the executive in charge of the fugitive slave community Dawn, Bibb was entrusted with large sums for the maintenance of the community. Ms. Shadd discovered that in addition to misappropriating funds, Bibb was also acting as a dictator in running the community. No one took seriously her charges against Bibb.

In the midst of these struggles Ms. Shadd published a tract that even former supporters Delany and Douglass ignored. *Notes on Canada West* was an investigation of the effects of the New Fugitive Slave Law of 1850.[31] In 1852 the subject matter was not novel, and blacks were trying in various ways to protest the law. Her breach came in her discussion of emigration as a response to the law, specifically when she raised the topic of a return to Africa. She evaluated five potential regions where blacks might seek refuge. Mexico and the West Indies were dismissed as possible havens. According to Shadd too many Americans, in Texas particularly, were voicing plans to annex all or part of Mexico. In the West Indies, Shadd asserted, despite emancipation in the British territories, slavery remained a reality throughout the region. Even in the British islands the ethnic mix of emancipated blacks, contract laborers, Indians from the subcontinent, and Chinese workers was potentially explosive.

She gave high marks to Vancouver Island. It had available land, could easily be defended, and had economic potential. Blacks could maintain themselves with an economy based on provisioning oceangoing vessels. It was also far enough away from the slavocracy, but its attractive features were also its major drawbacks because, for example, reaching Vancouver Island required more resources than most blacks had. Thus, Canada West, Ms. Shadd asserted provided the best haven for fugitive blacks. On Africa, Ms. Shadd volunteered that ultimately it was going to be the place of choice for blacks leaving America.

A conspiracy of silence seems to have met the pamphlet. Unlike her earlier work, no black newspaper reviewed *Notes on Canada West*. Ms. Shadd had touched the most delicate nerve in the topics discussed in the black press. The issue of Africa and colonization had been fought in the media and had split the community several times. Colonization directly contributed to the demise of *Freedom's Journal* in 1829. The leading black papers following the *Journal* took a definitive anticolonization stance. The *Notes on Canada West* response illustrated the power of the black press. In suppressing the discussion of blacks leaving the United States, black editors erred on the side of conformity and suppression. On the issue of colonization during the early 1850s the black press failed to lead in the enlightenment of its readership.

Despite its silence on Shadd's pamphlet and its option for conformity rather than broad discussion, the press had been involved in the colonization topic. No paper founded in New York following *Freedom's Journal* could afford to ignore the issue. Black editors organized to fight ACS which to them was synonymous with colonization.[32] Space was regularly devoted to refute the positive claims of the colonizationists, black or white. So powerful were black editors that an individual espousing a full impartial discussion of topics could be rebuffed. For *Freedom's Journal* and *The Rights of All,* such repression of competing views may be understandable. Before the early 1830s liberal whites had been taken in by ACS. Even those who advocated the end of slavery saw ACS as a positive institution. Among those supporting colonization were Benjamin Lundy, William Lloyd Garrison, the Tappen brothers, and Gerritt Smith. Not only did these whites have finances and influential friends, but Lundy and Garrison were veteran newspapermen. Moreover, the Lundy and Garrison papers were supported by numerous blacks.

Friends of the community were functioning as enemies of the group's best interests, thus making the task of black editors even more difficult. Blacks saw no middle ground and did not feel they could engage in a luxury: a debate on the merits of colonization. From the black editors' point of view there were no merits to the colonization scheme. If a wayward black wished to take advantage of the offer to relocate he was to be pitied and perhaps tolerated. The more important concern for the editors was to prevent the collective from supporting ACS and further succumbing to the colonizationist argument. In this instance, black editors chose to continue an unrelenting attack on colonization, and simultaneously promote the virtues of America and the idea that blacks merited full citizenship rights. Although it may appear that a disproportionate amount of time, energy, and space was given to the issue, it must be remembered that colonization was third only to slavery and discrimination as the major menace to black life. ACS/colonization was simultaneously invigorating and debilitating, but it was not the sole issue moving the black press.

V

In its very first issue *Freedom's Journal* had set an editorial policy to which the black press remained committed throughout the antebellum period. Several common themes emerged in 1827 and were refined over the years to become staples in the black press.[33] Certainly of overwhelming importance to black editors was the quality of life for the black community. Lacking its later statistical emphasis, quality of life for nineteenth-century black editors concerned the issues of self-determination and self-definition. Running through all the issues discussed in the black journals were the twin questions of "Who are we?" and "What do we want?" Interestingly both questions initially were answered in a similar way. Black Americans were Americans, and as such were entitled to all the rights, privileges, and responsibilities of citizenship. They were, at any rate, meeting many of the obligations of citizenship. Chief among these were forms of taxation without representation.

The editors seldom failed to point to the historical irony of their position compared to the founding fathers of America. Citing the revolutionary rhetoric allowed editors to establish a continuity of service to the nation's historic struggle. Editors such as Cornish, Russwurm, and later, Phillip A. Bell, extolled the community's contribution as soldiers protecting the infant colonies. Black participation in the nation's wars was not only a necessary military tactic but also a proud memorial to blacks. Even when their participation was initially rejected, blacks persevered in their efforts to serve the nation. Frequently cited were the exploits of black soldiers and sailors in the revolutionary war and the War of 1812. In the latter context, the decisive Battle of New Orleans was frequently featured.

Self-definition and self-determination also were fostered by the editorial policy first used by *Freedom's Journal* to conduct a scientific study of slavery.[34] From the editors' point of view the topic encompassed an examination of slavery from the ancient world to the present. It involved the discussion of slaves in the Old World who had been allowed to develop their talents, and pointed out that most societies found ways to reward slaves for their services to the state. Slaves became valued advisors to political leaders; some also won freedom for military valor. Most ancient societies, according to the editors, recognized slaves as possessing personalities at law and allowed slaves greater civic responsibility than they had in America. The result of the editorial policy supported the call of the black press for immediate emancipation and unconditional freedom for black Americans. Unless immediate freedom became a reality, editors argued America would continue to feel the consequences of its system of oppression. Racial conflicts would continue to permeate American society and call into question its progress and enlightenment. Enlightened nations, the editors said, tended to move away from a dependence on a slave labor force or on discriminatory treatment of its minorities. Whether accurate or not, this line was constantly circulated by the black press.

Economic critiques of slavery were not the norm in nineteenth-century American thinking, but correspondents and columnists would address the issue frequently in the black press. One of the most favored ways of discussing the economics of slavery was to compare the productivity of free and slave labor. The editors cited views of the comparison between the two labor systems from a variety of sources. Even Russia, which certainly could not make a claim to Western enlightenment, offered examples that free labor was more productive.[35]

Although the economic critique of slavery was not systematically developed, the correspondents writing on slave versus free labor demonstrated a good deal of ingenuity pursuing the topic. In addition to citing the enlightenment of backward Russia, several well-known thinkers, who were certainly not friends of the race, had their ideas on the issue repeated in the black press. The views of eighteenth-century Scottish historian and philosopher David Hume on the subject of slave and free labor costs were reiterated for the black readership. Hume saw slave labor as more expensive than free labor.[36]

The dissemination of Hume's views was an inspired choice. In the 1750s, at the beginning of the rhetorical stage of the American Revolution, Hume had been one of a number of European thinkers discussing progress and political economy.[37] These men explored the tension between economic progress and liberal human nature. Progress had a dynamic of its own which could not be arrested. It not only threatened man's liberal humanitarian values but also threatened his alienation from the soil and from his personal identification with work. Progress would, it was feared by some, result in overcrowded urban conditions, an exploited laboring class, and a debilitated and debauched merchant class. Thirty years later during the war, American patriots debated the same issues. Thus, Hume's ideas were a known quantity to American political thinkers. Probably equally important for black editors were Hume's derogatory views about black capacities.[38] Even given his perceptions of blacks, Hume was still of the opinion that free exploited labor was more efficient than enslaved labor. If white labor freed from bondage was less expensive than enslaved white labor it logically followed, according to the editors, that black free labor would produce the same results. A less expensive, more efficient work force would be of general benefit, and black editors speaking through one of the Western world's major economic thinkers, stated as much. Unfortunately, neither the black readership nor white politicians followed the *Journal*'s lead in stimulating general discussion of Hume's ideas.

A week after the Hume column appeared, the *Journal* devoted more space to the issue of slave versus free labor. This time the editors reprinted portions of a pamphlet by an Englishman James Anderson.[39] Anderson was a prolific writer on the question of slave labor costs and the capacity of slave labor. His works were not based on scientific testing yet they had a basis in fact. As an honorary member of the Bath and Manchester Philosophical and Agricultural Societies, he was in a position to make observations about agricultural work and articulate enough to weave his findings into an abolitionist plea. Anderson's pamphlet reiterated many of the philosophical concerns of the *Journal*'s editors. Both Russwurm and Cornish would heartily agree with Anderson's position that:

> We are thus led to perceive that it is Liberty alone which produces industry, and excites all those generous feelings, that exalt man above the other animals on this globe: while slavery as necessarily debases the mind, and enervates, and in some measure destroys all active bodily exertions.[40]

Anderson's ideas embodied his principle of self-love which animated all free men. Its absence in slaves was, he argued, "cruel, inhumane but [also] impolitic and absurd." [41]

Moreover, Anderson made two further points that Russwurm and Cornish wished to see given wider distribution. One, it was Anderson's contention that the question of the productivity of free over slave labor had never been fairly investigated. According to Anderson, both antislavery and proslavery factions maintained their differing perceptions about labor without proof. Proslavery advocates thought it would be too costly to have labor provided by free men. Representatives of free societies would not subject men to slavery unless it was more productive. In the colonies, Anderson argued, free labor was so scarce that labor rates were artificially high. It was well-known, he observed, that laborers in piece-work economies produce more and enjoy a greater standard of living than those who work by the day, but even day laborers produce more than slaves. Two, part of the solution to the problem, for Anderson, was that abolitionists must add to their moral aversion to slavery, arguments of economy and political expediency.[42] Part of the new attack on slavery involved trying to arrive at some calculations of the cost of labor. Using a formula that combined the elements of slave purchase price, slave life expectancy, annual maintenace, and number of annual work days, Anderson arrived at the following conclusion: the cost of slave-produced goods was higher than the earnings of the average English wage earner.

Not content only to demonstrate the economic backwardness of slavery, Anderson also attacked the failure of political initiatives against slavery. He pointed out to readers that none of the disastrous rumors about conflict with the American colonies had been realized. England had not lost its commercial empire or America as a customer. The ruinous arguments notwithstanding, politicians needed to eliminate slavery as a legitimate institution in civilized society. In fact, the end of slavery would produce good results in that manufacturing would be stimulated. He pointed out that slavery contributed to the ability of Poland and Turkey to establish manufacturing.

Although Anderson advocated gradual emancipation, an idea that was not favored by the editors of *Freedom's Journal*, they published his arguments about how the process could be handled. Their motivation is clear: Anderson's gradual emancipation plan was far in advance of anything being discussed in the American political and economic debates. Anderson placed a heavy emphasis on laws to protect blacks "while they acquired property and habituated themselves to competitive work habits." [43] In the ten year period necessary to complete Anderson's proposal he stipulated a five-and-a- half-day work week. He also suggested that slaves be able to contract for extra labor. Male slaves should be allowed to purchase land and wives. A reasonable land policy would stimulate agricultural exploitation of new areas. Accompanying the economic and work factors Anderson proposed must be a provision for a christian education. Not only would education help slaves work toward becoming freemen but also it would, according to Anderson, ensure other good effects.

Despite the lack of interest in the Hume and Anderson columns the editors followed up the slave/free labor debate in September.[44] This time the angle of observation was slightly different. Adam Hodgeson, who had corresponded earlier with the editors on the issue, used South American slavery as his focal point. He compared it to feudalism and concluded that neither was efficient nor free. Nor was either system, according to Hodgeson, very progressive in a world of enlightened political ideas. In the 1780s a group of black slaves had argued that the

Spanish system of slavery was more humane than its American counterpart, but Hodgeson was not interested in reviving the argument of Spain's liberal system of bondage. Instead he was more interested in demonstrating that South American slavery and feudalism were inefficient and expensive. He was equally interested in examining the proposition of paying slaves. Paying slaves, he argued, would lead to a twofold positive result. Slaves would immediately become better workers and the increased productivity would offset the master's payment of wages. Before this September column Hodgeson had explored similar ideas in a long letter to Jean Baptiste, president of Haiti. Hodgeson's letter first appeared in the *Journal* on 19 August 1827 and ran until its completion 31 August 1827.[45] Unfortunately, the *Journal* did not remain at the leading edge of the antislavery economic arguments. Articles similar in nature to those Hodgeson, Anderson, and Hume appeared only sporadically after September 1827.

Although *Freedom's Journal* continued after the departure of Samuel Cornish, it was by some accounts significantly reduced in its political fervor, particularly on the issue of opposing the American Colonization Society.[46] Unlike the Reverend Peter Williams who was silenced for his criticism of ACS, John Brown Russwurm had reasons for rethinking his opposition to African colonization. Among the more intriguing, but little verified, reasons was Russwurm's own feeling that he suffered unfairly because of his mixed racial parentage.[47] This same charge surfaced earlier as part of the disillusionment of Rev. Daniel Coker. Whether these examples of intraracial color phobia are accurate, they were important measures of the frustration experienced by some black leaders.[48]

After the demise of *Freedom's Journal* both Russwurm and Cornish felt compelled to return to newspaper work. Cornish, certainly smarting, with many others, over Russwurm's defection, tried to fill the void by editing and publishing *The Rights of All*.[49] Originally envisioned as a weekly, it became a monthly organ because the needed finances could not be raised. Published between May and October 1829, *Rights* had only six issues. It continued the attack on ACS, but with the exception of scapegoating Russwurm, no new perceptions about colonization appeared. Although beyond the scope of this work, Russwurm's journalistic career continued in Liberia when he founded *Liberian Herald* shortly after his arrival in Africa.

New Yorkers, Cornish chief among them, kept their commitment to providing a black newspaper alive through the 1840s. In January 1837 Phillip A. Bell founded *The Weekly Advocate,* a paper dedicated to the people. Samuel Cornish's association with the paper came a month later and he quickly became the shaper of the paper's editorial policy. Within months he changed the paper's name to *The Colored American.*[50] Not only did *The Colored American* become the longest running black newspaper, but it also returned with a vengeance to attacking the ACS. Before it ceased publication in December 1841 other notable blacks worked on the paper. By 1840 Phillip A. Bell, former agent for the paper, had replaced Cornish as its editor. Even Bell's talents and amazing energies could not keep the paper afloat. For the remainder of the antebellum period New Yorkers tried their hand at journalism and several short-lived papers and magazines found brief life.[51]

Not until the advent of *The Anglo-African* in July 1859 did the crusading zeal of *Freedom's Journal* and *The Colored American* re-emerge in New York City newspapers. Founded by the brothers Thomas and Robert Hamilton, this organ asserted that the question of slavery was leading the nation toward an irrepressible conflict.[52] More than any of its predecessors, *The Anglo-African* sharply debated the escalating antiblack attitudes represented by the New Fugitive Slave Law of 1850, the Dred Scott case (1857), the Kansas Civil War, and other political actions generated by recalcitrant southerners. Almost every issue reminded its readership that blacks were capable fighters and would assist in any direct confrontation against slavery. Some of *The Anglo-African's* militancy stemmed from a general escalation of black rhetoric probably dating to Henry Highland Garnet's 1843 Buffalo convention speech. His speech projected an implicit assertion that blacks would fight for and defend their liberty. By 1851 many of Garnet's contemporaries, initially opposed to his radical stance, "would welcome the intelligence that slaves had commenced the work of death in pursuit of their liberation."[53] Moreover, black individuals and communities were successfully opposing the implementation of the coercive Fugitive Slave Law. The New York City newspapers of the 1840s and 1850s were displaying a matching aggressiveness.

VI

Unlike New Yorkers, blacks in Philadelphia and Boston did not develop an antebellum newspaper tradition. Boston never had a black paper that rivaled even the least of New York's black journals. In 1861 when *The Pine and Palm* began publishing in Boston it had three peculiar qualities. One, it was a transplanted sheet. James Redpath had purchased *The Anglo-African* from Thomas Hamilton in 1860. He changed its name to *The Weekly Anglo-African* and in 1861 changed it again and moved its operation to Boston.[54] Two, it was dedicated mainly to the cause of Haitian emigration and was not a broad-based attack on Afro-American disabilities as its predecessors had been. Finally, Redpath was white. While earnestly committed to helping blacks go to Haiti, his overall assessment of blacks was negative.[55] Despite these characteristics *The Pine and Palm* sold well among blacks.

As with the Boston paper, Philadelphia's black paper the *Christian Recorder* was a late transplant. It first appeared in Pittsburgh under the title the *Christian Herald.*[56] By 1856 it had moved operations to Philadelphia. As the official organ of the AME church the *Recorder,* like *The Pine and Palm,* was more limited in scope than most other black newspapers. Both were attached to either a specific ideology or a specific institution rather than a broad-based community view. Yet the issues being a transplanted, white ownership and having a narrow focus were not the decisive reasons that Philadelphia and Boston did not develop a black newspaper industry.

Several more compelling reasons help explain the lack of black newspaper in Philadelphia and Boston. First, in both cities there were powerful black individuals opposed to complexional institutions and activities. Boston's William Cooper Nell and Benjamin Roberts had fought for integrated schools in the city, and led the assault on barriers to black and white cooperation.

This group's counterpart in Philadelphia consisted of William Whipper, William Still, Robert Purvis, and Stephen Smith. Second, not only were these individuals able to influence black public opinion, but they commanded much of the financial assets that a fledgling black press needed. Their failure to invest in the local black press signaled the enterprise's doom.

Third, these same blacks, particularly, Nell, Whipper, and Purvis, were closely tied to powerful whites. While supportive of black agitation whites such as William Lloyd Garrison, Arthur Tappen, and James Redpath simultaneously could be paternalistic, manipulative, and ambivalent about blacks. Redpath questioned black capacity to excel, even exist, in a white- dominated society. At least part of Garrison's objection to Frederick Douglass' newspaper venture must have been fear of competition with his own *Liberator.* While it is inaccurate to label Garrison a racist, like other white abolitionists and newspaper people he experienced some difficulty dealing with aggressive, independent black males.[57]

Fourth, blacks in both cities were deeply committed to supporting Garrison's *Liberator* and Redpath's *Pine and Palm.* Nell, Whipper, and Purvis were adamant in their support of Garrison and his paper.[58] Moreover, Garrison courted black support. He asserted that the paper would represent black interests and opened its pages to a diversity of black views. In addition, William Cooper Nell had a long and beneficial apprenticeship with the *Liberator.*

Black support for *Pine and Palm* was substantial because of both cities longstanding contact with Haiti. In Philadelphia the business sense and energy of Jacob C. White, Jr., materially benefitted the paper's circulation. Redpath and White engaged in a lengthy and sometimes testy correspondence about conducting business. Typical of their exchanges was a letter of 3 June 1861.

> . . . Please send 360 copies of this week's issue of The Pine and Palm . . . The extra copies of no. 1 I gave into the hands of the carriers for gratuitous distribution with a view of increasing circulation of the paper. Enclosed is an obituary notice for insertion. . . . I paid Mr. Lawrence for advertisements monthly, deducting 20 per cent. What day do you go to press?[59]

Later in the month, White was informing Redpath that circulation would be down temporarily as people were leaving the city on summer vacations.

By August of 1861 A. E. Newton, writing for Redpath, was soliciting White's ideas for raising circulation. Later in the month, upon returning from vacation, White raised critical issues about the low circulation. He suggested that the outbreak of the Civil War and the emphasis on Haitian emigration were to blame. There is one curious note in White's letter of 21 August 1861. He denies knowledge of any Philadelphia agent for *The Weekly Anglo-African* and suggests the *Pine and Palm* might get a headstart in the subscriptions race.[60] Why White chose to be duplicitous is not clear. Since both men were corresponding with George Lawrence about their distribution problems it was clear Redpath could get the information from Lawrence that White was the agent for the rival newspaper.

Later, as a matter of fact, Lawrence interceded in a dispute over the *Pine and Palm* accounts between White and Redpath.[61] The year 1862 was a particularly rancorous time for Redpath and White. They exchanged letters that barely maintained a minimum civility. White took Redpath to task about shipping arrangements. He had, he said, been greatly inconvenienced and materially affected by late arrival of papers.[62] In June and August White received two letters written in the same style from Redpath. The paper had fallen on hard times and economy measures were necessary. White was informed that papers no longer would be sent free after 26 August.[63] Before apologizing for his brevity Redpath asked White to get his bills up to date.

The *Christian Recorder,* although under the capable editors Rev. J. P. Campbell and later Elisha Weaver, encountered many problems in its early years. Weaver seems to have established a surer footing for the paper during the war years.[64] During the war, the paper spread into the South and West, and ultimately the regional editions eclipsed the original paper in Philadelphia.

Finally, blacks in Boston and Philadelphia overwhelmingly supported Garrison's *Liberator.* In Boston the support and identification of mutual interests sometimes made it appear as though blacks were too accommodating to whites. For example, many people came to think of the African Baptist Church as the abolitionist church, forgetting its position as the first black church in the city. Moreover, in an attempt to settle the conflicts within the church, its name was changed to First Independent Baptist Church of the People of Color, of Boston. The name change suggests a greater identification with black American ethnicity. It was also symptomatic of the diversification that had been taking place within the black community. African Baptist's monopoly of the black leadership position in Boston was broken and more choices were available to blacks seeking reform outlets.[65]

Loss of consensus also was signaled by the name change and its accompanying circumstances. Given the multitude of causes to support and the energies devoted to the school integration struggle, the cohesion necessary to support a black newspaper could not be achieved. While the emergence of diversity was a positive development for it helped to create many points of attack on black disabilities, it may have inadvertently stifled black journalism in Boston and Philadelphia.

Several attempts were made to overcome the obstacles to homegrown journalism despite the limited chances of success. Several newspapers briefly circulated in Boston.[66] While their existence is to be noted, their brief tenure does not materially change the interpretation here. The attempts by Benjamin Roberts, in fact, accent the dilemma of black leaders not only on the subject of newspapers, but also across the whole spectrum of reform activity and cooperation with whites. Roberts was one of the principals in the fight to integrate Boston's schools, and his daughter provided the test case for the litigants.

He also shared with other blacks the idea that they had to organize, control, and underwrite their own reform activities.[67] At another level his dilemma was compounded: Garrison could not be denounced as a racist, but his actions may have as effectively prevented black initiatives.

In the absence of Garrison and the *Liberator,* would blacks have developed their own successful newspaper? There are no clear answers. It is not clear that Boston had a large enough black population to sustain a paper. Unfortunately, Philadelphia, with its larger black population and no Garrison in residence, does not offer a different answer. Blacks in the City of Brotherly Love did not develop their own paper until late in the period. Publishing a black newspaper in antebellum America was in part a gamble. Yet it was a gamble that engaged the community because its spokespersons saw a paper as a viable part of the foundation of their community.

Even given their uneven development black newspapers were a viable part of the platform for change. The papers coming out of New York were eagerly sought by the black agents, advertisers, and readers.

What they found were stories, history, current events, and common themes dedicated to describing black life in the United States and sometimes in communities abroad. More important they found a voice to champion their lives, their efforts, and their need for access to a better life. Among the common themes emerging throughout the period in the black press were the discussion of slavery in the South and sometimes the history of slavery in other places. In addition, northern discrimination was constantly under attack in the pages of *Freedom's Journal, The Rights of All, The Colored American,* and the other papers coming out of New York. The newspapers carried on their mission of informing blacks and others about black life, black activities, and black aspirations. The newspapers were an important influence on the development of a national black public image. The New York editors succeeded in creating a consistent but not monolithic public image. In the years between 1827 and 1865 the papers founded in New York also attempted to shape an ideal for blacks to emulate. Given the limited resources, the constellation of functions needing the attention of the black newspapers may have been too much. In spite of all the difficulties, however, black editors continued to view newspapers as a viable part of the platform for change.

While New Yorkers were the only blacks that succeeded in producing newspapers the community effort was not missing. Blacks in Philadelphia and Boston rushed to be agents, boosters, and advertisers in the papers. Richard Allen, Jacob White, Sr. and Jr., Benjamin Roberts, David Walker, and others functioned to bring the papers to the black population, making the distribution of black newspapers national. The community's thirst for newspapers continued even when no papers were being published in the three cities. At such times the black community relied on papers published outside the three cities or on white papers that attempted to address the issues that blacks found most important.

Despite their uneven development the antebellum black newspapers left a heritage of crusading journalism for future black generations. This heritage included a place of significance in the platform for change for antebellum blacks; and the role of black newspapers in shaping, influencing, and trying to lead black public opinion remained a staple in black political awareness until well after World War II. Black newspapers, like many of their white counterparts in contemporary America, fell victim to the greater advertising potential of televisions and perhaps to diminished interest in the print media in the late twentieth century.

In keeping with the theme of the interrelatedness of the five activities making up the platform for change the issue of the place and significance of black newspapers continued to surface both in connection with the convention movement and with the development of the ideology of emigration. In the following chapters discussion concerning newspapers that will emerge will demonstrate not only the black commitment to newspapers but also will show how they were part of the flow of the community organizaing and building process.

Notes

1. William H. Robinson, *Phillis Wheatley and Her Writings* (New York: Garland Publishing, Inc., 1984), 27-32; M.A. Richmond, *Bid the Vassal Soar: Interpretive Essays on the Life and Poetry of Phillis Wheatley (ca.1753-1784) and George Moses Horton (ca. 1753-1883)* (Washington, D.C.: Howard University Press, 1974), 20-21; William H. Robinson, *Black New England Letters: The Uses of Writing in Black New England* (Boston: Trustees of the Public Library of the City of Boston, 1977), 26-63.
2. Ibid., 34; Robinson, *Black New England Letters,* 44-46; Kenneth Silverman, "Four New Letters By Phillis Wheatley" *Early American Literature* 8, no. 3 (Winter 1974): 256, 268
3. Leonard P. Curry, *The Free Black in Urban America 1800-1850: The Shadow of the Dream* (Chicago: University of Chicago Press), 49-80; James Oliver Horton and Lois E. Horton, *Black Bostonians: Family Life and Community Struggle in the Antebellum North* (New York: Holmes and Meier Publishers, Inc., 1979), 67-81.
4. "A Man of Color," *Freedom's Journal* (18 May 1827); Julie Winch, *Philadelphia's Black Elite, Activism, Accommodation, and the Struggle For Autonomy* (Philadelphia: Temple University Press, 1988), 41, 42; William H. Pease and Jane H. Pease, *They Who Would Be Free: Blacks Search For Freedom, 1830-1861* (New York: Athenaeum, 1974), 114-15.
5. Pease and Pease, *They Would Be Free,* 115-16; "Report of the Committee on a National Press and Printing Establishment for the People of Color," *North Star* 14 January 1848.
6. Gregory U. Rigsby, *Alexander Crummell: Pioneer in Nineteenth Century Pan-African Thought* (Westport, Conn.: Greenwood Press, 1987), 10; *Freedom's Journal,* 16 March 1827; Bella Gross, "Freedom's Journal and The Rights of All," *Journal of Negro History* 18, no. 3 (July 1932): 241-42.
7. Peter Williams *Letter* to Thomas Tucker, New York Manumission Society, 10 June 1816.
8. Rigsby, *Alexander Crummel,* 15; Gross, "Freedom's Journal," 242.
9. *Freedom's Journal,* 16 March 1827, 3.
10. Ibid.
11. David E. Swift, "Black Presbyterian Attacks on Racism: Samuel Cornish, Theodore Wright and Their Contemporaries," *Journal of Presbyterian History* 51, no. 4 (Winter 1973): 441, and Frederick Cooper, "Elevating the Race: The Social Thought of Black Leaders, 1827-1850," *American Quarterly* 24, no. 5 (December 1972): 604-6, are too limited in their assessment of *Freedom's Journal.*
12. Henry G. LaBrie, ed., *Perspectives of the Black Press: 1974* (Kennebunkport, ME: Mercer House Press, 1974), 1-3; Roland E. Wolseley, *The Black Press, U.S.A.* (Ames: The Iowa State University Press, 1971), 17, 18; Robert L. Allen *Reluctant Reformers: Racism and Social Reform*

Movements in the United States (Washington, D.C.,: Howard University Press, 1983), 18.

13. *Freedom's Journal,* 13 April 1827, 17.
14. *The Rights of All,* 18 September 1829, 26.
15. *Freedom's Journal,* 16 March 1827.
16. Ibid., 3; 25 April 1827, 38; Donald M. Jacobs, "David Walker: Boston Race Leader, 1825-1830," *Essex Institute Historical Collections* 107, no. 1 (January 1971): 95-6.
17. *The Colored American,* 1 April 1838, 3 and 24 June 1838; I. Garland Penn, *The Afro-American Press and Its Editors* (New York: Arno Press and the New York Times, 1969), 42.
18. A North Carolina slave, Horton wanted to use the proceeds from the sale of his poems to purchase his freedom. See *Freedom's Journal,* 29 August 1828, 179; see also Richmond, *Bid the Vassal Soar,* 81-198 for biographical details on Horton; and Jacobs, *David Walker,* 97.
19. Penn, *The Afro-American Press,* 91-99.
20. See *The Colored American,* 15 April, 17 June, 4 November 1837; and Penn, *The Afro- American Press,* 35-47.
21. *Liberator,* 6 October 1837.
22. *The Colored American,* 7 July 1838.
23. *The Colored American,* 26 August, 9 September, 10 February and 24 March 1838.
24. *Freedom's Journal,* 16 March 1827; Martin E. Dann, ed., *The Black Press, 1827-1890* (New York: Capricorn Books, 1971), 33-7; Lee Finkle, *Forum For Protest; The Black Press During World War II* (Rutherford, New Jersey: Fairleigh Dickinson University Press, 1975), 17; Gross, "Freedom's Journal," 241-42; Penn, *The Afro-American Press,* 22-5.
25. Joseph Harris, *Africans and Their History* (New York: New American Library, 1972), 11-26; William Leo Hansberry, *Africa and Africans As Seen By Classical Writers,* Joseph E. Harris, ed. (Washington, D.C.: Howard University Press, 1977), 336-40.
26. Letter *Freedom's Journal,* 16 March 1827; Gross, "Freedom's Journal," 260.
27. *Freedom's Journal,* 10 August 1827; Gross, "Freedom's Journal," 260.
28. Lawrence J. Friedman and Arthur H. Shaffer, "Mercy Otis Warren and the Politics of Historical Nationalism," *The New England Quarterly* 48, no. 2 (June 1975): 197, 206-7.
29. Jim Bearden and Linda Jean Butler, *Shadd: The Life and Times of Mary Shadd Cary* (Toronto: NC Press, Ltd., 1977), 128-130.
30. Ibid., 128-30; and Martin R. Delany, *The Condition, Elevation, Emigration and Destiny of the Colored People of the United States* (New York: Arno Press and The New York Times, 1969), 131.
31. Mary Ann Shadd, *A Plea for Emigration; or Notes on Canada West in its Moral, Social, and Political Aspect: with Suggestions Respecting Mexico, West Indies, and Vancouver's Island for the Information of Colored Emigrants,* (Detroit: George W. Pattison, 1852), 8-24.
32. Dann, *Black Press,* 39-41; Penn, *Afro-American Press,* 31; and Gross "Freedom's Journal," 256.
33. Ibid., 42-44, 246-51; Penn, *Afro-American Press,* 33-37; Gross, "Freedom's Journal," 257-59.

34. *Freedom's Journal,* 16 March 1827; Gross, "Freedom's Journal," 261.
35. *Freedom's Journal,* 24 August 1827.
36. David Hume, "Slave Labor," *Freedom's Journal* 17 (August 1827): 89.
37. Drew McCoy, *The Elusive Republic: Political Economy in Jeffersonian America* (Chapel Hill: The University of North Carolina Press, 1980), 17-27.
38. Harris, *Africans and Their History,* 17.
39. *Freedom's Journal,* 24 August 1827, 83; James Anderson, *Observations on Slavery Particularly with a View to it Effects on the British Colonies in the West Indies* (Manchester: J. Harrop, 1789), 7.
40. Anderson, *Observations on Slavery.*
41. Ibid.
42. Ibid., 9-12.
43. Ibid., 16-21; James Anderson, *Addenda: Containing Answers to Some Objections That Have Been Urged Against the Abolition of Slavery* (Manchester: J. Harrop, 1789), 26-38.
44. Adam Hodgson, "Compares South American Slavery to Feudalism" *Freedom's Journal,* 7 September, and 14 September 1828, 101, 105.
45. Hodgson, "Letter to Jean Baptiste" *Freedom's Journal,* 10, 17, 24, and 31 August 1827.
46. Gross, "Freedom's Journal," 248, 278-79; Dann, *Black Press,* 16, 17; Samuel Cornish, *The Rights of All,* 29 May 1829, 2; Carter Bryan, "Negro Journalism in America Before the Emancipation," *Journalism Monographs* 12 (September 1969): 9. The Gross, Dann, and Bryan assessments are challenged by my reading of *Freedom's Journal.* Russwurm continued to use the pages of the paper to attack ACS until late in the paper's last year. See Donald M. Jacobs, ed. *Antebellum Black Newspapers: Indices to New York, Freedom's Journal (1827-1829), The Rights of All (1829), The Weekly Advocate (1837) and The Colored American (1837-1841)* (Westport, Conn.: Greenwood Press, 1976), 161-62.
47. Winch, *Philadelphia's Black Elite,* 42-43; John B. Russworm *Letter* to R.R. Gurley, May 1829.
48. John B. Russwurm *Letter* to Rev. R. R. Gurley 26 February 1827, *Journal of Negro History* 10, no. 2 (April 1925): 156; Carter G. Woodson, ed., *The Mind of the Negro As Reflected in Letters Written During The Crisis, 1800-1860* (New York: Russell and Russell, [1929]1969), 3.
49. Dann, *Black Press,* 17; Gross, "Freedom's Journal," 270-72; Jacobs, *Antebellum Black Newspapers,* 161-62.
50. Jacobs, *Antebellum Black Newspapers,* 207.
51. Other New York City papers included Thomas Hamilton's *The People's Press* (1843); David Ruggles; *The Genius of Freedom* (c1845-46); and Willis Hodges; *The Ram's Horn* (1847).
52. *The Weekly Anglo-African,* 3 December 1859.
53. Frederick Douglass speech, 31 May 1849 cited in Waldo E. Martin, *The Mind of Frederick Douglass* (Chapel Hill: The University of North Carolina Press, 1984), 167. See also John Blassingame, ed., "Slavery, The Slumbering Volcano: An Address Delivered in New York, New York, 23 April 1849," in *The Fredrick Douglass Papers: Speeches, Debates, and Interviews, 2, 1847-54* (New Haven: Yale University Press, 1982), 153.
54. Penn, *The Afro-American Press,* 86-87.

55. Michael Meyer, "Thoreau and Black Emigration," *American Literature* 53, no. 3 (November 1981): 386-87; David M. Dean, *Defender of the Race: James Theodore Holly Black Nationalist Bishop* (Boston: Lambeth Press, 1979), 37.

56. Martin R. Delany, *Condition, Elevation, Emigration and Destiny of the Colored People of the United States* (New York: Arno Press and The New York Times, 1969), 127-28; Dann, *Negro Press,* 19-20; Penn, *Afro-American Press,* 73-81. See Winch, *Philadelphia's Black Elite,* 119, 122-24 and Winch, *Leaders of Philadelphia's Black Community,* 532 for references to *The National Reformer,* a monthly publication of the American Moral Reform Society in 1839. See *Liberator,* 20 July 1831, 107 Reference to Junius C. Morel and John P. Thompson, and their plans to publish a black newspaper entitled *The American,* and also *Liberator,* 7 July 1841 and 24 July 1841, for announcements of intentions to publish two other black papers in Philadelphia, the *Pennsylvania Freeman* and *Colored American.*

57. Maria Weston Chapman, "The Buffalo Convention of Men of Color," *Liberator,* 22 September 1843, 151; Donald Jacobs, "William Lloyd Garrison's *Liberator* and Boston's Blacks, 1830-1865" *The New England Quarterly* 44, no. 2 (June 1971): 263-67; *The Colored American,* 18 April 1840, 2, and James Oliver Horton, "Generations of Protest: Black Families and Social Reform in Antebellum Boston," *The New England Quarterly* 69, no. 2 (June 1976): 251.

58. Jacobs, "William Lloyd Garrison's *Liberator,*" 260-62. "Meeting in Philadelphia," *The Liberator,* 12 March 1831, 43.

59. Jacob C. White Jr. *Letter* to James Redpath 3 June 1861. George Lawrence was a black New Yorker involved with the finances of several papers including *The Weekly Anglo-African* and *The Pine and Palm.* All letters in the White-Redpath correspondence are in the Leon C. Gardiner Collection, Box 12G manuscripts, Historical Society of Pennsylvania.

60. White *Letter* to James Redpath 21 August 1861. See also White *Letters* to Thomas Hamilton, George Lawrence and Robert Hamilton, 2 and 16 April; 6 May 1861 and 1 January 1862 requesting papers to sell, clearing accounts for *The Weekly Anglo-African.*

61. George Lawrence *Letter* to Jacob C. White Jr., 25 June 1862.

62. White *Letter* to James Redpath, 6 January 1862.

63. Redpath *Letter* to Jacob C. White Jr., 23 August 1862.

64. See *The Christian Recorder* Manuscripts Collection, Pennsylvania State University Library.

65. Delany, *Condition, Emigration, Elevation, and Destiny of the Colored People,* 127-29; Dann, *Black Press,* 19, 23, 30, 65; and George A. Levesque, "Inherent Reformers-Inherited Orthodoxy: Black Baptists in Boston, 1800-1873," *Journal of Negro History* 60, no. 4 (October 1975): 514.

66. Jacobs, *Garrison,* 276; Delany, *Condition, Emigration, Elevation, and Destiny of the Colored People,* 128, and Dann, *Negro Press,* 19, 30, 65.

67. "Editorial" *The Colored American* 8 (July 1837): 2.

5

The Convention Movement: Public Forum for Black Ideas and Black Leaders

Two catastrophic events a dozen years apart ushered in the fourth element in the nineteenth -century black platform for change: the convention movement. The first of the events was the founding of the American Colonization Society in December 1816. Immediately, blacks came together in cities across the country, including southern locales, to protest the emergence of the organization.

In January 1817 the most important of these meetings took place in the city of Philadelphia.[1] While the meetings in other cities are evidence of a high level of black political awareness, the Philadelphia meeting set several precedents. It was the largest meeting of blacks ever assembled in the United States but, more important, blacks utilized the Philadelphia meeting as the mode of response years later when they found themselves facing another menacing circumstance.

The second call for a national conclave was generated by the 1829 riot and the ensuing expulsion of large numbers of blacks from the city of Cincinnati. Richard Allen, in his preeminent position as the bishop of the African Methodist Episcopal Church, had the power and authority and the historical experience to call such a meeting. When blacks met in the spring of 1830 in Philadelphia they were setting in motion a series of annual meetings that would run through the late 1830s.[2] After a suspension of about eight years the conventions began to meet again in the 1840s and continued until the post-Civil War years. Here we trace the genesis, the development, and the demise of the convention movement and evaluate its importance to the black platform for change.

These conventions were the calling together of black leaders from across the country to discuss problems of mutual concern to all blacks. They represented the collective deliberation about the problems facing the community but more important they represented attempts to provide solutions to those problems. Of great importance to black leadership was the opportunity to address local and federal authorities about black grievances. When coupled with black newspapers, the conventions were part of a two-pronged attack on black social and political inequalities. Understandably, with black leaders representing every region and every shade of opinion, solutions were sometimes difficult to achieve. Nevertheless, even blacks opposed to the conventions had to acknowledge their existence and power. The conventions were the arenas and leaders who expected to be legitimate representatives of the people had to be in attendance.

Even if specific conventions were captured and manipulated by one political faction, the convention format mirrored the search for change in status being pursued in the black community. Although the convention movement eliminated neither slavery nor discrimination, on balance, black leaders considered conventions a viable means to attempt to achieve stability, acceptance, and equality in America. The meetings dramatized the issues around which blacks wanted the community to coalesce. In addition, they informed blacks and whites of black dissatisfaction and often pointed the way to possible solutions. They served as training grounds, second only to the church, for developing young black leaders. Most important, the conventions provided closure for the community; the meetings were a relatively safe place to fight factional battles without destroying needed community unity.

I

In 1817 black leaders were without an effective means to register their disaffection with the emergence of the American Colonization Society. At the time they lacked any newspaper or national political organization that could command attention. In fact there was even an absence of a nationally recognized political leader. At the local level there were a number of black leaders who were known to blacks in other cities but not necessarily to white political authorities. Moreover, the ability to protest against ACS was made more difficult because the whites who founded ACS were politically well-placed.

Additionally, blacks were committed to a historically positive perception about Africa and equally committed to their potential for being good Americans. To protest too loudly against whites suggesting the African return might call into question much of the positive Afro-American assertions about Africa. Given the absence of an apparatus to protest against ACS and their own ambivalence about leaving the United States, the Philadelphia blacks, who constituted the most organized and recognizable group, had to find a way to gather more precise information on ACS and how best to respond. Further complicating the black response was the fact that several of the influential whites in the organization had some knowledge of and prior connections with several of the black Philadelphians, such as Absalom Jones and Richard Allen. The whites in touch with Allen seemed sincere in their concerns for the welfare of blacks and they couched those concerns in religious rather than political terms.

One such white individual was the Reverend Robert Finley of Basking Ridge, New Jersey. Much of the impetus for the founding of ACS rests with the efforts of the Reverend Finley. A well-meaning Presbyterian clergyman, Finley was deeply concerned about the plight of northern free blacks, particularly those in his vicinity. Since emancipation had not significantly changed their status and because Finley thought blacks unsuited for life in a free society dominated by whites, he began his crusade to find them a place where they might fare better. Finley was aware of and had corresponded with Paul Cuffe to ascertain Cuffe's feeling for Finley's developing plans of black repatriation. Cuffe gave his qualified blessing to Finley's enterprise and also supplied Finley with the names of his black allies who were members of the African Institution, a London-based organization experimenting with blacks in Sierra Leone. Once he had finished his work of forming ACS in Washington, Finley planned to meet with leading blacks to get their approval of his scheme and to enlist their aid in publicizing the society's aims.

Although a clergyman, Finley was well connected with the Washington elite. He had conducted discussions with President James Madison, a friend from their student days at Princeton. Madison had firsthand knowledge of the Sierra Leone project through dealings with Paul Cuffe in 1815. Madison approved the idea of black colonization but was constrained by the War of 1812 from giving federal financial assistance. His position and knowledge were of support to Finley. In addition, Finley had the support of his brother-in-law Elias B. Caldwell, clerk of the United States Supreme Court. Also at the December meetings was Bushrod Washington, nephew of the first president of the United States, who accepted the presidency of ACS. Joining Washington as executives of the new organization were politically ambitious new politicians such as Henry Clay, General Andrew Jackson, Daniel Webster, and older ones such as John Randolph. Francis Scott Key, author of the national anthem, was also an active participant in founding ACS.

In a series of meetings on 21 and 28 December 1816 Finley and his cohorts constructed the first white organization dedicated to the relocation of blacks to Africa. Finley's organizing efforts were assisted by the steady interest of the white news media. His ideas were circulated by papers in New York and Philadelphia. Most were supportive of Finley's plan and concentrated on the philanthropic thrust rather than on the disruptive aspects of his proposal. For most whites there was no menace in the proposed removal since most believed blacks lacked the capacity to deal with the rapidly modernizing America. Finley's humanitarian prouncements, however, saved many whites the trouble of revealing their individual negative perceptions about the black presence in America.

While whites concentrated on Finley's philanthropic posture, blacks kept abreast of the pronouncements of Henry Clay and John Randolph. Both men used the pages of big city newspapers to make clear that the "society had no intention of interfering with slavery."[3] Blacks focused on the two men's remarks concerning the removal of the free blacks. They agreed with Clay and Randolph that removal would stabilize the institution of slavery by reducing the problems of slave control. As reported later by James Forten, blacks were much frightened by the assertions of Clay and Randolph.[4] Still, they were willing to give Finley an audience and hear his proposals.

The massive coverage of Finley's activities in the Philadelphia papers kept the menace of the organization before the black public. Philadelphia journals reprinted several of Finley's offerings in the *National Intelligencer.* These articles outlined Finley's basic feelings about the nature of white prejudice against blacks. He noted that in an age when more democratic impulses were becoming hallmarks of American politics, blacks were not the beneficiaries of these changes. He spoke of the opportunity in Africa for blacks to explore their political future free of white obstruction.

Blacks may have been more sympathetic with Finley because he seemed to understand certain debilitating features of American life for blacks. For example, he discussed the discrimination that faced New Jersey blacks once slavery ceased to exist. He could even entertain that black polities in Africa would combat the African slave trade at its roots. While the English abolitionists had promulgated a similar idea for several decades no American thinker had dared to broach such sentiments. Black leaders resonated with Finley's observations although they were not the official policy of ACS. They could not, however, condone the organization's depiction of them as criminal, parasitic, and lacking the capacity to govern with whites.

The black interactions with Finley leave open a historical speculation of major significance that neither white nor black activists seems to have answered. What was to be the nature of any black polity emerging out of either black or white schemes of the African repatriation? We can never know whether Finley perceived that a black political entity free to operate in its own sphere would be the equal of white nations. Judging from the lack of political relations between the United States and Haiti, blacks would have continued in an inferior status with whites even at the nation state level. None of the white political leaders espousing black relocation and expressing it as an opportunity for blacks suggested the possibility of diplomatic relations with the new African nations.

Blacks themselves, especially at this early date, had not worked out clearly, formulations about the nation-state. From a twentieth-century perspective it is stunning that no one was asking such questions. Thus, it seems, black and whites shared to an astonishing degree a lack of political vision about what could eventuate from the African return. Both seemed motivated by reducing as much as possible the nuisance factors involved in their relationship. For whites it was an opportunity to rid themselves of a troublesome presence while assuring that a sufficient black work force remained. For blacks relocation seemed to carry the major implication of fleeing the inequality of life in America and its attendant disabilities.

Despite the fact that some major philosophical directions were missing, there were questions on the minds of blacks and Robert Finley in January 1817. Blacks needed to know what had transpired in Washington and how the ideas of ACS would be implemented. Finley needed to know what level of support he could receive from blacks to further the society's goals. Thus, on his return from Washington to Basking Ridge he called on black leaders to ascertain their responses to the ACS proposals. The atmosphere was highly charged, not only because of the newspaper accounts, but also because of the differences between black leaders and many blacks in the community. At the time of the meeting between Finley and black leaders the splits had not yet surfaced. Black leaders such as Richard Allen, Quomony Clarkson, and James Forten assumed that they spoke for the community's interest when dealing with Paul Cuffe and the African Institution. Several Philadelphia blacks accompanied Cuffe on his 1815 voyage to Sierra Leone, but the majority of blacks who were opposed to the African return had not found an outlet for their views.

Most of what we know about Finley's meeting with black leaders is limited to Finley's accounts and the brief letter of James Forten. Forten's missive to Paul Cuffe describing the meeting and subsequent activities of blacks along with Finley's accounts allow us to reconstruct a credible version of the meeting. The blacks were animated, according to Finley, and he describes them as supportive of his plans. Understandably, he may have read more support into their verbalizations than they intended to convey.

His possible misjudgment could also be attributed to the fact that at some level he was speaking with the already converted. The black leaders he knew, had cooperated with the African Institution and were assisting that organization with its exploration of the African return. He also may have been misled by the personal respect he was given by the black Philadelphians and by the deference to him as a symbol of white power. Neither Forten nor Finley addressed the questions raised by the assertions of Clay and Randolph. Black leaders certainly had opinions about their characterizations and about the justifications for their removal. Finley may have avoided those troublesome aspects as they did not seem to represent his major motivations for ACS. Instead both parties concentrated on those areas where agreement already existed.

For example, when the animated Forten asserted that blacks would become a great nation on the order of Haiti, Finley could respond favorably to the assertion while not agreeing with all its particulars. His view concerning blacks governing themselves when away from whites was already on record and his opinion of Haiti as a nation state may have paralleled his opinions of blacks' capacity to govern within a white polity. Forten's assertions that blacks would not remain forever in bondage were not counter to Finley's ideas, and he intuitively understood why Forten and other blacks used Haiti as their example. The Haitians had seized their liberty in a long and bloody revolution, the very thing Finley and his ACS associates wished to avoid.

Finley and his black host did not differ substantially in their perceptions of the frustrations faced by free blacks. Forten addressed the continuing dissatisfactions of being a free black with aspirations. He observed, according to Finley, "that neither riches nor education could put blacks on a level with whites."[5] Moreover, the more wealth and awareness that blacks acquired the more frustrated they became. Forten and Finley also agreed on the assumption that if blacks and whites remained in the same state whites would always prevail. Finally, they seemed to affirm the choice of Africa as the site most advantageous for black development.

Simultaneously, according to Finley, Richard Allen expressed himself in terms favorable to some of the ACS proposals. Characterizing Allen as speaking with warmth throughout the meeting, Finley's recall was that the bishop favored African colonization. The subtlety in Allen's response may not have been conveyed to Finley even after the meeting, when he corresponded with members of ACS.[6] Allen proclaimed himself so much in favor of the African return that if he were young he would consider going himself. Further, Allen spoke warmly of the colony of Sierra Leone and especially of Paul Cuffe. The distinction that Finley failed to see was that the Sierra Leone and Cuffe plans had neither the negative characterizations of free blacks nor the desire for the complete expulsion of blacks from America. Cuffe and the African Institution presented a voluntary plan of creating a black refuge and therefore was receiving the assistance of several black leaders. Again, the unexpressed different assumptions were ignored in favor of what appeared to be a consensus of purpose.

Having satisfied himself that blacks were in basic agreement with his plans, Finley left Philadelphia to work for greater acceptance of ACS's plans. The meeting between Finley and the black leaders had taken place at the Reverend Absalom Jones's church and the apparent consensus may be attributed to the narrow sample of blacks who attended the meeting. They were all leaders and all involved in some degree with Paul Cuffe's efforts. Differences of opinion among blacks never surfaced in the meeting with Finley.

II

Yet the different opinions did surface shortly after the meeting with Finley when the blacks themselves discussed ACS at Richard Allen's church. Several differences in this meeting are immediately apparent. First, more than three thousand black males gathered at the church to give their responses to the emergence of ACS. Not all of these men were from Philadelphia but the historical record is mute on where the men came from or how they were informed of the gathering. One of the ironies of black American life and history can be glimpsed in this meeting. Although one of the first and possibly the largest black group voluntarily assembling in America at that time, it was completely ignored in the white media, and blacks organizing and attending this historic gathering did not keep minutes of the proceedings. Our evidence for the meeting rests largely on the Forten to Cuffe letter. Second, the opinions of the assembled mass of blacks departed significantly from the leadership's responses to ACS and their depiction of the good motives of Robert Finley and some other more philanthropic members of the society.

The assembled blacks made no distinction between ACS and certain aspects of Finley's personality: they unanimously rejected the whole scheme. Those leaders who had participated in the discussions with Finley must have been slightly taken aback. There seems to have been an aggressiveness at the meeting that forced Allen, Forten, and others to remain silent about sentiments they had shared with Finley. They neither made a forceful attack on ACS nor defended Finley as a humanitarian. Despite its aggressive rejection of ACS and its designs, the meeting was anticlimactic. No standing organization with the responsibility for coordinating black responses nationally emerged from this first meeting. Unlike earlier incidents in the community, such as the 1793 yellow fever epidemic, no public defense of the community or criticism of ACS was printed and distributed. Two things did result from the meeting: an eleven member steering committee was formed and there was a renewed dedication to keeping the pressure on ACS. This responsibility would be carried out by continually publicizing the menacing aspects of ACS and warning black leaders not to cooperate with the organization.

By the summer of 1817 the steering committee's efforts resulted in a second protest meeting. On 10 August 1817 with James Forten as chair and Russell Perrott as secretary, blacks in Philadelphia met. The results of their deliberations are seen best in an address co-authored by Forten and Perrott. Given this opportunity to speak to the existence of ACS, the authors began by listing the benefits enjoyed by black Americans in the United States. To whites, Forten and Perrott acknowledged their participation in the manumission of blacks.[7] Moreover, the authors explained that blacks had been exposed not only to Christianity and its blessings but also to industry and integrity. From these benefits the writers, and the blacks they spoke for, had no wish to depart. Blacks wished to secure prosperity for their families, prosperity based on their own application of work and thrift. They were content with present conditions, they said. Their contentment was based, in part, on the opportunities for improvement which the Constitution and laws gave to all. It was therefore painful, they noted, that the scheme for colonizing came from men whose name and power automatically commanded respect.

While the authors do not use the words self-determination, such an idea is clearly implied. Forten and Perrott asked their audience to note that blacks did not ask to be colonized. To force colonization on blacks was not in their best interests. In addition, Forten and Perrott could foresee no future circumstances in which forced colonization would be beneficial to the black community. The portrait of the United States given in the address is certainly more positive than most black Americans would agree with. Forten and Perrott state that blacks would not consider separating from America. As the objects of ACS's intentions black leaders declared they were in the best position to determine if its aims met their needs. Seeing no benefits to the free blacks, Forten and Perrott denounced the ACS plans. They further requested that the scheme's designers renounce the plan and they asserted their "determination not to participate in any part of it."[8]

Not only could the two men address self-determination for free blacks but also felt themselves to be especially prepared to protect enslaved blacks. The speakers declared themselves to be in even greater opposition to ACS plans and its effects on slaves. Perhaps Forten and Perrott were naive or disingenuous when they claimed that abolition was progressing in the United States. They seemed to accept the slow gradualist evolution of antislavery sentiment in the United States. Both speakers knew that no radical national abolitionist organization had yet emerged nor had the philosophical shift from gradualism to immediatism taken place. Blacks also knew that many existing manumissionists supported ACS. Blacks were in the position of having to guard against attacking their benefactors while questioning their benefactors' associates. Thus, Forten and Perrott made the most positive interpretation on rather limited evidence. They even speak approvingly of the opportunities for instruction and improvement afforded to slaves by gradual emancipation, but they denounce the way that ACS coupled emancipation with relocation. They suggest that relocation as a part of manumission was little more than intimidation. They also note that bondage had already separated southern and northern families, a break that could not be restored if freed blacks were sent to Africa. According to the authors the slaves, unprepared because of their lack of education, would find little happiness in Africa, an idea frequently asserted by ACS spokesmen. Since slaves had not been educated in the arts or industry, any colony they inhabited would suffer and Christianity, another favorite of ACS publicity, would soon disappear.

If those slaves who were manumitted would suffer by relocation, the authors of the address claimed that those remaining would also suffer greatly. By various devices, slave masters would remove the most dangerous slaves through manumissions and colonization. The resulting diminution of leaders would make slaves easier to control, would remove the threat of insurrection, and year after year the stability of the institution of slavery would be guaranteed. Forten and Perrott end their address by noting what they considered to be the final state for Afro-Americans should ACS succeed in its design: misery, sufferings, and perpetual slavery.[9] Although the address was powerful and the blacks who supported the address were also powerful, it had little impact on official attitudes toward ACS or its continuing activity.

Those individuals on the steering committee continued to fight ACS but their gains were minimal. Until 1827 they had no newspaper or white spokesperson of sufficient authority to command attention. Finally, in 1827, blacks organized their first newspaper and, understandably, part of its editorial policy was an expose' of ACS. Although the newspaper, *Freedom's Journal,* represented a first-strike weapon against ACS, even it succumbed to the colonization controversy. Oddly enough, when a powerful white, William Lloyd Garrison, endorsed what a number of black opponents had been saying for more than a decade, more men of authority began to take notice.[10] Despite the fact that several influential procolonization white abolitionists denounced the organization following Garrison's publication, the organization continued to menace black community life. Blacks continued to take sides over the colonization issue. The convention format proved to be enduring and provided for black Americans a forum for discussing important issues throughout the antebellum period.

III

The convention format was not used in a conscious and sustained manner, however, until the 1830 meeting following the 1829 Cincinnati riot. Unlike when they convened the 1817 mass meeting, in 1830 John Gloucester, Richard Allen, and James Forten envisioned annual conventions to discuss black problems and solutions. From 1830 through 1835 and again from 1843 to 1865 black leaders turned to the convention format because they felt it allowed the widest range of opinions to be expressed on a subject and it reached the greatest range of leaders active in the country. Unlike the call for the 1817 meeting, the men calling the 1830 meeting for Philadelphia envisioned several days of discussion and deliberation. There also seemed to be a hidden rivalry between blacks in Philadelphia and New York surrounding the question of which group would call the meeting first. No such rivalry was apparent in 1817. The 1817 event was a mass meeting attended by most, if not all, black males in Philadelphia. The impetus for the 1817 meeting had come from two sources: the anxiety of blacks over newspaper accounts of ACS' founding and the small group of black leaders who had attended an informal discussion with the Reverend Robert Finley.[11]

Despite the differences between the 1817 and 1830 events, they are linked in several important ways. First, both call for public discussion of problems confronting the black community. Second, both issued resolutions that they hoped would be guidelines for collective action. Third, both selected committees to carry out the decisions of the deliberations. Fourth, the leadership in both incidents was similar. Finally, discussions of ACS were significant at each meeting.

The precipitating incident for calling a convention in 1830 was an attack on the civil liberties of blacks in Ohio followed by a riot against the blacks of Cincinnati. Such a physical attack, which resulted in a loss of life and property, was a much different basis for calling a convention than the founding of ACS, which stated only principles on which white men could agree to deport blacks. While it antedates the antiabolitionist riots of the mid-1830s, the Cincinnati riot was symptomatic of those confrontations.[12] Whites in Cincinnati were alarmed at the growing self-assertion of blacks, particularly in employment pursuits and political agitation. Further, there appeared to be a rise in antislavery sentiment coupled with new challenges to old line white political leadership. The account of the Cincinnati riot has been told elsewhere.[13] What concerns us here is the reaction to Cincinnati manifested by black leaders in New York and Philadelphia.

In 1859 a black newspaper commemorating the 1830 meeting noted with some irony that the call to meet was not issued by a major black leader. According to the paper, black America in 1830 was blessed to have giants such as Richard Allen, Christopher Rush, Peter Williams, Jr., William Hamilton, James Forten, Frederick Hinton, Samuel Cornish, and Phillip A. Bell. Yet the idea to call the convention came from the unknown Hezekiah Grice of Baltimore.[14] Mr. Grice, the paper stated, desired a national conclave to discuss the issue of emigration and the desirability of targeting Canada for relocation. What is missing in the

Anglo-African report is the state of agitation in New York and Philadelphia over the plight of the Cincinnati blacks and the continuing power of ACS. In 1829, before the riot, black Philadelphians, Junius C. Morel, and Peter Gardiner held a meeting to respond to black Ohioans' calls for support against new legislation attempting to force blacks from the state. Some Ohioans were in favor of emigrating to Canada to avoid American racism. Morel's and Gardiner's meeting was to garner support of the black Ohioans' plans.[15] Thus, the tangled nexus for the first national convention incorporated the following issues: aid to stricken blacks in Ohio, the necessity of discussing the idea of emigration with special reference to Canada, maintaining the offense against ACS, and the striving for national supremacy between blacks in New York and Philadelphia.

The *Anglo-African* report relied almost exclusively on the rivalry issue. It reported that Grice had distributed a circular to black leaders around the country calling for a national convention. Five months later, in August 1830, he received a response from Richard Allen to come to Philadelphia to discuss his proposal. Once there, according to Grice, he was shown a flyer approving his plan that was being circulated by New Yorkers Peter Williams, Peter Vogelsang, and Thomas L. Jennings. Bishop Allen is reported to have said, "we must take some action immediately, or else these New Yorkers will get ahead of us."[16] Bishop Allen, Benjamin Paschal, Cyrus Black, Junius C. Morel, and James Cornish constituted the committee that heard Grice's plan and subsequently called for a meeting in Philadelphia on 15 September 1830.

Hezekiah Grice had thus set in motion one of the pillars of black community activity, the convention movement. He was little known outside of Baltimore and did not participate strongly in the movement once it started. Although young, Grice had kept abreast of problems facing blacks those obstacles that hindered emancipation. Moreover, he had met and discussed a variety of issues with two of America's most active antislavery advocates, Benjamin Lundy and William Lloyd Garrison, both of whom at the time, were also staunch supporters of ACS. About the time that Grice met Garrison, the latter had just finished David Walker's *Appeal*. On balance, Garrison agreed with Walker's assessment of slavery in the United States, but felt it was the wrong time to express such aggressive sentiments. Grice, then, troubled by his own assessment of life in the States desired a convention of colored men to discuss the vexing problem of emigration.

When the group gathered in Philadelphia the agenda was threefold: discuss emigration in general; exploration of Canada as a relocation point; and how to assist Cincinnati's blacks. As it turned out the third point was the least discussed item during the convention. Instead, the gathered delegates gave major emphasis to examining Canada as a refuge for American blacks. The delegates met secretly from 15 September until 20 September. This was necessary as there were rumors circulating that ruffians would try to stop the meetings. There is no direct evidence of threats, but the Cincinnati case, the Providence case in 1820, and what would ensue in New York and Philadelphia in 1834 probably justified the caution.

Once publicly assembled the delegates lost no time choosing officers and giving their enterprise a name. The Reverend Richard Allen was named president of the convention. This was a fitting recognition of almost forty years of activism in the black community. Dr. Belfast Burton of Philadelphia and Austin Steward of Rochester were selected as vice presidents. Junius C. Morel became secretary and the assistant secretary was Robert Cowley of Maryland. After the elections the first order of business was the recommendation to form a parent society. It would be the immediate responsibility of the officers of the Parent Society to appoint an agent to reside at or near the place where land would be purchased in Upper Canada.[17] The business of naming an agent was not successfully concluded at the deliberations.

Although the number of delegates was far below the three thousand black men in Philadelphia in 1817, the list of attendees was impressive. Seven states sent at least one delegate. Delaware was represented by Abraham D. Shadd. From Virginia free black interests were represented by Arthur M. Waring, William Duncan, and James West, Jr. Hezekiah Grice, James Devour, Aaron Willdoon, and Robert Cowley were the Maryland representatives. Pennsylvania, naturally, had the largest delegation consisting of Allen, Morel, Belfast Burton, Cyrus Black, William Whipper, Peter Gardiner, John Allen, James Newman, Charles H. Leveck, and Frederick A. Hinton. New York had three delegates in attendance: Austin Steward, Joseph Adams, and George L. Brown. Conspicuously absent New Yorkers included Peter Williams, Peter Vogelsang, and Thomas L. Jennings. These three were the Philadelphians' major opponents in the jockeying to lead the convention movement.

Despite the absence of the politically conscious New Yorkers the assembled delegates completed several serious tasks. The most important single accomplishment was the crafting of the "Address to the Free People of Colour of These United States." It begins with a reference to the Declaration of Independence reminding readers that all men are born equal, and endowed with the unalienable rights of life, liberty, and the pursuits of happiness. The address ends with a plea to brethren throughout the United States to cooperate with the Parent Society by forming societies of their own. If these directives were impractical to comply with blacks were instructed to contribute funds and/or send one delegate to the convention to be held in June 1831.

This brief address touched on the staple topics of black agitation. Immediately, ACS was singled out for condemnation. Again, as they had in 1817, the delegates made allowances for misguided philanthropy on the part of some ACS supporters. "Not doubting the sincerity of many friends who are engaged in that cause, yet we beg leave to say, that it does not meet with our approbation."[18] They indicted the system of enslavement, the exploitation of black women, and the injuries to Africa. Reasserting their claims to American nativity, the delegates warned that they would never accept the redress of leaving the United States.

Next the address calls attention to the enactment of laws, such as those in Ohio, which forced blacks to leave their homes, to suffer in overcrowded cities, and to be the victims of unemployment. To continue to subject blacks to these conditions, the address said, is barbaric and unchristian. The realities of overcrowding, forced removal, and unemployment suggested to the delegates that there was the need for some form of relief, but no relief was forthcoming except that designed by ACS and rejected by the majority of blacks. Thus, the delegates focused on the idea of examining the possibilities of voluntary relocation in Canada. The delegates supported the establishment of a settlement in British Upper Canada and sent out a call to philanthropic individuals to support such a settlement. It was implied, of course, that this was a wiser, more humane solution than ACS's African colonization.

While the delegates were more attracted to Canada than to Liberia, they overstated the receptivity of Canadians to a black exodus. As in other periods the bleak prospects for blacks in America led men, who should have learned from earlier historical experience, to be overly optimistic. Just six years before, in 1824, the same leadership had responded enthusiastically to plans of Haitian relocation despite signs of its unsuitability to absorb large numbers of blacks.[19] Now in 1830 they were putting Canada in the most positive light. Canadians were not concerned, the address stated, about color differences and blacks would be entitled to the same rights and responsibilities as other citizens. Language, climate, and soil would be familiar enough to black Americans not to cause a problem. The delegates further stated that quality land was available in abundance for a dollar and a half an acre. Economically blacks would be well situated in Upper Canada. Produce raised in the colony attracted good prices assuring farmers of a good return for their labor. Finally, the delegates called for black mechanics and builders to come as part of the exodus. Their task would be to erect buildings and by their efforts help design a stable black community. The address read more like a promotional brochure than a hard political/economic assessment of Canada.

While the promotional tone of the address is counterproductive, another aspect of the address is equally disturbing. Although its drafters

note that blacks seemed to choose the urban environment, they continued to promote Canada as a positive rural experience. They had failed to
note that blacks found urban areas, even with their attendant problems,
more attractive than rural settings.[20] In hindsight, the address is ambiguous. It simultaneously promotes the rural life and tantalizingly extols the
virtues of the urban area. When it addresses economics the address sees
black recovery tied to yeomen farmers not urban laborers, but when it
addresses education, which it does briefly, the vision is urban. The
drafters never seemed to have noticed the dichotomy of their views.

The address closed by introducing the topic of solidarity and cooperation. First, the draftees direct a mild criticism to blacks for their failure to
pursue more lasting goals and activities.[21] Black leaders must help the
community engage in activities that will raise the moral and political
standing of all blacks, the address warned. Paramount among these tasks
for moral and economic uplift were the agricultural and mechanical arts.
Agriculture would provide a degree of independence and the mechanical
arts, in connection with the sciences, would contribute to a new standing within America.

The work of the convention societies suffered a keen blow with the
death of Bishop Richard Allen in 1831. He had provided some form of
leadership to the community since 1787 and had experienced different
levels of oppression as well as different levels of resilience within the
community. His leadership was not without controversy. As possibly his
final expression of community leadership, the convention movement
exemplified the positive and the negative of nineteenth-century black
authority. The controversial aspects of Allen's personality and the convention movement are contained in both the rivalry between competing
sets of black leaders and the fact that they had to strike an independent
but similar course of action while simultaneously indicting ACS for promoting the removal of blacks from America. Even after Allen's death the
task for black leaders involved the tightrope act of differentiating their
plans of finding a black refuge from those suggested by ACS. Although
leaders were forced to recognize the necessity for a place of solace they
also had to assert their rights to American citizenship. The balancing act
resulted in sharp debates and a keen focus on the language used to
inform the black community about acceptable grounds for leaving the
United States and also acceptable terms to describe the place of refuge. It
could not appear, for example, that any area could replace the United
States as the desired home of American blacks. Although leaders stressed
the equality of blacks recognized in Canadian law, they were equally
quick to stress the desirability of achieving that equality within America.

Moreover, for most leaders Canada or Haiti was the expedient, not the
desired choice. During the second annual convention held in Philadelphia
in June 1831 the delegates continued to argue over balancing the same

themes with which Richard Allen had struggled since 1811. In 1811 Allen supported Paul Cuffe in his attempts to interest blacks in Sierra Leone. Later, in 1824, Allen had assisted in exploring repatriation to Haiti. In both cases he expressed his ambivalance about staying in the United States.

IV

In 1832 the delegates reassembled in Philadelphia and reaffirmed the first general convention's plan to purchase lands in Upper Canada. Simultaneously, they noted that conditions in the United States still necessitated the Canadian asylum. On the following day, Wednesday, 6 June, the delegates returned to the issue of Upper Canada. The minutes describe an animated discussion taking place. The discussion became lively over motion to continue support of Canadian settlement; but some delegates were concerned that the motion would be construed as relinquishing their claim to rights as Americans.[22] The issue divided the convention. William Hamilton of New York, Abraham Shadd of Delaware, Thomas Jennings of New York, Phillip A. Bell and J.W. C. Pennington, both of New York, John B. Vashon of Pittsburgh, and Samuel Johnson of Lewiston, Pennsylvania, saw the motion as inaccurately conveying black sentiments. Junius C. Morel, one of the earliest advocates of Canadian resettlement, defended the motion and stated that support of Canada did not suggest any lessening of zeal for America. Morel's interpretation was supported by the entire Maryland delegation of Samuel Elliott, Robert Cowley, and Samuel Hiner. He also received support from Aaron Roberts of Trenton, New Jersey, Thomas Banks, also of New Jersey, and fellow Philadelphian Benjamin Paschal. To break the impasse' Abraham Shadd offered the following amendment:

That members of the Convention take into consideration the propriety of affecting the purchase of lands in Upper Canada, as an Asylum for those of our brethren who may be compelled to remove from these United States.[23]

Neither Benjamin Paschal nor Thomas Coxsin of New Jersey liked Shadd's amendment. They countered by making a motion to form a committee and submit the Canadian amendment to the panel. Robert Cowley, William Hamilton, Junius C. Morel, John Peck, and William Whipper were appointed to a committee which was given a Thursday reporting date.

The committee did not report back until Friday morning, 8 June. Its report was signed by only three members of the committee—Whipper, Hamilton, and Peck. A minority report signed by Morel and Cowley was also submitted. Long discussion of the motion did not produce satisfactory closure. Not until the afternoon session was the issue resolved by voting down the minority report. By motion of Thomas L. Jennings the committee was expanded by two more people: Thomas Coxsin and Benjamin Paschal. On Saturday morning, 9 June the newly expanded committee submitted its finished report. It was the most comprehensive report of the convention and it commenced by dividing the original motion into its three component parts. Then the report went on to describe objections to the amendment. Declaring the minority motion to be premature the committee instead put to the delegates the three separate inquiries contained in the motion.

1. Is it proper for the Free People of Color in this country, under existing circumstances to remove to any distant territory beyond these United States?

2. Does Upper Canada possess superior advantages and conveniences to those held out in these United States or elsewhere?

3. Is there any certainty that the people of color will be compelled by oppressive legislative enactments to abandon the land of their birth for a home in a distant region?[24]

The committee had established the clearest statement of the issues surrounding relocation and emigration.

Following the statement of the three inquiries the report went on to discuss the historical background of the questions and the convention. Committee members admitted that the expulsory legislation in Ohio in 1829 had not only stimulated blacks to leave the state but also triggered the call for the first convention. Those responsible for calling the convention were duly acknowledged. Their insight in recognizing the limited knowledge of Upper Canada was praised, as was their sending of agents who corroborated the positive perceptions but cleared up the issue concerning the purchase of property. They found that United States citizens could not purchase property in Upper Canada for transfer to other individuals. Without resolving the issues of land purchase the first convention did recommend to blacks generally and particularly those in Ohio the wisdom of seeking asylum in Upper Canada. While not abandoning the issue of emigration, the obstacles surrounding property purchase convinced the first convention to turn its attention to raising the status of blacks within the United States.

The committee noted that circumstances in the South had changed so drastically that two things were clear to the delegates in 1831. One, the situation of blacks was more precarious than at any time since the

Declaration of Independence. Two, the reactions of southerners provided more inducements for blacks to leave their native land. The committee then proceeded to respond to the three inquiries stated earlier. If, the drafters said, the first inquiry was true then blacks should make no provision for the intellectual, moral, or political elevation in the United States. Moreover, they argued that should the content of inquiry one be accurate, then the blacks' benefactors would abandon their efforts to assist blacks here. In addition, white benefactors might question both the courage and the wisdom of a people who would leave their home to dwell among strangers. The draftees then returned to a theme contained in the Forten and Perrott report of 1830: if some blacks left those left behind would be even more severely persecuted. Therefore, in response to inquiry one, they recommended that all possible monies should be used to promote the interests of blacks here. On inquiry number two the drafters concluded that legislative protections were better in Canada than in the United States presently. As proof of their analysis the drafters cited a report in the leading antislavery paper of the times.[25] Benjamin Lundy's report outlined the progressive nature of Canada's civil liberties statutes.

Like a number of white benefactors, Lundy posed problems for his black contemporaries which they were reluctant to speak about openly. They praised him for being antislavery and paid homage to the fact that he was often a lonely crusader in the cause. Like many of his white allies, however, he had severely restricted perceptions about black capacities to live in a multiracial society.[26] His solution to white prejudice, like many of his white fellows, was to counsel blacks to leave the United States. Blacks politely ignored his negative perceptions and his advice on that score, and extolled him for his antislavery work. After admitting the positive nature of Canada's laws, the drafters concluded that the convention should assist blacks seeking asylum in Canada by collecting monies and appointing agents for potential settlements.

In response to the third inquiry the drafters asserted that only time would tell whether blacks would be compelled to quit the United States. This response is probably unsatisfactory to the twentieth-century mind, depending as it does on divine intervention. For the drafters, however, the tone was more correct than discordant. The language of religious imagery and millenialism dominated the early years of the nineteenth-century American reform movement. Not only were blacks seeking political equality caught up in this language but so were reformers as seemingly different as Charles G. Finney and Lyman Beecher.[27] Finally, the committee submitted a resolution revised as follows:

> That this Convention recommend the establishment of a Society, or Agent, in Upper Canada, for the purpose of purchasing lands and

contributing to the wants of our people generally, who may be, by oppressive legislative enactments, obliged to flee from these United States and take up residence within her borders. And that this Convention will employ its Auxiliary Societies, and such other means as may lie in its power, for the purpose of raising monies, and remit the same for the purpose of aiding the proposed project.[28]

While the Canadian issue took much of the convention's time ,other striking issues were introduced, debated, and resolved. Among the more interesting items on Thursday, 7 June were letters from Major General Andrew Jackson and his aide-de-camp, Thomas Butler, addressed to the free colored inhabitants of Louisiana, in 1814. John B. Vashon of Pittsburgh introduced the letters and hoped the delegates would approve his request to have three thousand copies printed and distributed at large. Like other delegates, Vashon knew that Jackson was a vice president of ACS, but his 1814 letter, which amounted to a proclamation, expressed sentiments in "accordance with those of every philanthropist in theses United States."[29] A lengthy debate ensued over the merits of including the proclamation in the minutes. Eventually Vashon's resolution was voted down. He then pursued the matter of printing and distributing the three thousand copies. Again, lengthy and provocative debate took place. Vashon was forced to withdraw the motion as the debate had carried through to the hour of adjournment.

This same convention had in attendance a number of whites, all of whom projected themselves as the friends of the blacks. Several whites made their appearance on Monday afternoon, 11 June 1832. Rev. Simeon S. Jocelyn of New Haven and Rev. Mr.Harrison from the Island of Antigua addressed the convention on issues of social uplift and education. This was not the first time whites had been in attendance but it was near the end of such practice. The most crucial enterprise that whites and blacks had tried to work on jointly through the convention movement was education. The specific educational issue was the task of opening a manual labor college for blacks in New Haven. At the 1831 convention the idea of the school was ably argued by William Lloyd Garrison, Arthur Tappen, Thomas Shipley, and Jocelyn. Working with black members of the convention the whites hoped to raise $20,000 to open the college. Together with the blacks, Garrison, Tappen, and Jocelyn had worked a positive profile for the city of New Haven. They reasoned that New Haven was better suited to host the school for the following reasons:

the site is healthy and beautiful; the inhabitants are friendly, pious, generous, and humane; laws are salutary and protecting to all, without regard to complexion; boarding is cheap and provisions are good.[30]

In addition, both blacks and whites noted that the city carried on an extensive West Indian trade. It was hoped that sons of wealthy black islanders would find the school attractive and enroll. Samuel E. Cornish was unaminously elected general agent to collect funds for the projected institute, Arthur Tappen was appointed treasurer to receive funds, and provisional committees to assist in the collection of funds were organized. These committees contained some of the most vocal and active blacks of the time. Boston's committee included the Reverend Hosea Easton, Robert Roberts, James G. Barbadoes, and the Reverend Samuel Snowden, all of whom contributed to the platform for change. In the mid-1830s, Easton would be a leading advocate of elevating the race and the liberation philosophy of the chosen people. Roberts and Barbadoes, in the 1840s, would share common interests in educational agitation and creating newspapers in Boston. The Reverend Samuel Snowden had been the pastor and confidant of David Walker before Walker's untimely death in 1829.[31]

New York's provisional committee consisted of Rev. Peter Williams, Boston Crummell, Phillip A. Bell, Thomas Downing, and Peter Vogelsang. All of these men in their careers pursued a number of issues vital to community consciousness. Williams, Crummell, and Vogelsang engaged in activities such as founding organizations, funding newspapers, and creating separate black churches, and were also involved in several emigration schemes. Phillip A. Bell became a leading black newspaperman ultimately founding papers on both the East and West coasts. In the 1850s, Downing, became one of the most vocal supporters of Afro-American citizenship and an equally vocal opponent of African emigration. Other committees were organized for Washington, D.C.; Lancaster, Pennsylvania; Newark, New Jersey; Wilmington, Delaware; and Baltimore. A great deal of energy and enthusiasm went into ensuring the success of the proposed black manual arts college in New Haven. Although the idea of the black college received strong support, it ultimately failed in the face of a determined backlash from the white citizens of New Haven.

The collapse of the college was still a year away and in 1831, the convention continued to respond enthusiastically to white participation and to new black initiatives. White participants were honored not only for their presence but also for representing the interests of the black community. A resolution noted:

> . . . that the editors of the Genius of Universal Emancipation, The Liberator, and the African Sentinel are our tried and true friends, and fearless advocates of our rights and promoters of our best interests, [and] are entitled to a prominent place in our affections.[32]

Prior to the resolution on the white newspaper editors another resolution congratulated Junius C. Morel and John P. Thompson and requested the convention delegates to help insure their proposed newspaper venture.

At the 1832 convention some of the enthusiasm of 1831 had come into direct collision with economics and prejudice. Morel and Thompson never got their paper off the ground and no other serious attempts to create a black paper in Philadelphia reached fruition until the mid-1850s. Instead, black Philadelphians supported a number of black and white organs published elsewhere. The delegates in 1832 were sobered by the virulent racism of New Haven whites who opposed the black college. Although the delegates voted to continue their efforts to found a college in New Haven or elsewhere, their deliberations were devoid of the old enthusiasm and positive assessments of future sites. Unlike in 1831, the only white man present during the 1832 discussion was Simeon Joyceln, and his participation was limited to his well-received history of colored schools, not a continued defense of establishing the college.

The delegates decided to retain Samuel Cornish as the agent to collect funds and to retain Arthur Tappen as receiver of such funds. If Cornish were unable to continue in service an appointment to fill the position would be made by the executive committee of New York State. Phillip A. Bell, in his minority report, pointed out that when the opposition of New Haven's white citizens became manifest, those in attendance in 1831 had expected a series of actions that did not take place. One, they expected a suspension of collecting funds, until, two, a pamphlet could be prepared by Joycelyn addressing how to respond to New Haven's obstacles. When collection of funds was resumed there was so little support that it was determined to abandon funding until the 1832 convention met.

While William Lloyd Garrison and Thomas Shipley were not defending their 1831 advocacy of the manual arts college, they were in attendance in 1832. Their services were valuable to the assembled delegates. Both men rebutted the claims of the Reverend. R. R. Gurley, an ACS representative.[33] Gurley had become, since the death of Robert Finley, the leading society member with the responsibility to placate black fears. Gurley addressed the convention on its second day, 5 June 1832, during its afternoon session. Gurley's address was lengthy and eloquent and was meant to correct inaccurate perceptions about ACS's work. Immediately after, Garrison responded by demonstrating that indeed the ACS continued to work against the best interests of blacks. Garrison's speech was followed by a black participant, Pittsburgh's John B. Vashon. Finally Thomas Shipley, another white participant from 1831, criticized Gurley's representation of ACS. A day later, on 6 June,

Garrison provided the critique of a speech given by Rev. Mr. Patterson, another ACS official. Garrison's remarks were substantially what they had been the day before in response to Gurley.

The Canada and ACS issues were expected at the convention and the response to them was basically the same: advice for continued perseverance on the part of delegates and the community at large.

New issues also made their way, albeit sometimes briefly, into the discussions. Three that would figure more prominently in future conventions and in community life were introduced on 12 June, as the convention neared its end. First was the topic of black public processions. It would become commonplace in the 1830s for local authorities to place restrictions on black participation during national holidays. It was almost equally common for blacks to organize parallel celebrations that antagonized whites and often led to violent attacks on blacks.[34] The delegates, therefore, recommended that the people of color discontinue public processions not only on holidays but on any day. There was no dissent among the delegates concerning the recommendation. That this was meant to protect the community from gratuitous violence is beyond question but some little suspicion might attach to the motivations of the men who seconded for the motion. Both William Whipper and J. W. C. Pennington were opposed to separate or "complexional" activities. Separate black parades or 4th of July orations acknowledged and perpetuated black exclusion, according to Pennington and Whipper. It was better, from their point of view, to forgo celebrations if they could not be multiracial. Since both were committed to multiracial activities, their energy and enthusiasm for the conventions began to wane when white participation decreased.[35]

William Whipper also introduced, by motion, the second new item: a call for temperance and total abstinence from the use of spirits. This limited motion foreshadowed Whipper's involvement in a more comprehensive program of moral uplift after 1835. Once introduced into convention deliberations the moral reform emphasis began to challenge the political orientation of the first conventions. By 1834 the battle lines had been clearly drawn between the political agitators and the moral uplifters. This emergence must be seen in the larger context of the American reform movement. Just as divine intervention was seen as a resolution of earthly ills, individual moral regeneration was, for some, a precondition to beneficial societal changes. Blacks were not immune to the reform impulses surging through American society, nor should they have been since reform leaders saw the problems attendant upon drinking as disproportionately affecting the working class. Since the socioeconomic status of most blacks was working class or lower, Whipper and others attempted to combat drink by temperance agitation, the same as whites.

Coupled with the concerns for the working classes' welfare was the third motion introduced at the Wednesday afternoon session. Thomas Coxsin's motion asked the convention to seek means to improve the condition of black mechanics. Interestingly enough, this issue was not debated at length nor did the delegates pass the motion. Instead it was referred to committee, but "its fate" is unclear. Certainly, black mechanics were by ritual and systematic discriminatory statutes being forced out of the trades.[36]

One possible explanation for the seeming inaction on the motion is that the reform period itself seems devoid of any real look at economic and class issues in American society. Instead, most reformers concentrated on the moral uplift of society, thinking once that had been achieved all other things would assume their natural place. More important, attempting to alleviate economic problems might, in fact, have led to an analysis detrimental to cherished notions of American society. For example, the middle-class agitators might have had to recognize the limited value of defining poverty instead of making concrete economic proposals. Furthermore, they might have had to delay indefinitely their own class rewards in American society if they pursued too closely the deviations between American ideals and American realities.[37] Finally, an economic analysis may have brought to the surface even greater ethnic and class antagonisms for middle-class agitators to confront which would rival those already existing between blacks and whites.

The failure to grasp the significance of economic arguments is borne out in the convention address. Nowhere in that oration does anything close to economic analysis make an appearance. The expected topics all appear: Canada, ACS, slavery, discrimination, the college, and proclamations that suggest blacks are eligible for citizenship. On the matter of where and when to hold the next convention there was no dissent from the choice of Philadelphia on the first Monday in June 1833.

Before adjournment, Hezekiah Grice's name was mentioned. As the representative of the Legal Rights Society of Baltimore, Grice tried to convince the delegates to consider a series of inquiries about black status in America. In a later age, we would say that the delegates waffled. They withheld their support of Grice by not considering his questions but paid him a compliment by thanking him for providing valuable information. This lack of guts is probably one of the things that soured Grice on the convention movement, an activity that he had helped to initiate. Hezekiah Grice did not attend another convention. Instead, by 1834, he was in Haiti and over the years rose to a position of prominence within the government.[38]

On the first day of the 1833 convention the delegates spent their time with housekeeping issues, defining delegate status, the adoption of rules and regulations, and appointment of committees. Wednesday morning, 5 June the convention began discussion of significant items. One of the very first issues involved a set of inquiries about how well the previous conventions' resolutions and directives had been carried out. The questions were really an attempt to assess the impact of the two previous conventions. Uppermost in the delegates' minds was the question of whether the last convention had any effect on improving the condition of the colored people. They were equally interested in whether any manual labor school would be established, if so, where, and what progress had been made toward that goal. Third, the questions asked if any resolutions of the Canadian Report Committee had been put in operation. Finally, the inquiries requested a clear statement of sentiments regarding colonization. The committee consisting of William Whipper, John Peck, Henry Sipkins, Robert Cowley, and William Douglass were not asking delegates to debate the issue or arrive at conclusions immediately. What they put forward was an agenda item that said we need to assess our effectiveness. Again, it was the moralists' egos that led this small skirmish. Spurred by the inquiries, the assembled immediately appointed committees to bring their findings to the body on each issue. Responsibility for reports was more clearly established in 1833 than it had been between 1830 and 1832.

The moralists were also those most committed to interracial solutions and so went on record once again to support William Lloyd Garrison. This time the convention not only commended his abolitionist activity but also voiced its support for his upcoming trip to England.[39] In addition to stumping for the New England Antislavery Society, Garrison had also committed himself to lay before the British public two other topics: aid for the manual school, and the dissemination of accurate information about the ACS.

On Friday morning, 7 June, Mr. Buffum spoke to the convention about a high school in Canterbury, Connecticut, for black females operated by Miss Prudence Crandall. Buffum's presentation included an excerpt from a letter by Arthur Tappen urging blacks to support the school. Little did the delegates suspect that Miss Crandall's school would be forced to close by the racist elements that prevented the establishment of the manual arts college in 1832.[40] Still, the idea of the manual arts college persisted, and this convention, like its predecessors, heard another report, on founding the school elsewhere. This report given on Saturday, 8 June, stated that two efforts were proceeding simultaneously in New York and Philadelphia. Although not as ecstatic as initial reports in 1831 the prognosis seemed good for the two schools to actually begin operation. Ten thousand dollars had already been pledged in Philadelphia and it was proposed that the school be placed under the supervision of the Society of Friends.[41] The

Canadian report was equally positive in that Mr. Austin Steward was asked to stay on as the agent for the Wilberforce Settlement in Upper Canada.

The temperance committee report was given Monday morning, 10 June. It was one of the longest reports in the history of the convention movement. It began by noting the progress of the American Temperance Society. It hailed the million people in the United States who had taken the pledge of total abstinence. It also hailed the six hundred American ships that were operating at sea without grog. The drafters of the report strongly recommended the founding of the Colored American Conventional Temperance Society whose annual meetings would be held in conjunction with the convention meetings. The report called on all blacks, with a special emphasis on influential blacks, to promote the new society and its goals. The report was as much fire and brimstone as it was fact.

Contained in the report were ringing calls for total abstinence and lurid references to early graves for the intemperate.[42] Following the submission of the report a committee of three was selected and empowered to draft a constitution in order to form the new group. Those appointed to the committee were William Whipper, Frederick A. Hinton, and Thomas Jennings. The report and the appointment of Whipper marked his personal ascendancy and the growing importance of issues with which he was associated within the convention movement: moral reform and interracial participation.

As late as Tuesday, 11 June the delegates were receiving correspondence from interested parties such as Simeon Jocelyn reporting that Prudence Crandall's school was weathering the opposition in Canterbury. Like Buffum a few days earlier, Jocelyn urged support from the black community as a way to stem the opposition. Later, in the report on African Colonization, the Crandall school again is mentioned. The delegates learned that the selectmen of Canterbury had called on representatives of ACS to advise them in the matter of Miss Crandall's school. In light of nineteenth-century sexism which, unfortunately, black males also practiced, the committee's response to the intrusion of ACS is very interesting. Not only did they condemn the selectmen and the ACS but they castigated their lack of progressive educational ideals. Both parties were scored for "preventing innocent and unprotected females from receiving the benefits of a liberal education, without which, the best and the brightest prospects of any country or people, must be forever blasted."[43] At least one other gesture to women as equal participants in the struggle occurred during the convention. Shortly before adjournment on 13 June Robert Purvis moved that the convention commend Miss Lydia White for her work in the free labour movement and for the successful running of her free labour store.

Purvis' motion recommended patronage of her store at 42 North Fourth Street in Philadelphia. The motion passed unanimously.

As in previous conventions the abolitionist press was singled out for its support of black causes. Among those papers cited were the *Genius of Universal Emancipation*, the *Liberator*, *Emancipator*, *Genius of Temperance*, and the *Abolitionist*. Benjamin Lundy was mentioned several times and his work with the *Genius of Universal Emancipation* was cited approvingly. The conventional address, signed by Abraham D. Shadd as president, was a hard-hitting piece of polemicism. Shadd's last item of business was to announce that the delegates voted to meet in the city of New York, on the first Monday in June 1834.

The fourth annual convention met in New York City beginning Monday, 2 June 1834. William Hamilton, president of the convention, gave the longest opening address on record, up to that time. Hamilton touched all the relevant themes that had surfaced in the previous conventions. He first spoke to the issue of inequality and caste in the United States. Hamilton thought it sad that United States society was divided and as such could reflect neither happiness nor civilization. On the topic of happiness within a society Hamilton cited the findings of a French explorer of Africa and his thoughts on the Hottentots as a balanced, compassionate society. The present state of society necessitated that Afro-Americans combine and work on their own particular needs. Hamilton, of course, strongly indicted the ACS. Its continued existence spoke to the continued need for blacks to meet in conventions. He spoke out against slavery and cheered that black agitation was limiting the power of ACS and helping to promote an antislavery movement. The moment was optimistic and hopeful and this convention would, Hamilton suggested, continue to display to the world the quality of black character. He also lightly noted past convention debates and hoped that the proceedings would be pleasant and refined.

On Monday, 9 June 1834 the delegates directed the publishing committee to publish, as part of the minutes, the proclamations of Major General Andrew Jackson and his aide-de-camp, Thomas Butler, issued in September 1814. Both proclamations elevated blacks to a status equal to white citizens and white soldiers. Blacks were addressed as "sons of Freedom," "Americans," and as having "intelligent minds" not led astray by false representations.[44]

Butler's oration spoke of informing the president and the American public about the blacks' noble participation. It is easy to understand why John B. Vashon, earlier in 1831, had wanted to inform the black and white communities that a vice president of ACS had at a crucial historical juncture turned to blacks to support national aims. None of the black delegates in 1831 or 1834 had to add the proviso that if blacks could be considered citizens and noble saviors at a time of national peril, then citizenship should be theirs despite the prounce-ments of ACS. Jackson's and Butler's proclamations put the lie to the negative characterization circulated by the organization.

Several reports were submitted to the delegates on subsequent days following the decision of the publications committee. Among other com-mittee reports was one supporting the New England Antislavery Society. Then, mindful of the workload necessary to clear the convention's charges, the delegates appointed a committee to condense the remaining reports. This group took under consideration twenty five reports includ-ing those on moral reform, manual labor schools, ACS, teacher training, libraries, and literary societies. The committee reported that the dele-gates could be well satisfied with their guardianship of the black commu-nity. They had provided useful insights to most of the problems confronting black Americans and, in those instances where the conven-tion did not provide a resolution, it at least provided a platform for airing views. On Thursday morning, 12 June the convention issued a lengthy Declaration of Sentiment. It touched on all the concerns the gatherings had discussed since 1830. The tenor of the declaration was that all obstacles to black equality need be removed before the United States could be considered Christian and progressive. The declaration sternly admonished the community:

> Let no man remove from his native country, for our principles are drawn from the book of revelation, and are incorporated in the Declaration of Independence, "that all men are born equal, and endowed by their creator with certain inalienable rights, that among these are life, liberty, and the pursuit of happiness."[45]

This convention also finished the task of completing the constitution to guide deliberations at future meetings. The committee overseeing the constitution included Peter Vogelsang, William Hamilton, Samuel Van Brackle, James Bird, and John Closson. They set out guidelines for names, where and when the convention should meet, the size of state and local delegates, the process of credentialing delegates, the matter of finances, selection of officers, and what forms and rules would govern until the constitution went into effect. As the convention neared its end, William Whipper again made several motions connected with moral reform. Again, this put Whipper's person and his causes in a position of notoriety, ensuring in part that delegates reviewing the minutes could not forget the issue or the man. One motion addressed specifically the area of moral reform: It referred back to the Declaration of Sentiment and recom-mended the establishment of moral reform societies suggested in that doc-ument. His second motion to recommend temperance on the principle of total abstinence spurred a series of other motions on the subject. Thus,

Whipper's strategically placed ideas of moral reform closed the 1834 convention and were in place to dominate the attention of the 1835 convention. Finally, the fact that the 1835 convention would be held in Philadelphia additionally strengthened Whipper's hand. He could expect to draw support from his many comrades in the City of Brotherly Love.

V

Immediately upon the opening of the convention of 1835 there was a motion by Augustus Price, of Washington, D.C. and seconded by the Reverend Stephen Smith, of Columbia, Pennsylvania (a longtime Whipper cohort) to organize the American Moral Reform Society. The motion touched off a hot debate; it even had a call from Junius C. Morel for a reading of the minutes of 1834. This was necessary as Price had referred to the Declaration of Sentiment for authority to make his motion. Morel and others were not convinced that the declaration had called explicitly for structuring a moral reform society. Defending the motion Edwin P. Atlee, a Philadelphian, made a strenuous speech concerning the condition of blacks in America. He and his supporters believed that conditions cried out for a moral reform society articulated in the motion. After much debate Price withdrew his motion and a substitute was offered by Frederick A. Hinton and again seconded by Stephen Smith. The new motion stated it was the sense of the convention to form a National Moral Reform Society. Almost immediately William Whipper moved that a committee of five be appointed to prepare a constitution for the National Moral Reform Society.

Despite this carefulness with language the next reference to a moral reform society boldly designated it the American Moral Reform Society.[46] On Thursday morning, 4 June William Whipper moved the convention recommend the formation of auxiliary societies of the American Moral Reform Society (AMRS) throughout the United States. None of the assembled delegates objected to Whipper's use of the title that had been attacked and voted down on the first day of the convention. From that initial motion on Thursday, Whipper and his cohorts steamrollered the convention with business concerning the AMRS. An address was to be prepared to the American people announcing the formation of the society. Another motion, also passed, required each auxiliary to contribute five dollars at each annual meeting to assist the society in its aims. Later that same morning the committee report on manual labor colleges included the announcement that the American Moral Reform Society would be the agency to collect money and designate the site of the college. The motion passed by a vote of ten to nine. In principle the AMRS had replaced the annual convention. Continuing the barrage of motions Whipper moved that AMRS establish its own press.

That afternoon a motion was introduced that the convention appoint a five-man committee to nominate officers of the AMRS. Before the issue could be resolved the meeting was adjourned. The first item of business of Friday, 5 June was the motion which passed with the seating of Whipper, Smith, Robert Purvis, Samuel Van Brackle, and Francis Lippins. Before the morning session concluded, Whipper reported that the officers nominated for the AMRS were fellow Philadelphians, John P. Burr, president, and Rev. Morris Brown, Frederick A. Hinton, John B. Roberts, Stephen H. Gloucester, Joshua Brown, and Thomas Butler. Later the convention voted that each delegate be a committee to promote the interests of the AMRS. The backers of AMRS had succeeded in dictating their narrow interests to the convention. Other business was conducted, of course, but none had the impact of the AMRS.

An address to the American people was given to the convention and included in the minutes was a statement to let the American public know of AMRS's existence. The address, coupled with the constitution and the officers of the AMRS was the longest in convention history. The officers were not those nominated earlier. Instead, they were more geographically diverse but still dominated by black Philadelphians. James Forten was chosen senior president, and only two of the four vice presidents were not Philadelphians. The offices of treasurer and three secretaries were all held by Philadelphians. The minutes contain no official adjournment and no call for a convention for 1836.

VI

What had the early conventions accomplished? How did the three cities under study lead the convention movement? Does the idea of a national consciousness percolating out of New York, Boston, and Philadelphia break down in view of the convention movement? From the above discussion it is obvious that New York and Philadelphia played key roles in the convention movement between 1830 and 1835. It was, after all, the leaders in the two cities competing with each other to host the meeting that brought about in the first call for a convention by black Philadelphians. Moreover, the rivalry continued for several years and was of such intensity that several active New Yorkers refused to participate as long as the Philadelphians held the power. Those New Yorkers who did attend the early meetings participated fully and continued to try to have the convention meet in their city. Although a convention did not meet in New York until 1834, each year before that an increasing number of New Yorkers played significant roles. Peter Vogelsang, for example, served on a variety of important committees such as credentials, constitution, conventional address, Canada, emigration, and ACS. Although they were not winning the fight to host, their attendance and participation were appreciated by their fellow delegates.

When New Yorkers finally hosted a convention in 1834 William Hamilton, convention president, pioneered a new innovation: the president's opening address. Subsequent presidents used the device, as Hamilton had done, to focus delegates on the sense of national purpose with which the business was to be conducted. It served as a gentle reminder that narrow sectarian concerns were not the preferred topics of discussion. It likewise attempted to set a standard of debate and argument without rancor for the delegates. In light of the tone that conventions took after 1835, the gentle reminder did not work. In several conventions, following the resumption of the meetings in 1843, the debates became personal and acrimonious.

The presidential address was only one example of a national consciousness both guiding and emerging in the deliberations. When delegates convened they had in mind providing succor for the community under siege. This involved Canadian refuge not only for blacks in Ohio but also for slave and free blacks everywhere in the United States. Once the issue of Canadian relocation was introduced it opened the broader topic of emigration. Unlike the earlier attempts, in 1817, for example, at discussing the potential, not the reality of emigration, which were local or regional in nature, the convention delegates tried consciously and consistently to shape a national policy for black relocation. As a part of this effort it was as important to create an ideology for relocation as it was to pinpoint a resettlement target. The delegates understood clearly the risks for all blacks in the emigration solution. It would be easy for whites to misinterpret black schemes of relocation as an admission that they neither desired nor merited American citizenship. The delegates felt that if free black emigration succeeded the slave population would be in greater peril. Thus, the convention leaders envisioned themselves as a national directorate of black interests. In conjunction with emigration, of course, was the specter of the American Colonization Society. This organization so reflective of white national power could only be successfully countered by a national black response which the convention represented.

Even the issue leading to the demise of the early movement was seen by its advocates as having national import. Beginning in 1833 the Philadelphians most responsible for the moral reform impulse kept trying to assert their ideas for black moral reformation on and through the national body. In its early stages, although supported by friends and cohorts of William Whipper, black moral reform was not narrow and sectarian. It aimed at the moral rejuvenation of the black community through temperance, education, and uplift. Far from a Philadelphia scheme, black moral reformation was part of the trend of morality as politics then sweeping the United States. Like white reformers generally, black moral reformers disdained political and economic solutions to societal ills in favor of moral regeneration. It might be argued that black leaders in their focus on morality were exhibiting a degree of their Americanness, which could be lost on observers as the conventions largely pursued explicitly black activities.

Despite the fact that a single issue, moral reform, effectively halted the early convention movement, the early conventions achieved a number of remarkable goals. First, the convention provided the first national public forum for an articulation not only of black problems but also of potential resolutions. Second, the meetings allowed black leaders from across the United States to come together, which had not occurred prior to the convention. Third, the structure of the meetings, annual and national, fostered a broad-based program to combat black disabilities.

In a certain sense the meetings represented a first, sometimes tentative, united exploration into political agitation for the black community. At the early stage the obvious issues of slavery, discrimination, and inequality of opportunity were the major foci. These issues were debated over and over in succeeding conventions but even the repetitions proved to be an asset, because each succeeding discussion brought more sophistication and maturity to the issues under consideration. Blacks were growing in their political consciousness and were finding outlets for this new maturity. By 1835 they had created an omnibus indictment of American society. Moreover, the indictment, if heard and heeded by white Americans, would benefit them as well as black Americans. In other words, the convention worked on projecting a vision of a united, egalitarian, Christian commonwealth, a vision as profound as any being propagated by white reformers in the antebellum period.

In the hiatus between 1835 and the next convention of 1843, the AMRS attempted to exert its hegemony over leadership in the black community. Instead, it rankled many black leaders including at least one of its original officers. By 1837 Samuel Cornish was so out of sympathy with the aims of AMRS that he waged an intensive campaign against its influence.[47] Cornish's objections are representative of the opponents of the AMRS. Among the society's activities that Cornish and others objected to were its criticism of exclusively black organizations; its focus on moral reformation while ignoring political and economic change; and its insistence on interracial participation even in the face of massive white indifference to their interracial rhetoric. By 1841 the AMRS had ceased to exist for all practical purposes. It had not supplanted the convention movement and for the next two years there were frequent calls to revive the conventions.

An apparatus for reestablishing the conventions existed in the form of state conventional societies that had been set up as early as the first convention. Once revived the conventions, beginning in 1843, were in several ways significantly different from their 1830-1835 predecessors. Most obvious, the action shifted away from the New York, Boston, and Philadelphia. Yet these cities still retained a major influence after the proceedings. For example, Henry Highland Garnet, initially operating out of Troy, New York, but later out of New York City, continued to be a major force in the conventions through the Civil War. The same illustration could be offered about Frederick Douglass. Although living in Rochester, New York, for a period of time he was closer ideologically to the Boston clique than to black New Yorkers; and although 1847 he was often at odds with black Bostonians William Cooper Nell and Charles Lenox Remond after 1847, Douglass was an agent of the continuing presence of the nuclear cities.

Garnet and Douglass often were disruptive influences in the second-stage conventions. The degree of their personal and ideological animosity had not been demonstrated in the earlier conventions. At Buffalo in August 1843, Garnet and Douglass found themselves on opposite sides of the issue concerning militant slave action versus moral suasion. Douglass led the opposition to Garnet's *Address to the Slaves of the United States of America* and contributed to its defeat on the convention floor.[48] Later during the middle to late 1850s Douglass took exception to Garnet's stance on emigration. From 1858 until 1861 he opposed the African Civilization Society, Garnet's emigration and Christianization organization, on the grounds of its affiliation with the dreaded ACS. Their confrontations are another marker differentiating the two phases of the convention movement.

New York, Philadelphia, and Boston were only partially eclipsed in the revival period after 1843. Conventions continued to meet in the three cities but these locales never recovered the preeminent positions they held in the early convention period. This is probably due to a number of causes, among them the growth of the Afro-American leadership cadre. Partly due to the success of the convention movement, more black males came into leadership positions after the mid-1830s.

Even cities away from the mainstream, without large black populations, mounted calls for conventions after 1843. These were successful efforts partly because they addressed specific issues or were the projects of particular leaders. Because the meetings were in locales such as Albany, Detroit, Cleveland, Chatham, and Rochester, the attendance was lower and the agendas were usually confined to a pet issue of the most popular leader in the area. The provincialism of the later conventions also meant that the deliberations would not receive fair coverage in the leading East Coast journals.

Provincialism and factionalization were major factors in the new convention movement so that counter conventions often were held when one faction felt it had been overlooked in the call to meet or disregarded during deliberations. Unlike the consensus of the earlier meetings the convention idea proliferated into specific and sometimes localized versions of the larger community's needs.

Because the participants in the conventions after 1843 were younger, better educated, and more politically sophisticated than earlier conventioneers there were more divisions as well as more explosive topics among them and during deliberations. The topics of slave action in the cause of abolition, the creation of a national black press, the pro- or anti-slavery bias of the Constitution, the merits of political action in the abolition struggle, judging the merits of the political parties' commitment to abolition, and the utility of continuing to seek white allies to support black causes, were more sophisticated political concerns than the topics discussed during the early conventions.

While a new political maturity marked the later conventions, it is inaccurate to suggest that the early conventions were assimilationist and therefore neither original nor successful.[49] Between 1830 and 1835 leaders from Boston, New York, and Philadelphia experimented with the form and set the agenda for the first ongoing black public forum in American history.

A certain degree of radicalism existed in the black American insistence on creating and sustaining a convention movement, but that radicalism was qualitatively different from some twentieth-century black political nationalism. The radical content is a position driven by the black assertion into the political discourse at a time when their voices were neither sought nor generally welcomed. It is not a challenge to analyze or create alternatives to the existing system.

Yet the assertions of the nineteenth-century conventioneers are considerably beyond the radicalism of twentieth-century racial politics. The majority of twentieth-century black political activists have eschewed radical political change that indicts the American creed for a politics of inclusion. With the exception of Marcus Garvey, most twentieth-century blacks have sought redress within the confines of the American political mainstream. Their nineteenth-century counterparts also advocated a politics of inclusion but at a time when they, like most Americans, were in their infancy in terms of political recognition and access. Most nineteenth-century political activists, black or white, were focused on making the new republic work, not in seeking alternatives. In the black case, the dangers were twofold: slavery and discrimination. Most black leaders felt that the end of slavery would evince a salutary effect on discrimination. That nineteenth-century blacks held to this hope is understandable because of the youth of the American political experiment. Their holding to a politics of inclusion was more understandable and perhaps more justified than later black radicals.

The substratum of conservatism should not blind us to the accomplishment of the black leadership in creating the convention movement. Its format has left an idelible mark on black politics well into the twentieth century. The ideas that commanded the most attention at the meetings were: creating a maunual arts college, founding a national press, debating the merits of emigration, defending black character and black lives, and how best to connect with the larger American reform movement. Although neither a national press nor a manual arts college resulted from the deliberations, the ideology of emigrationism was positively assisted by the convention format.

Notes

1. Louis R. Mehlinger, "The Attitude of the Free Negro toward African Colonization," *Journal of Negro History* 1, no. 1 (January 1916): 276-301; and William Lloyd Garrison, *Thoughts on African Colonization* (Boston: Garrison and Knapp), 1832.
2. Howard Holman Bell, ed., *Minutes of the Proceedings of the National Negro Conventions 1830-1864* (New York: Arno Press, 1969); William H. Pease and Jane H. Pease, *They Who Would Be Free: Blacks Search For Freedom, 1830-1861* (New York: Athenaeum, 1974).
3. William Loren Katz, "Introduction" to Garrison, *Thoughts on African Colonization.*
4. James Forten *Letter* to Paul Cuffe, 25 January 1817 cited in various sources, see Katz "Introduction" to Garrison, *Thoughts,* 7-9.
5. Isaac Van Arsdale Brown, *Biography of the Rev. Robert Finley* (New York: Arno Press and The New York Times, 1969), 123.
6. Ibid., 123-25.
7. James Forten and Russell Perrott, "An Address to the Humane and Benevolent Inhabitants of the City and County of Philadelphia" in Herbert Aptheker, ed., *A Documentary History of the Negro People in the United States, 1661-1910* (New York: Citadel Press, 1963).
8. Ibid., 53.
9. Ibid., 55.
10. Garrison, *Thoughts,* 11.
11. Brown, *Biography of Robert Finley,* 125.
12. Leonard P. Richards, "Gentlemen of Property and Standing," *Antiabolition Mobs in Antebellum America* (New York: Oxford University Press, 1970), 34-35.
13. Richard C. Wade, *The Urban Frontier: The Rise of Western Cities, 1790-1830* (Cambridge: Harvard University Press, 1959), 222-29; David Gerber, *Ohio and the Colorline* (Urbana: University of Illinois Press, 1976), passim; Carter G. Woodson, "The Negro in Cincinnati Prior to the Civil War," *Journal of Negro History* 1, no. 1 (January 1916): 4-7; Richard C. Wade, "The Negro in Cincinnati, 1800-1830," *Journal of Negro History* 39, no. 1(January 1939): 43-55; Henry L. Taylor, "On Slavery's Fringe: City-Building and Black Community Development in Cincinnati 1800-1850,"

Ohio History 95 (Winter-Spring 1986): 5-33, there is no mention here of the 1829 Riot, but Taylor provides a marvelous look at conditions that contributed to racial unrest in the Queen City.

14. "The First Colored Convention." *The Anglo-African Magazine* 1, no. 10 (October 1859), 305-6.

15. Julie Winch, *Philadelphia's Black Elite: Activism, Accommodation, and the Struggle for Autonomy, 1787-1848* (Philadelphia: Temple University Press, 1988), 66-67; Gary B. Nash, *Forging Freedom: The Formation of Philadelphia's Black Community, 1720-1840* (Cambridge: Harvard University Press, 1988), 245; Emma Jones Lapsansky, "'Since They Got Those Separate Churches': Afro-Americans and Racism in Jacksonian Philadelphia," *American Quarterly* 32, no. 1 (Spring 1980): 58-60.

16. "The First Colored Convention," 307.

17. Richard Allen, *Constitution of the American Society of Free Persons of Colour, For Improving Their Condition in the United States; For Purchasing Lands; and for the Establishment of a Settlement in Upper Canada also The Proceedings of the Convention, with Their Address to the Free Persons of Colour in the United States,* (Philadelphia: J.W. Allen, 1831), in Howard Holman Bell, ed., *Minutes of the Proceedings of the National Negro Convention 1830-1864* (New York: Arno Press and the New York Times, 1969).

18. Ibid., 10.

19. Floyd J. Miller, *The Search for a Black Nationality: Black Emigration and Colonization 1787-1863* (Urbana: University of Illinois Press, 1975), 232-50; Ludwell Lee Montague, *Haiti and the United States, 1714-1938* (New York: Russell and Russell, 1966), 66-80.

20. Leonard P. Curry, *Blacks in Urban America, 1800-1860: The Promise of the Dream* (Chicago: University of Chicago Press, 1981), 3-7.

21. Allen, " Constitution of the American Society," 11-12.

22. *Minutes and Proceedings of the Second Annual Convention for the Improvement of the Free People of Color in These United States* (Philadelphia: Martin and Boden, 1832), 10.

23. Ibid.

24. Ibid., 15.

25. Benjamin Lundy, *Genius of Universal Emancipation*, 10, 12 (27 November 1829): 91

26. Winthrop Jordan, *White Over Black: American Attitudes Toward the Negro 1550-1812* (Baltimore: Penguin Books Inc., 1968), 342-74.

27. Alice Felt Tyler, *Freedom's Ferment: Phases of American Social History from the Colonial Period to the Outbreak of the Civil War* (New York: Harper and Row, Publishers, 1944), 41, 336, 490; Ronald G. Walters, *American Reformers 1815-1860* (New York: Hill and Wang, 1978), 125-26, 146, 175-76.

28. *Minutes and Proceedings 1832*, 20.

29. Ibid., 12.

30. *Minutes and Proceedings First Annual Convention*, 6 (Philadelphia: J.W. Allen, 1831).

31. Herbert Aptheker, *One Continual Cry; David Walker's Appeal to the Colored Citizens of the World 1829 1830, Its Setting and Its Meaning,*

together with the Full Text of the Third and Last Edition (New York: Humanities Press, 1965), 45-53.

32. *Minutes and Proceedings First Annual Convention*, 11.

33. *Minutes and Proceedings Second Annual Convention*, 1832, 9.

34. John Runcie, "Hunting the Nigs" in "Philadelphia: the Race Riot of August 1834," *Pennsylvania History* 2, no. 39 (April 1972): 191.

35. Richard P. McCormick, "William Whipper: Moral Reformer," *Pennsylvania History* 1, no. 43 (January 1976): 37-44; Carleton Mabee, *Black Freedom: The Nonviolent Abolitionists from 1830 Through The Civil War* (New York: Macmillan, 1970).

36. Leonard P. Curry, *Blacks in Urban America: The Shadow of the Dream* (Chicago: University of Chicago Press, 1980); Leon Litwack, *North of Slavery* (Chicago: University of Chicago Press, 1961), see especially his chapter "The Economics of Discrimination"

37. Walters, *American Reformers*, 7.

38. *Anglo-African Magazine*, 306.

39. *Minutes and Proceedings of the Third Annual Convention for the Improvement of the People of Colour* (New York: The Convention, 1833), 9.

40. Litwack, *North of Slavery*, 153-87

41. *Minutes and Proceedings, 1832*, 14.

42. Ibid., 18-19.

43. Ibid., 27. On sexism in the black community, see Marilyn Richardson, *Maria W. Stewart America's First Black Woman Political Writer: Essays and Speeches* (Bloomington: University of Indiana Press, 1987); and Bert James Loewenberg and Ruth Bogin, eds., *Black Women in Nineteenth Century American Life: Their Words, Their Thoughts, Their Feelings* (University Park: Pennsylvania State University Press, 1976), 5, 184-85.

44. *Minutes of the Fourth Annual Convention for the Improvement of the Free People of Colour* (New York: by Order of the convention, 1834), 21.

45. Ibid., 29.

46. *Minutes of the Fifth Annual Convention for the Improvement of the Free People of Colour in the United States* (Philadelphia: William P. Gibbons, 1835), 9-15.

47. *The Colored American*, 26 August; 2 September; 9 September 1837 and 25 August; 15 September 1838 and 5 September 1841.

48. *Minutes of the National Convention of Colored Citizens: Held at Buffalo, on the 15th, 16th, 17th, 18th, and 19th of August, 1843 for the Purpose of Considering Their Moral and Political Condition as American Citizens* (New York: Pierce and Reed, 1843), 12-14, 17-19; and Harry A. Reed, "Henry Highland Garnet's 'Address to the Slaves of the United States' Reconsidered," *The Western Journal of Black Studies* 9, no. 3 (Fall 1982): 144-51.

49. Jane H. Pease and William H. Pease, "Negro Conventions and the Problem of Black Leadership," *Journal of Black Studies* 2 (September 1971): 30.

6

Emigrationism: Toward the Evolution
of a Nationalist Ideology

Of the ideologies that emerged in the black community between 1770 and 1865 perhaps none was more important than the idea of emigration: the return to Africa, or an exodus to a black-dominated polity. A curiously minority philosophy, it nonetheless maintained relevance for northern black Americans throughout the period. As black fortunes changed so too did the public advocacy of leaving America. Beginning, perhaps, as an expression of a slave corollary to revolutionary rhetoric, then changing to an assertion of frustration and despair, by the mid-1850s emigration had attained a nationalist tone and a significant hold on the black mind, but not one that translated into a large-scale following. The hold on the black American mind was a spiritual adhesion that could not be dislodged by politically conscious blacks even when they themselves could not take advantage of the idea.

The ideology of emigation posited that blacks should seek the solace of Africa first as a place of return for those who still remembered the homeland. Beginning in the postrevolutionary war period the ideology was discussed by blacks in several eastern seaboard cities. Many of those who strongly favored emigration had been born in Africa and their ideas ran counter to some of their contemporaries who had been born in America. In the earliest expressions of leaving America the black message was one of going home. Seldom did their petitions or arguments raise the specter of slavery or the other ills faced by blacks in America. Simultaneously, the American-born blacks generally believed that concessions would be made to their status in postwar America avoided committing themselves to emigration.

Later, during the national period as the revolutionary egalitarianism disappeared, several well-known American blacks sounded the call for leaving the United States. At this time the call came after the failure of the effort to redress black grievances in the new state or federal government. Relief from bondage and discrimination generated the black interest in the return to Africa. In addition, the calls to emigrate to Africa during the national period were also driven by the desire for religious freedom and commercial opportunities. Even in this second incarnation of emigration, only a minority of black leaders gave credence to the ideology. Most of the black working class simply ignored the call because they lacked the resources to take advantage of its offering. Throughout the antebellum period lack of resources, more than any other factor, characterized the limited black response to the African return.

While resources were a major factor in the African return, they were less crucial in emigration to other locales, particularly those within the Western Hemisphere. Thus, black leaders were able to attract a following for relocation schemes to Haiti during the entire antebellum period even when those same followers disdained the African return.

In its final phase emigration became a nationalist philosophy. It was promoted by a number of leaders who were interested not only in relief from slavery and discrimination, but also dedicated to establishing a black polity in Africa. More than their predecessors, the advocates of the African return after the mid-1850s hoped they could ultimately challenge the slavery-driven economy of America. Thus, in a relatively brief period of roughly seventy years, the focus of emigration shifted from the desire to return home to a full-blown nationalist philosophy.

I

One would assume that the conservative response to emigration stemmed from the lack of a developed nationalism among early northern blacks: the early advocates of a return to Africa were not themselves nationalists.[1]Their interest in Africa derived partly from a perception of the continent providing refuge and solace from American slavery. Still others viewed Africa as providing an opportunity for religious tolerance and missionary outreach. Even an individual such as Paul Cuffe with interests in commercial development had grounds other than nationalism for pursuing his African plans. Paramount among his ideas were a check on the slave trade, the establishment of Christian worship, commercial opportunities, and the respect for law and order. On the latter point, like Daniel Coker later, Cuffe was interested not only in having the opportunity to discharge the responsibilities of citizenship but also desired to live in a polity where justice was, indeed, color-blind.

Unlike Cuffe who had reconnoitered Sierra Leone, Daniel Coker had not previously visited the continent. Although motivated by desires for religious and political freedom, Coker's experience in 1820 makes clear the traumatic nature of the undertaking. While his journal does not directly address this fear, it emerges with force. Hitherto historians have neglected the degree to which the fear of the unknown may have prevented untold numbers of Afro-Americans from considering a return to Africa. An examination of Coker's work is long overdue and will be attempted here.[2]

Cuffe and Coker, who exhibited the most developed commitment to leaving and assisting other blacks to leave, spent considerable time pursuing emigration in Boston, New York, and Philadelphia. Neither depended principally on the three cities, but each was materially assisted through his connections with all of them. Within the three cities there were less well-developed counterparts to Cuffe and Coker, but this did not prevent black New Yorkers, Bostonians, and Philadelphians from supporting the efforts of both men. What emerged was a complex, if not a widespread or deeply felt, network of blacks working out the frustrations of living in America, and the improbability of establishing a new life in Africa. After the time of Cuffe and Coker, more acute pressures on black life subtly changed the rhetoric driving black desires to leave America.

By the mid-1840s and the early 1850s black individuals advocating the African return continued to advocate Christianizing and commercializing the continent but they also added the nationalist dimension. The calls for blacks to accept the challenges to govern themselves was considerably beyond the political consciousness of Coker and Cuffe. The 1850s nationalism was anchored to the ideas of black self-determination expressed in the establishment not only of a black refuge, but also a black political entity.

Ironically, when the advocacy of emigration was at its zenith in the 1850s , it was promoted by and also rejected by nationalists. This lack of consensus even among nationalists further added to the minority status of emigration. Much of the motivation for the opposition nationalists seems to have come from their need to maintain control over the black movement. These older, established leaders had waged twenty- or thirty-year campaigns against the ACS brand of colonization, which in their minds too closely resembled the black call for an African return. In trying to stifle public discussion of a return to Africa older leaders implied that cowardice was part of the reason for attempting a return. Unwittingly, however, they provided a vehicle by which the discussion became public knowledge. Unwilling to ignore the ideas of relocation totally, the established leadership did allow and promote relocation within the Western Hemisphere. They refocused on schemes to relocate blacks in Haiti and the development of newspapers and advocates kept the topic of relocation alive.

Once the Africa nationalists had gained such a concession it was only a matter of time before the return to Africa emerged as an issue of public importance. To the advantage of the supporting nationalists, Western Hemisphere relocation was debated and openly supported while secret councils were held to discuss Africa. Moreover, the Africa advocates were skilled managers and consolidated their position and their support. Like minded black leaders met in conventions away from the established centers of power where it was possible to discuss a return to Africa without interference. Distance provided protection not only from black opposition but also from white abolitionists, particularly the Garrisonians. Equally important for those blacks living near the western limits of the United States, movement, travel, and relocation constituted a rhythm of life and was therefore favorably received. Blacks in Canadian settlements also were more open to public discussion of African emigration than their counterparts on the East Coast of the United States.

Finally, to the advantage of the Africa supporters was the acceleration of antiblack feeling best exemplified in the New Fugitive Slave Law of 1850 and the Dred Scott decision in 1857. Both pieces of legislation galvanized the black community for action but part of the action, in addition to opposing the enactments, also forced black Americans to reevaluate America's willingness to grant full citizenship to blacks. Two profound results of that forced reevaluation emerged: the beginning of a black nationalist critique of the United States and an open attitude toward the African return. As the decade of the 1850s closed some blacks were in Africa attempting to implement the African exodus.[3] Intervening historical incidents such as the Civil War prevented the fullest implementation of the African return.

Yet, the lack of success does not detract from its centrality to black American consciousness in the antebellum period. It will be argued here that "back-to-Africa" was not a movement but something more powerful. It was an idea, a philosophy, which even in the face of tremendous opposition remained relevant for black Americans. In the crucible of American race relations the return to Africa directed and financed by blacks was a positive contribution to a platform for change.

Obviously, emigration was not the sole ideology emergent in the black consciousness during the seventy years before the Civil War. During the period a number of ideologies commanded attention in the black community: the social action gospel, elevating the race, the chosen people, and others. While all were important in their time, only one— elevating the race—sustained its importance throughout the period. None, including race elevation, led to a nationalist position vis-a-vis American society but all contributed immeasurably to the growth of consciousness which concerns us here.

Emigration had an attractive but fleeting popularity among those black leaders reaching a flash point of frustation, and it maintained a tenacity with the small group of adherents who seldom tired of touting

Africa as the cure for black American disabilities. Given the shifting and sometimes short-lived support and the continued minority espousal of emigration, the community forged and utilized several other liberation ideologies. That the other majority idealogies did not result in either greater acceptance of blacks in America or the creation of self-sustaining political ideas fostered the cyclical interest in emigration. Those ideologies are of interest not as a backdrop to emigration but because their existence speaks to the energy and imagination of the black leaders actively engaged in constructing the platform for change.

II

Possibly the most pervasive of the early ideologies, the social action gospel was promulgated by black clergy and non-clergy. Members of the black clergy were the earliest and most visible symbols of leadership in the community and thus had to provide more than spiritual sustenance. Even had they not been the major source of leadership, the needs of their constituency would have forced them to assume more than a narrow religious function. Few black religious leaders were formally trained or ordained and the community to which they ministered was largely illiterate. The nature of the flock often necessitated specific duties of black clergy with respect to recruiting, preaching, and representing the aspirations of the community. Little emphasis, therefore, could be placed on the written word or esoteric points of doctrine.[4] More useful was a talent for associating the community's survival needs with biblical references.

Much emphasis was placed on educational needs of black youth. Black clergy petitioned local boards of education to provide facilities for black schooling. Simultaneously, they sought white benefactors or patrons to support individual or institutional educational plans. In turn the black clergy was sought by black educators to provide money, space, equipment, and publicity when local officials were not forthcoming with aid. Their own limited education notwithstanding, black clergy perceived the need for acquiring an education. Moreover, they worked to demonstrate the natural connection of religion and education. Learning to read would ensure reading of the Bible, which in turn would enhance the spiritual nature as well as the economic opportunities of the individual. In the 1790s Richard Allen's continued support of Quomony Clarkson's educational goals was an indication of Allen's commitment to the social action gospel.

In Clarkson, Allen had a young man who was not only teaching in Mother Bethel but also seeking employment as a teacher in the Philadelphia system.[5] To this end Clarkson wrote letters illustrating his own literacy and qualifications to teach. His letters of support from Allen extend beyond mere character or employment references. The implication is clear that Allen equated the needs and goals of Clarkson with those of the entire community. Allen's social action gospel in education alone had at least three main nonchurch functions. One was to promote education for the general uplift of black life. Two, he made facilities available within his church. Third, he promoted the employment of black teachers and chided the authorities to take more responsibility for educating blacks.

In the area of recruiting membership Allen's actions reveal also a commitment to social action. Neither he nor any other black churchman had the luxury of waiting for individuals to present themselves for church membership. Instead, like Thomas Paul in Boston, they had to circulate throughout the community gaining members. Since most blacks were common laborers, the black preacher's day was the same. Allen's first opportunity to preach to a black audience was scheduled for 5:00 a.m. by the white trustees of St. George's Church. While there may have been some racism involved in the trustee's decision, the fact remains that Allen maintained early services even after acquiring his own church. The process of gaining members for black churches could not be confined to the pulpit, and once outside that pulpit black clergy had to speak to a number of nonreligious concerns.

In the decades immediately preceding the Civil War the black social action gospel was best exemplified by the Reverends Henry Highland Garnet and Samuel Ringgold Ward.[6] Both men's public roles were enhanced and influenced by the idea of the social action gospel. Garnet's energies and intellect engaged him in a number of American reform activities: peace, abolition, the free produce movement, and education. To these he added strictly black activities: newspapers, conventions, vigilance, elevating the race, combatting northern discrimination and, for a period, emigration. Perhaps his rejoinder, in a letter of 1843, to Maria Weston Chapman, that as a black man he was capable of making philosophic and policy statements without prompting from whites, is apropos of his social action ideology.[7] It is clear that being a clergyman did not exempt Garnet from speaking to the pressing problems of the day. From a black social action perspective, the problems necessitated Garnet's action.

Samuel Ringgold Ward, too, found that issues other than the sacred commanded his attention. It was readily apparent to all from his dress and his constant references to religious subject matter that he was a cleric. Yet his activities militate against a simple labeling of preacher. Simultaneously, he was an abolitionist, a political party organizer, newspaper promoter, education advocate, vigilance worker, and much-traveled orator. Like the notoriety Garnet achieved in the reaction to his 1843 convention speech, Ward, too, engaged in what some called non-clerical behavior. More aggressively than Garnet, Ward opposed the 1850 Fugitive Slave Law. His activity in the Jerry case caused a federal warrant to be issued for his arrest. Rather than face incarceration for opposing what he felt was an unjust statute, Ward fled the country.[8] He died in 1856, attempting to establish a new life in Jamaica.

Certainly not all black clerics were involved in the social action gospel and some who were not clerics found it easy to combine their secular mission with heavy sacred overtones. Several black public speakers issued calls to the community that were permeated with religious symbols and a focus on moral philosophy. In his annual addresses Prince Hall always equated the mission of the masons with that of the church. Biblical references abounded when Hall reported on the state of black America. The Philadelphian, Cyrus Bustill, made it clear that the accepted image of the black preacher combined the sacred with the secular in pursuit of community goals.[9]

III

While the social action gospel was based principally on action, other ideologies were identified by more direct means. Black activists never said they were advocating the social action gospel, but they did publicly proclaim that they were working for the elevation of the race. To do so meant putting the best image of the race forward at all times. It was arguably a conservative philosophy taking, as it did, its standards from Yankee Christendom. To stop the analysis at that point, however, does major disservice to black reformers. Faced with a society that equated all blacks with slavery or at best was indifferent to blacks, the shapers of race elevation were motivated by two basic goals. First, they wished to blur the differences between themselves and white Americans. This was particularly true when it came to judging black potential for citizenship, employment, integrity, education, and health and behavior standards. Second, they wished to have blacks, themselves, provide a more stringent evaluation of rights and responsibilities which they had not acquired.

To achieve the first goal, unfortunately to some later historians, black advocates sounded like they were advising the community to copy white norms.[10] Something more fundamental was at stake, however. Not only were blacks fighting to overcome the stigma of slavery but also they were attempting to gain social and economic mobility in a rapidly modernizing society. Success was defined by upward mobility and material acquisition, but these gains also carried, in their wake, disruptive aspects. Since black leaders felt slavery had already had a debilitating effect on the black family, they had to guard against family group disintegration. To promote the ideals of family life, quiet leisure pursuits, quality education, and responsibility, were overriding concerns. The task required uplifting blacks and assisting whites to recognize their own prejudices and to be attuned to recognizing and accepting black achievements.

In the hands of overzealous and conservative black leaders, elevating the race sometimes carried with it an overwhelming criticism of the black working class. For example, although both were generally close to poverty, Samuel Cornish and Alexander Crummell maintained a commitment to middle-class standards that was at best rigid and at worst, perhaps, misguided. Without Cornish's and Crummell's access to education and upper-class white acquaintances, their parishiners could not aspire to the leaders' well-intentioned but misplaced focus on impossible-to-attain standards.

A corollary goal for black advocates of race elevation was to impress upon their followers the need for a challenging, skeptical attitude regarding education. David Walker warned young blacks not to be taken in by their newly acquired penmanship. Education meant the ability to think, to reason, and later to teach others. Education would be the primary means to achieve the elevation of the race. Every opportunity to acquire an education must be diligently pursued, and no opportunity to display that education, as an incentive to others and as a step toward breaking the barriers between the races, could be ignored.

Thus early graduation celebrations were looked on as community celebrations. Speeches concerning the future of the black race in America were prominent. Special themes noted the similarities between the Afro-American struggle and past historical events. Particularly prized were speeches or essays finding biblical or classical allusions to black circumstances. Orations were not only for black consumption but were also heard by a number of white benefactors who tried to expose other whites to examples of black intelligence. Such sentiments account for the yearly displays and distribution of the final papers of the graduating class of the High School for Colored Youth in New York City.[11]

Even better examples of elevating the race in educational affairs were the invitations to former students to give graduation speeches. Octavius V. Catto's, "Our Alma Mater," is a classic example of the technique.[12] Catto was enthusiastic in reporting the achievements of young black scholars in Greek, Latin, Mathematics, and higher English studies. He was equally ecstatic about white observers and examiners who were exposed to the accomplishments of the race. White examiners energetically participated in the examinations and, in some cases, pronounced the results superb. A report in the *Philadelphia Press* noted that about one-third of the audience were respectable white fellow citizens. Catto told the crowd about the history of the Institute for Colored Youth, and also took the opportunity to note the school's illustrious graduates. Two had graduated from Penn Medical University and several were school administrators in the city. While the individuals were to be congratulated, Catto pointed out that the greater achievement was the effect of the institution on the lives of the collective. The institution was, he said, part of the revolution in American politics and education. An important function of the school and its graduates was to bring light and learning to the brethren once they were released from bondage.[13] Education, social responsibility, and elevating the race all found their place in graduation orations.

Graduation exercises were also the proper arena for political activists to criticize white school administrators' lack of commitment to black education. The Boston Common School Committee faced at least one annual confrontation at spring commencement. No white official, regardless of his rank, was immune from these attacks. In 1848 the governor of Pennsylvania, an honored guest at the Institute for Colored Youth ceremonies, was sternly rebuked by Jacob C. White, Jr. White reminded the governor that he was addressing an assemblage of educated black youth, and he should take the examples before him back to the statehouse and to political battles, to remind attackers of the race's achievement. This achievement, he stated, had been accomplished in the face of terrific oppression and with limited resources.[14] The chief executive, White noted, needed to set a more positive tone among his colleagues toward black education.

Not all advocates of elevating the race sought relief through reform or formal education. As with other social/political causes, black activists opted for a broad-based attack on black disabilities. Nonformal education as a way of elevating the race was also persistently followed. In this instance the promotion of reading rooms was a characteristic activity of black leaders. Given the limited resource base of most black communities some of the achievements in establishing reading rooms were quite remarkable. In 1836 the Colored Library Company of Philadelphia was founded. Within a few years it owned six hundred circulating volumes. More modest enterprises could be found in practically all black communities. In many instances reading rooms were conceived within an elitist mentality: for members of the upwardly mobile classes. The Colored Library Company confined the use of its reading room and circulating volumes to its membership, not the entire black population.

Programs were also presented at reading rooms which benefited those asserting the elevation of the race. Lectures, demonstrations, debates, poetry readings, and dramatic readings were regular offerings. These presentations were geared toward classical and formal subject matter but issues of contemporary political significance were not neglected. In 1830 a Philadelphia gathering discussed plans to purchase and sell a volume of George Moses Horton's verse. The proceeds were to assist Horton, a North Carolina slave, in buying his freedom. Although the desired level of funding for Horton never materialized the idea of reading rooms persisted. Frances Ellen Watkins Harper, a teacher, writer, poet, and lecturer in the 1850s, practically supported herself by giving readings in these locations. Particularly striking about the reading rooms were their universality, the broad range of topics discussed, and their connection to the philosophy of racial uplift.

IV

Simultaneous with the philosophies of elevating the race and the social action gospel, the ideology of blacks as the chosen people emerged. Unlike either the social action gospel or elevating the race idea, the chosen people theme was more limited chronologically and regionally.[15] Throughout the period from 1770 to 1865 black leaders made frequent references to black peoples' special relationship with God. Only in the Boston area, however, did the relationship briefly serve as the basis for a liberation philosophy. It seems to have been sponsored and pursued principally by a group of Boston clergymen. Moreover, their advocation of the idea seems to have been most overt during the years 1831 to 1836.

It is still difficult to determine why this philosophy was prominent in Boston. It is equally difficult to ascertain its precise origins or the reasons for its demise. Nonetheless, it is clear that Boston blacks worked earnestly to keep the idea of the chosen people in full public view. When seeking explanations for the existence of this phenomenon several interesting speculations emerge. They suggest much about black community awareness in general and about changes in Boston specifically.

The principal spokesmen for the chosen people idea were Boston blacks associated with the Massachusetts General Colored Association. In Boston the association emerged as part of a new assertion of independence from older leaders and their white supporters. Association members were the more radical sons of fathers who had composed black leadership since the Revolution. Committed to the ideals of the "era of good feeling," the fathers worked closely with white benefactors such as the Reverend Dr. Stillman and the Reverend Dr. Baldwin. Unlike their fathers, the sons chafed at white paternalism and a quiet but intense philosophical struggle ensued. The younger men correctly perceived that Stillman and Baldwin by the mid-1820s no longer represented majority feeling among Boston Baptists. In a sense younger whites were doing the same as blacks in the association, pulling away from their elders' ideals of race relations.

In 1829 David Walker's publication and his subsequent death placed a severe strain on the fragile black/white relationship. Always a proponent of black independence, Walker was part of the trend that also challenged the continuing leadership of Thomas Paul in the African Baptist Church. Walker's *Appeal,* published in 1829 with its severe criticism of the church and white paternalism, exacerbated tensions among Boston's blacks. When Thomas Paul died in 1831, his death strained the racial alliance more profoundly than did either Walker's writing or Walker's death.[16] Almost singlehandedly, Paul had kept alive the prosperity of African Baptist Church while simultaneously nurturing the connection with Stillman and Baldwin. Robbed of Paul's support, continuation of the era of good feeling lost its urgency for blacks.

In this turbulent context the younger blacks became more public with their discontents. Their assertion of the chosen people theme is more complex than simply a revolt against the fathers. This new philosophy embodied a rejection of the church and its tacit support of slavery and discrimination. To assert that blacks were the chosen was an appeal to history, the Bible and the highest authority. Nonslave owners and slaveholders alike were put on notice that they could not abuse, indefinitely, the special friends of God. Divine retribution, they warned, would ultimately support the righteous by destroying its enemies. After the death of David Walker, Scipio Dalton seemed to be the most avid advocate of calling down the wrath of God on white Christians. By so doing, Dalton signaled the end of black dependence on white paternalists. Although black/white cooperation in Boston continued, especially during the later abolition period, the era of good feeling among black and white clergy had ended.

Abolitionist spirit in Boston holds another clue to the demise of the black emphasis on the chosen people theme. Boston abolitionists, particularly William Lloyd Garrison, did not make the sharp distinction between legal and social equality that many whites did. Moreover, Garrison's intimacy with the black community and his radical stands on the church, ACS, and restrictive laws, appealed to the younger members of the association.

By 1836 the New England Antislavery Society had hired its first black paid agent: Charles Lenox Remond. While Remond's hiring did not put to rest all black concerns about discrimination within the abolition movement, it was a visible commitment to sharing leadership and broadening the participation of blacks. These greater opportunities for blacks plus a strong ally against the church makes the demise of the chosen people ideology more than coincidental. True, Garrison was white, but he was not counseling the black community about strategy or smoothing paths within church councils as Stillman and Baldwin had done.

Although the era of good feeling was particularly characteristic of the relationship between black and white Baptist in Boston, it may have stifled the independent development of black leaders. Thus, one of the positive results of the end of the era of good feeling was the breaking of African Baptist's monopoly of leadership and black public opinion in Boston. Intraracial struggles undoubtedly siphoned off energy and time, but in the case of the Massachusetts General Colored Association the conflict was fought over the ground of self-determination. In short, the confined appeal of the chosen people idea can be attributed to the special nature of black struggles in Boston. Not only did sons have to challenge the power of their fathers but they had to confront and break the hold of white benefactors and Thomas Paul, for years the most respected black leader in Boston.

Such was not the case in Philadelphia, where blacks had moved away from dependence on white paternalism as early as 1793. In their coauthored pamphlet Richard Allen and Absalom Jones made three things clear. One, that blacks made their own decisions about assisting the city in a time of crisis. Two, that blacks assisted, even in view of their own vulnerability, which white laymen and the medical profession were ignorant of and therefore denied. Third, the blacks had sufficient and able spokesmen to defend the community's interest and integrity. Allen's and Jones's continued collaboration is indicative of the greater diversity and cooperation of leadership in Philadelphia. Neither Allen nor Jones monopolized black leadership in Philadelphia as had Paul in Boston. Ecumenism was a factor in Philadelphia: Presbyterians Samuel Cornish and John Gloucester worked with Jones and Allen as did several nonclergy such as James Forten, Russell Perrott, Jacob Tapsico, and James Wilson.

Although diversity of leadership existed, it alone could not and did not prevent confrontations. Allen, particularly, became embroiled in controversies. What is important about Philadelphia's unity is that it gave clearer evidence of black decision making and their freedom from having to placate white benefactors. While the chosen people idea did not make an appearance in Philadelphia, the other liberation philosophies did.

Taken together the social action gospel, the chosen people, and the elevation of the race represent the fecundity of the black mind in generating ideologies for liberation, but they did not represent all of the of ideologies current in the antebellum black North. While they may have enjoyed more public acceptance than emigrationism they were not, individually or collectively, as significant. Although addressing self-determination for blacks the above ideologies, unlike emigration, continued the call for blacks to work within a white-dominated polity.

Also unlike emigration these three ideologies remained rooted in the moral suasionist tone of American reform and the chosen people idea depended on divine intervention while it criticized the church. All three, however, lacked the tenacity of emigration which had a quality that invited black Americans to investigate repeatedly the African return.

The idea of African return was also unique in that it evolved to fit the dynamic and changing nature of the black struggle. More important, in the last decade before the Civil War the African return advocates had fashioned a new platform for future black generations. Out of their activities came the first black political critique of the American political economy and a nationalist resolution to black problems.

V

That evolution, however, took almost a century because the earliest calls for the African return were appeals for refuge based on morality, commerce, and Christianity. A clear impetus for the early espousal of the African return was the rhetoric of the American patriots during the revolutionary war. As the patriots accelerated their agitation against British hegemony, they made constant use of the term slavery. These utterances were not directed at the bondage of blacks. Instead it was the patriots' characterization of their political connection with Great Britain. Given the political background of New England slaves, it was inevitable that a black spokesperson would seize the opportunity to address their needs in revolutionary language.

Such an opportunity came on 20 April 1773.[17] On that date the representative of the town of Thompson received a brief petition "in behalf of our fellow slaves in this province."[18] It immediately strikes the revolutionary tone but with a specific focus on black problems. The petition called for an end to the institution of slavery and suggested that those Americans opposing a discussion of the topic were not only unpatriotic but also corrupt.

The juxtaposition of slavery and corruption reveals how closely slaves were listening to the revolutionary debates. Corruption of British civil servants was the second most popular theme in revolutionary agitation. After revealing their familiarity with revolutionary rhetoric, the petitioners address some of the perplexing issues inherent in their status. Among these was the thought of financial/economic dislocation that could follow in the wake of ending slavery. Therefore, the petitioners disclaim any demand for remuneration for past services. Such demands would, they allowed, "be highly detrimental to our present masters."[19] In the event that masters would not be moved by their disclaimer, the four slaves provided an additional political/economic alternative: they suggest creating a mechanism where slaves could earn money toward their manumission.

The radical nature of their petition notwithstanding, the signers make it clear that they were not trying to usurp the legislature's authority. While acknowledging their obligations to the officials, the slaves reminded them that their demands were based on natural law. Slave spokesmen had neatly associated their cause with revolutionary rhetoric on three grounds: the equation of slavery not with political status but with black bondage; the corruption of opposition to manumission; and associating black demands with the theory of natural rights.

Still, the petitioners were not finished putting their demands in the most positive context. They alluded to the possibility of divine intervention but, they cautioned, their attempts to gain freedom would be done peaceably because they submitted to the will of the wise and righteous Governor of the universe.[20] As slaves they perhaps knew that it was better to render unto Ceasar that which was Ceasar's. Thus, in addition to obeying divine will they promised to respect new regulations and laws relative to them.

When the slave demands appeared most conciliatory is also when the tone of the petition changed. They will respect laws and regulations "until we leave the province."[21] Further, the legislature was informed that they "determined to do so as soon as we can from our joint labours procure money to transport ourselves to some part of the coast of Africa, where we propose a settlement."[22] In the midst of arguing, however briefly, for natural rights and English liberties, it is unmistakable that these petitioners' would opt for self-determination in Africa rather than remain slaves.

Thus, the idea of a return to Africa advocated by black men became a conscious, publicly stated desire. We can make no claim for the originality of the petitioners' thinking vis-a-vis an African colony. Since at least 1714 there had been frequent references to repatriating blacks within and outside the American mainland. All such plans before 1773 represented white thought and had at least a modicum of paternalism, if not racism. Unlike the white plans, the 1773 petition made an indictment of the English system, revolutionary rhetoric, and slavery as well. Since the record is mute on slave deliberations before and after the petition was rejected, its unqualified acceptance by historians is probably risky. Yet several strong conjectures can be forwarded to support the authenticity of this black assertion. First, had this been one of the frequent white efforts about separating the races it seems likely that greater resources and more organization would have been used. It is more likely that white patriots would have orchestrated a more vocal and supportive reception for the petition. It would have probably contained white signatures and a representative number of signers would have attended the session when it was presented.

Second, had the representative of Thompson initiated the petition he would have been more diligent and defended it during the session. Instead, the petition was tabled without discussion. It seems unlikely that the energy used in organizing and writing the petition would be dissipated without even a cursory defense. Finallly, the issues are explosive enough and confined enough to suggest that the petition was genuinely of black origin. Patriots and loyalists were slaveholders and the petitioners made little distinction between the two. Manumission would have created economic problems which the slaves acknowledged, but their solution was not compensation to masters which white manumissionists usually proposed. Rather the slaves asked for limited remuneration, a provision more favorable to black self-interest. Working even one day a week for wages would have increased black economic resources and also strengthened their participation in decisions regarding their status. Such a happy set of circumstances did not follow in the wake of the 1773 petition.

There is no evidence that this petition stimulated other slaves to act for the back-to-Africa plan. More important, though, the idea was in the public domain and its first black expression had been executed. Certainly, one of the spurs to the 1773 petition was the political flux and the uncertainties of the revolutionary period. For black Americans the postrevolutionary period presented similar uncertainties. The war had been won, the Union was being established, and slavery was ending in northern states but there was no universal conferring of citizenship on blacks.

Instead the newly independent Americans vacillated. Several of the former middle colonies legislated gradual emancipation plans. These plans offered little beyond eventual freedom: a freedom that could be blocked by unscrupulous masters. In states where slavery was abolished before the end of the war, free blacks' prospects were little better. Citizenship was severely circumscribed: all the new states limited blacks in their exercise of the franchise. Postrevolutionary America was still a society in flux for blacks. Where Bestes, Holbrook, Joie, and Freeman had stood revolutionary rhetoric on its head, the postrevolutionary blacks in bitter frustration reiterated a call for the African return.

Significantly, the call came from New England, the most racially liberal sector of the new Republic. In 1787 Prince Hall, usually a supporter of American ideals, issued a call for emigration. In January of that year, seventy-three "African Blacks" including Hall, again petitioned the Massachusetts General Court.[23] A striking difference from the 1773 document is immediately apparent. Whereas the slaves felt some obligation to flatter the legislators and to couch their demands in revolutionary rhetoric, those devices are absent from the Hall petition. Instead they went to the heart of the matter:

> We, or our ancestors have been taken from all our dear connections, and brought from Africa and put into a state of slavery in this country; from which unhappy by the new constitution which has been adopted by this state, or by a free act of our former masters. But we yet find ourselves, in many respects, in very disagreeable and disadvantageous

circumstances; most of which must attend us so long as we and our children live in America.[24]

Continuing to focus on specific black needs the petitioners stated an "earnest desire to return to Africa."[25] They would be more happy and comfortable in their own environment and they might, it was asserted, be of some use to their brother Africans.

Not content to simply point out their desire to go to Africa, the signers detailed a plan of execution. They proposed that arable land in Africa be acquired for settlement. Those Afro-Americans desiring to settle the land would form themselves into a civil society united by a political constitution. Significantly, religious dimensions of the exodus were also suggested: those wishing to go should form a religious society or church and have one of their number ordained and resettled with the group. Since blacks lacked the resources to carry out such a plan the petitioners said:

These must be furnished with necessary provisions for the voyage; and with farming utensils necessary to cultivate the land; and with the materials which cannot at present be obtained there and which will be needed to build houses and mills.[26]

Hall and his cohorts were requesting the types of assistance that were standard inducements of the British, at the end of the war, to blacks who had served their cause and wished to leave the States. With the exception of freedom these were the basic benefits given to British veterans. Moreover, in 1772, Hall's plan had been the basis of British philanthropy in supporting the establishment of the colony of Sierra Leone. From his close association with British officers during Boston's occupation, Hall may have indeed been very familiar with their program. Moreover, American preoccupation with the return or compensation for those blacks who left at the war's end made the subject a matter of public knowledge.

Unable or unwilling to sustain the nationalist pose they had struck with the mention of political constitutions, the signers turned their attention to two other issues. First, they spoke to their plans being a means of Christian missionizing and enlightenment to Africa. Schemes of black missionary involvement had circulated in Boston during the 1770s. The signers were aware of such discussions and possibly hoped to gain support from white individuals and organizations. Second, the petitioners envisioned the establishment of a commercial network between Africa and the United States. Such a network would help Americans recoup the finances necessary for the project.

Although the proscribed status of Massachusetts free blacks in the 1780s made appeals to revolutionary rhetoric a dead letter, the Hall petition, like its predecessor, mixed assertion with humility. Only the last two paragraphs resort to flattery:

> We therefore humbly and earnestly apply to this honorable Court, hoping and praying that in your wisdom and goodness, you concert and prosecute the best method to relieve and assist us either by granting a brief for a collection in all the congregations in this state, of in any other way, which shall to your wisdom appear most expedient.[27]

Not only are the last paragraphs flattery but also they speak to lack of resources and lack of power to effect change.

In addition to the lack of power, rejection must have been part of the wellspring of despair providing the impetus for Hall's action. In 1786, the year before the petition, Hall's offer of military support against Daniel Shay's rebellion was rebuffed by Governor Bowdin.[28] Several other rejections at this time may have had a direct bearing on Hall's temporary flirtation with the back to Africa movement.

In 1780 when British occupation troops left Boston the American masons refused to acknowledge Hall's African masonic Lodge. In 1786 the white masons were staunchly opposed to Shay's rebellion and their support was accepted by the state government, but Hall's offer was rejected. Moreover, since 1784 Hall had been waiting for the London masonic order to issue his international authorization. It was finally received in the spring of 1787. By that time, Hall had participated in a number of abortive attempts to redress black grievances through petitions.

Thus the 1787 back-to-Africa stance of Prince Hall seemed directly linked to his frustrations over the intransigence of American racism rather than a fully developed political position. In the spring of 1787, with his charter in hand, Hall's outlook became more positive. He continued zealously to attack southern slavery and northern discrimination, but he never returned to an eposusal of African emigration as a possible solution to black problems. Instead he directed his energies against discrimination in education, against the slave trade, and to building the masonic order. After 1787 Hall's major public pronouncements were contained in his annual *Charge* to the members of the lodge.

Although the 1792 and 1797 addresses of Prince Hall do not mention the African return, they do present compelling evidence of the broad-based philosophical foundation of black liberation strategies. In 1792 Hall seemed particularly interested in the elevation of the race through the use of history. Most of his brief oration chronicled the ties between the African motherland and Christianity. Since the speeches were immediately published and sold, the distribution of his sentiments was much wider than the membership of the lodge. Later, in 1797,

Hall's speech anticipated some of the arguments used by blacks in the development of the chosen people theme. In addition to noting the relationship between Africa and Christianity, Hall also pointed out what he believed was the special status of blacks with Christ. Suffering, patience, and righteousness, he counseled, would create divine intervention on behalf of Afro-American aspirations.[29]

Hall's abortive return-to-Africa idea was, in part, too localized. While black Bostonians were aware of the efforts of blacks in Newport and Providence, Rhode Island, they were unable to enter into a broad coalition that might have made their efforts more successful. The failure to unite may be attributed to several conditions. One, Newport and Providence blacks with strong white support had been exploring emigration options as early as 1773, which made them reluctant to subordinate their concerns or share their resources with groups from other cities. Two, noted white clergymen in Newport, Samuel Hopkins and Ezra Stiles (later president of Yale), formulated plans to educate several blacks for evangelizing Africa.

The plans of Hopkins and Stiles met with general approval among Newport blacks and this good black/white working relationship made blacks less interested in pursuing outside liaisons. In addition, the black missionaries of the Hopkins, Stiles scheme would serve as the advance party for a general black exodus.[30] Second, the revolutionary war halted Hopkins's plans. Subsequent to the war, blacks themselves began taking the lead in shaping the return to Africa. Third, following the war new whites who were not residents of Newport, Providence. or Boston, particularly William Thornton of Antigua, were met with skepticism that had not surfaced against Stiles and Hopkins. Thornton had plans to emancipate his own slaves and take them to Africa. In working out the logistics of his emancipation plan, Thornton had found British abolitionists/proprietors of the Sierra Leone colony only lukewarm to his plans. Fourth, blacks were reluctant to commit themselves to a colony where they would be coerced into becoming British subjects. British politicians at Sierra Leone made it clear that all American blacks had to respect British common law. Fifth, blacks in Newport, Providence, and Boston formulated slightly different plans for funding, locating sites, and developing colonies.

The one consistent idea held by all three groups was an insistence on not melding with indigenous Africans, British blacks, or each other.[31] Probably the most important barrier to unified action was the fact that blacks thought they had sufficient support for their individual plans. With the end of both the war and slavery blacks seemed to expect more from whites.

After the war blacks returned to the exploration of the African return. Old activists such as Newport Gardner and Salman Nubia, who had founded the (Newport) African Union Society in 1783, continued their involvement. In slightly more than a decade two significant changes had occurred among black leaders advocating emigration: the new leaders were younger and, more important, they were at least second generation black Americans. Gardner, Nubia, Bristol Yamma, and John Quamine were native Africans. Yamma and Quamine were two of the blacks involved in Hopkins's and Stiles's prerevolutionary plans.

The younger blacks, while charged with a fervor for the African return, were almost equally affected by their perceived claims to American citizenship. Richard Allen, Absalom Jones, and Henry Stewart of Philadelphia's Free African Society provided the new organizational thrust. Simultaneously, they were also involved in a sharp conflict concerning equality within the Methodist Episcopal Church. Ultimately, this contest dominated the Philadelphians' energies and forced them, in part, to honor their African ancestry, but to work toward acceptance in their new birthplace. Although Stewart toured Boston, Newport, and Providence for the Free African Society, the organization was at best lukewarm to African return proposals. By 1793-1795, just when Newport and Providence blacks were showing new life, the Free African Society of Philadelphia was moribund and neither Allen nor Jones was still a member.

Ultimately Newport and Providence succeeded in sending James McKenzie as an advance man to Sierra Leone. A friend of Bristol Yamma's, he was neither as charismatic nor as close to Hopkins and, therefore, failed to obtain the backing of the earlier activists. Finally, in 1826, Newport Gardner, aged eighty, and Salman Nubia, aged seventy, returned to Africa and lived there briefly until their deaths.[32]

VI

Years later Paul Cuffe, although less committed to divine intervention than Prince Hall, utilized religion as one of the cornerstones in his own back-to-Africa program. Having attended Quaker services with his father and mother as a youth, he maintained the practice into his maturity. In 1808 he became a formal member of the society. One of his sons went to a Quaker school in Philadelphia. Later he put up most of the money to build a Friends Meeting House in Westport, Massachusetts.[33]

It was shortly after his formal acceptance, as a Friend, that Cuffe began corresponding with the white Philadelphian James Pemberton, a Quaker and merchant. Like Cuffe, Pemberton was interested in emancipation and Africa. He introduced Cuffe not only to other likeminded Quakers in Philadelphia, but also to powerful English supporters. Among the Englishmen who had formed the African Institution were noted abolitionists William Wilberforce, Granville Sharpe, and Thomas Clarkson.[34]

Not all of Cuffe's new acquaintances within the African Institution were white. Two influential blacks, one resident in Philadelphia—James Forten—were also Cuffe correspondents. For all of these men religion was an initial impulse guiding their interest in Africa. In addition, as blacks, Cuffe and Forten were motivated to attack the disabilities of free blacks as well as slaves and Africans.

With the insistence and the discussions of Pemberton and Forten, Cuffe crystallized his own back-to-Africa plans. For more than two years Cuffe's relationship with the Philadelphians centered around bringing civilization, Christianity, and commerce to Africa. Although Cuffe continued to speak in humble Quaker terms, he was fired with zeal to see Africa for himself so that he could gauge more accurately its potential for receiving black Americans and its potential for development.

Following the death of James Pemberton, Cuffe corresponded most frequently with John James and Alexander Wilson. It was natural that when he was ready to leave the States he would meet with his Philadelphia friends. In November 1810 he stopped there en route to Sierra Leone. While in the city discussing his voyage a minor confrontation occurred with John James. James solicited Cuffe's interest in taking a load of corn to Cadiz to make a profit on the trip. Cuffe's response left little doubt that he was about the business of investigating Sierra Leone and "not for profit or gain."[35] Finally, on 1 January 1811, with the good wishes of the African Institution, Cuffe sailed from Philadelphia.

Although of limited formal education Cuffe had been broadened by travel and business experience. This made it possible for him to compile an astute journal of his impressions of Africa. As the first black American's direct observation of Africa, Cuffe's journal deserves to be better known. One of the qualities of his account is the economy of expression used to convey a positive assessment of the colony. As Cuffe states, he did not attempt a hard scientific evaluation. Instead, he advised, "I merely wish to convey a brief account of the situation of the colony as I found it, hoping the information may prove serviceable and interesting to some of my friends in the United States."[36] He gives a brief description of the colony's establishment and the motivations of its guiding force, the Sierra Leone company. Cuffe makes it clear that the objects of the Company coincide with his own and those of the African Institution.

Among the positive objectives of the company were cultivation of the soil and the pursuit of trade with other countries. At the time of his visit, Cuffe reported, several agricultural experiments were showing promising results. Sugar and cotton particularly had prospered in the environment. A promising geographical feature that Cuffe noted was the Sierra Leone River. He informed his readers that the river "passes through the country, and the land for a great extent on each side is fertile, and with a

climate well calculated for the cultivation of West India and other tropical productions."[37] The straightforward modest tone must have belied
Cuffe's true excitement. He hoped that agricultural production and
trade would displace the slave trade in African commercial relations.
Curiously, Cuffe does not develop these points. Instead he outlines other
features of the colony.

As of April 1811, Cuffe reported the population included the following:

	Men	*Women*	*Children*
Europeans	22	4	2
Nova Scotians	188	294	499
Maroons	165	195	477
Africans	_20_	_43_	_37_
	395	537	485[38]

There were 1,917 enumerated people plus 601 Kru men (native
Africans). The Kru men were not yet citizens but were an important
source of labor to the colony's inhabitants.

Cuffe's pamphlet conveyed a feeling of industriousness about the settlement and an important interest in encouraging further immigration.
Several respectable inhabitants had presented a petition to the governor
which they hoped would stimulate future migration. A specific interest
was shown in a convincing more farmers to come to Sierra Leone. A second item in the petition solicited persons with vessels to come to the
colony to establish commerce. Encouragement was also given to people
who had expressed a desire to establish a whaling industry. Business and
economic opportunity, Cuffe seemed to say, were awaiting new arrivals.

Moreover, even in the positive business environment, Cuffe was
quick to point out that people had not neglected their education. Seven
or eight schools operated in the colony: one served adults and others
provided education for about twenty children. The settlers did not
ignore other aspects of developing their community, either: six places of
public worship existed. In addition Cuffe found a society to promote the
Christian religion, and an Institution for the Relief of the Poor and
Disabled.

Concerning the governing of the colony Cuffe delineated the various
courts and laws regulating the colony. British law prevailed and included
manumission and the protection of freed slaves. When describing the
court structure Cuffe specifically noted the jurors for only one court. The
Court of Quarter Sessions had a jury made up of Europeans, Nova
Scotians, and Maroons. At some levels, at least, Sierra Leone operated as
a free and open interracial society. The impact of this could not be lost
on black American readers. Although he was later proved to be too optimistic, Cuffe seemed to be saying that the opportunities for a better qual-

ity of life existed for blacks in Sierra Leone. Whether the colony represented a balanced multiracial polity is not the important consideration.
Even in the one example of the Court of Quarter Sessions, it was significantly beyond the political liberty available to blacks in America. Yet in
his customary low keyed way Cuffe's account simply states his observations without drawing distinctions between the colony and the United
States.

Moreover, the bulk of Cuffe's report addressed the potential for developing a religious commonwealth on the west coast. Despite its title the
Account contained more than his observations of Sierra Leone: also
included were "Advice" to the people of color in the United States and
an "Address" from abolition societies in the States. These two additions
contained the same religious and social deportment themes that occupied much of Cuffe's attention. Simultaneously, Cuffe praised the
colony's settlers for establishing worship societies and solicited help and
continued guidance from Afro-Americans. In his address Cuffe also
touched on the special relationship between God and Ethiopia.

The main emphasis of Cuffe's writings, however, were on counseling
people to meet on a regular basis, manifest a community spirit, strive for
sobriety, and give guidance to the youth. A like-minded group of
colonists, whose ideas were contained in the Cuffe report, spoke specifically to the inquiry of Christians holding slaves. Their short epistle is
packed with political power, the religious language notwithstanding.

> Dearly beloved brethren in the Lord, may the power and peace of God
> rule in all your hearts, for we feel from an awful experience the dis-
> tresses that many of our African brethren groan under. Therefore we
> feel our minds engaged to desire all the Saints and professors in Christ
> to diligently consider our cause, and to put our cause to the Christian
> query whether it is agreeable to the testimony of Jesus Christ for one
> professor to make merchandise of another. We desire that this may be
> made manifest to all professors of all Christian denominations who
> have not abolished the holding of slaves.[30]

This brief epistle constitutes perhaps the earliest assertion of Africans on
slavery directed to their Afro-American brothers.

The final section of Cuffe's account contained more advice to blacks
on how best to elevate the race. A degree of paternalism is apparent, the
same paternalism that Cuffe seemed to share with other black leaders.
Taken from the January 1796 abolition society meetings in Philadelphia,
this final section included nine points for black Americans to follow to
convince their detractors of black worthiness. In short the first observations about Africa by an Afro-American interested in promoting the
African return was hardly a nationalist statement. Cuffe did assess the

commercial possibilities in agriculture and shipping, but they weighed less than proper conduct and worship. In light of Cuffe's own astonishing success his limited references to commerce are surprising, but the *Account* reinforces the idea that Cuffe was fired by the African return, not by the promise of profit or gain.

On 11 May 1811, after four months in the colony, Cuffe sailed for England. It was his hope to meet with English members of the African Institution to lobby their continued support for his African project. The London branch was the original group of British abolitionists that had befriended black activists in Philadelphia and New York and helped them to form their auxiliary. It was the black American branch that introduced Cuffe to its London benefactors. In addition to helping with the African return, the powerful London branch also tried to help Cuffe further his commercial operations. He needed it as an ally because the Sierra Leone government had refused Cuffe licenses to engage in trade.

Several reasons account for the refusal of the Sierra Leone government. The first objection was based on the discomfort of the British merchant elite that ran the colony: they were not willing to engage in competition with outside merchants. Cuffe's nationality was also a factor in their rejection of his request for licenses. British merchants had no desire to share their trade with an American since they had been locked out of the American trade by several embargoes issued by the American government in years immediately preceding the War of 1812. As important as it was for the London branch to support Cuffe's commercial ventures, the first object was to secure financial and moral support for the African return.

Over the next four months traveling between Liverpool and London, Cuffe met and impressed the leading English abolitionists. Among those who met with and responded favorably to Cuffe's plans were Thomas Clarkson, William Wilberforce, Granville Sharpe, and others. They performed a very important service for Cuffe while he was in England. Immediately upon arrival in Liverpool Cuffe's ship *Traveler* was searched by a British press gang. Aboard they found Aaron Richards, an African who had apprenticed himself to Cuffe. Claiming Richards as a British subject, they took him into custody. Later in the day Captain Cuffe succeeded in gaining the release of two other crewmen who had also been taken. The authorities, however, refused to release Aaron Richards.

Although concerned about his plans for African repatriation and his licenses for trade in Sierra Leone, Cuffe pressed his friends to secure the release of his apprentice. The Cuffe journal reveals many moments of anxiety about Richards's incarceration. Cuffe sought the aid of Richard Rathbone and Thomas Thompson, both prominent Liverpool merchants and members of the African Institution. William Allen, Cuffe's closest

English friend, was also asked to intercede for Richards. On 23 July 1811 Thomas Clarkson succeeded in obtaining information that Aaron Richards was being discharged by the Vice Admiralty Court. Richards finally returned to the *Traveler* in Liverpool on 2 August 1811.

The Richards affair notwithstanding, Cuffe sought out many members of the African Institution to press his case on the African return. William Dillwyn, who had been informed of Cuffe's ideas earlier in 1809 by James Pemberton, met with Cuffe during August 1811. Through William Allen and Dillwyn other introductions and audiences were arranged. Among the new supporters were Zachary Macaulay, William Rathbone, Jr., Joseph Lancaster, Cornelius Hanbury, Stephen Grellet, the Duke of Gloucester, Joseph Gurney Bevan, James Cropper, and William Roscoe. In short, Cuffe met and was supported by the most prominent English abolitionists of the day. Finally, on 27 August 1811 Cuffe met with the African Institution committee chaired by the Duke of Gloucester, which authorized continued support for Cuffe.

His business in England at an end, Cuffe sailed, on 20 September 1811 on a return to Sierra Leone. This second trip was less pleasant than his first trip. He encountered several shady English businessmen and two of his crew were sickly, including a recalcitrant Zarcharia White. Among other things White had challenged the authority of Cuffe on several occasions yet Cuffe never lost patience. Moreover, some government officials began to suspect Cuffe's motives and they followed him during much of his daily business activity. On 15 February 1812 the *Traveler* left Greetown Harbor for the return to the United States. Within three days, however, Cuffe's ship was back at port.

During the interval he had been stopped and boarded several times by officers of the British warship *Abina*. Captain Tidwell was suspicious of the presence of Aaron Richards and two other African youths: George Davis, ten years old, and Moses Jenkins, aged seventeen. On 18 February 1812 Governor William C. Maxwell gave permission for Cuffe to take all three youths to the United States. The evening of 19 February Captain Tidwell came and made a "a handsome apology" and Cuffe was ready to get under way again. Before weighing anchor one final and annoying act took place: Samuel Hicks, one of Cuffe's original crew members, left the ship "without ever returning again."[40]

During Cuffe's absence from the United States Great Britain and America had commenced the War of 1812. When he entered American waters on 19 April 1812 his ship and cargo were impounded at New Bedford. From that date until 1 May Cuffe set about completing two tasks. His first, of course, was to gain the release of his ship and cargo. After making personal representations to President James Madison, the *Traveler* and her cargo were released.

Cuffe's second task was considerably more difficult. He had hoped to interest the United States government in supporting his back-to-Africa scheme. Several nonintercourse acts prohibited trade contacts between the Americans and the British. As he had done in England, Cuffe began working through influential people to accomplish his ends.

Subsequent to the release of his ship, Cuffe received correspondence from the African Institution that spurred his efforts. Thomas Clarkson and William Allen, acting for the institution, outlined their plan to Cuffe from London on 1 July 1812. They first made it clear that the institution had secured a grant of land in Sierra Leone for Captain Cuffe. He was advised that he could work the land himself or let it to others for cultivation. Further, Cuffe was told the grant could be increased after the initial portions had been peopled and developed.

Next the correspondence touched on Cuffe's own settlement in the colony. Several alternatives were put forward. Permanent residence was not necessary; the institution seemed to favor a situation where Cuffe could live for a period in the colony while making periodic visitations to maintain contacts with England and America. It suggested that perhaps some members of his family could be settled in the colony. It was clear, however, the determination of residence was solely up to Cuffe.

Next Clarkson and Allen pursued conditions relating to the settlers Cuffe would take to the colony. They must be willing to place themselves under the British government. Since he had been in the colony it was felt that Cuffe could speak with authority about freedom, religious toleration, and other matters. Prospective settlers had to be free people of good character and industrious. Important in the eyes of the African Institution was that settlers should also be persons skilled in the useful mechanical arts of cultivation of tropical produce. Farmers were needed, the sponsors said, because the Nova Scotians were mostly carpenters and handy craftsmen.

After describing the qualities they wished the settlers to possess, the sponsors addressed the question of numbers. They made it clear that they were not suggesting large numbers of people. "To carry over a colony is not intended; nor is it necessary to carry over as many as would work the whole grant of land made to you . . . ."[41] It would be better that a few choice persons be selected. The institution specified perhaps a dozen or eighteen would be sufficient. Cuffe was notified that the institution was prepared to financially assist this venture; the exact level of funding, however, is not mentioned although it is stated that poorer settlers would be assisted with passage money and agricultural supplies. Clarkson and Allen end their letter by stating that the whale fishery was a matter for future consideration but they wished Cuffe to give his full attention to the land grant and the settlers.

Spurred by this correspondence Cuffe sought a method to get around the nonintercourse regulations. Remembering that his influential English friends had acquired his licenses and secured release of Aaron Richards from a reluctant government, he decided to lobby the American government for special consideration. At the same time William Allen and others took similar courses of action with the British government. This time, however, positive results were not forthcoming.

Undeterred by this setback Cuffe expanded his plans and continued lobbying the United States government. In January 1814 Laban Wheaton of Massachusetts introduced in the House of Representatives a memorial authorizing the president to permit Cuffe to depart the United States with a vessel and cargo for Africa and to return. A Senate memorial to the same end was defeated in committee in March by a seenty-two to sixty-five vote. Although personally captivated by Cuffe, President Madison was in the midst of conducting a war and was unable to offer official or unofficial assistance.

In the interim, between Congress's defeat of his proposal and the end of the war, Cuffe attempted to rebuild his business. The war had a critical impact on his trading ventures. For a period he returned to farming around Westport. Yet his commitment to returning to Sierra Leone did not abate. He continued to write to the English African Institution and was a frequent speaker to groups of free blacks in eastern seaboard cities. In Philadelphia, New York, Boston, and Baltimore he told such groups about the potential of the colony and of the interest in receiving black American settlers.

James Forten, of Philadelphia, like Cuffe a successful merchant and involved in maritime business, headed the Philadelphia African Institution. This Philadelphia group was, perhaps, the most influential black group in the city. Like its London counterpart the Philadelphia Institution actively supported selective emigration to Sierra Leone and Forten had earlier provided Cuffe with letters of recommendation. Immediately following the declaration of peace, Forten wrote Cuffe expressing support for the plans: "I approve very highly of your proposition of building a ship for the African trade by men of color, and shall lay it before the Society when next we meet; and write you their opinions."[42]

Simultaneously, the Reverend Peter Williams in New York City functioned like Forten in his assistance to Cuffe. As head of the New York branch of the African Institution, Williams arranged speaking appearances for Cuffe. Through Williams's correspondence Cuffe was in touch with blacks interested in going to Sierra Leone. As early as 1812, Cuffe had met with Daniel Coker and George Collins when both were teachers at the Baltimore African School. Later, in 1820, Coker would make his own decision to emigrate to Sierra Leone.

All this activity expanded the scope of Cuffe's plans. He had been authorized to receive resources from his London supporters for a limited number of settlers. By November 1815, however, the number of persons willing to go had exceeded that authorization. To meet this contingency some of the passengers instituted their own solicitation for funds.

Boston November 15 1815 Whereas William Guinn with his wife and two children, Perry Lockes with his wife and three children, Samuel Hewes [Hughes ?] with his wife and four children, Thomas Jarvis with his wife and one child, Peter Wilcox and his wife and five children, and Robert Rigsby with his wife and one child, all free black people, now resident in Boston, are about to embark on board the brig Traveler, Paul Cuffe owner and master, bound to Sierra Leone in Africa, with the intention of settling there——and whereas the emigrants find themselves unable, without pecuniary assistance, to defray the expenses of their necessary outfits, sea-stores and passage money, and hereby humbly beg the aid of the wealthy and charitable. We the subscribers, wishing success to the laudable enterprize of the said William and his aims associated, to promote their wishes agree to pay the sums by us respectively subscribed:

W. Guinn	4
P. Lockes	5
S. Hewes	6
T. Jarvis	7
P. Wilcox	7
R. Rigsby	3
	32

Jos. May [43]

Such solicitations produced little financial support.

On 10 December 1815 Cuffe sailed for Sierra Leone. Between 15 November and the sailing date six new passengers were added to the list making a total of thirty-eight men, women, and children who went to Sierra Leone. The trials and tribulations of the settlers is beyond the scope of the present work.[44]

Cuffe left the colony on 4 April 1816 to return to the United States. His intention was to return to Sierra Leone in 1817. Several important factors, however, intervened. First, Cuffe's thinking on the African return was undergoing a metamorphosis. Some time in 1816 his ideas to changed from a selective emigration to a large scale exodus from the United States.

His vision of relocation did not retain its pre-1816 clarity. At one point Cuffe even suggested a two site relocation: continuing the Sierra Leone project as well as establishing a colony in Louisiana for those who wished to separate from whites but also remain in America.[45] Some of the confusion in Cuffe's later thinking could be attributed to his own ambivalence. He was committed to the idea of equality in America but at the same time the virulence of American racism was moving him to regard Africa as more than a refuge for a select number of blacks and as a solution to the black/white conflict. Second, Cuffe's wife, a woman of American Indian ancestry, was opposed to going to Africa; Cuffe expressed that he was unwilling to separate her from her people. Finally, by the year 1817 Cuffe's health began to fail and he died on 17 September 1817. Even then, according to his great grandson, Paul Cuffe was planning his third voyage to Sierra Leone.

Perhaps as important as Cuffe's failing health and his changing perceptions was the emergence of the American Colonization Society. Organized in December 1816 the group altered forever the black American attachment to the African return. Composed principally of southern politicians and sympathizers, this group masked its racist intent by posing as friends and benefactors of blacks. The ACS public image was helped by the number of liberal northern whites who initially supported its cause. Even the London African Institution was taken in by the ACS rhetoric.

The ACS wreaked havoc on black activists such as James Forten and Paul Cuffe. Both men were active supporters of the African Institution's lofty aspirations for blacks: African repatriation. Neither, however, could condone the negative, degrading assertions that ACS made about the free black population. ACS compounded the problem by attempting to co-opt black leaders in support of their program. Although the menacing nature of ACS was clear to some black Americans their initial reactions were slightly confused. For example James Forten, like Cuffe, began shifting his emphasis about the African return. First he supported individual voluntary plans and later became quite critical of ACS and still later turned away from the African return altogether.

From late 1816 on Samuel J. Mills and Robert Finley sought Cuffe's advice on a number of points concerning Africa. They asked if Cuffe would be willing to act as an agent of the society. He in turn gave them the names of Rev. Peter Williams and James Forten, black members of the African Institution. He wrote letters describing his voyages to Sierra Leone and, after ACS rejected sending American blacks to the British colony, Cuffe suggested they might explore possibilities in the Cape of Good Hope area. Finally, after Cuffe's death, ACS published excerpts from his letters making it look as though he wholeheartedly supported its aims. On 18 June 1818, ACS even published an imaginary conversation among William Penn, Cuffe, and Absalom Jones.[46] At the end of the discussion Penn and Cuffe convince Jones that deportation of free blacks to Africa was a desirable plan. Despite the negative reaction to ACS, Cuffe continued to try to convince black Americans that going to Africa was in their best interest; black American response, however, was never better than lukewarm.

VII

It was three years before another black American would venture to Africa. In three distinctive ways this second voyage to Sierra Leone underscores the collective perception and the continuing relevance of the African return to some blacks. One, the leader of the 1820 expedition, Daniel Coker, had been favorably impressed by Paul Cuffe's observations about Sierra Leone. Two, Coker and his followers in the Baltimore African Methodist Episcopal Church were in a crisis around 1815. Third, the Maryland Colonization Society was willing and able to assist Coker in his plans.

Coker's response to Cuffe's charisma was understandable but the nature of his crisis needs greater explanation. Emigrationist perceptions and actions were geared to overwhelming pressures in the black community. Usually the pressures were manifest in the intransigence of American racism. In the Coker case, however, the interracial conflict was exacerbated by an intraracial element. In 1815 a dispute accompanied the election of Coker as the first bishop of the AME Church; part of the negative reaction to Coker revolved around his mixed racial parentage.[47] In the five years following the convention the negative feelings had not subsided. Instead the Baltimore group factionalized and the conflict became more difficult to resolve. Not only was there an estrangement between the Baltimore and the Philadelphia AME members but local conflicts tested the solidarity of the black community. Buffeted by racism on the one hand and black intolerance on the other, Coker decided to emigrate. Clearly his decision and that of his followers was based on religious intolerance and not on nationalist perceptions. For Coker Africa was offering solace, and that was the primary impetus for all black Americans who advocated returning to Africa.

More important, the Coker trip demonstrated that the dangers inherent in such an undertaking were probably as prohibitive for black American aspirations as lack of resources. While Coker's journal is evidence of his faith in God and the high aspirations for his mission, it is also a daily account of traumatic situations.

On Sunday, 6 February 1820, immediately after departing New York, the first of a series of troublesome incidents occurred. Coker's group of about ninety persons plus three white Maryland Colonization agents had charted a ship named *Elizabeth*. On the first day their escort vessel, the U.S.S. *Cyane*, lost contact and was not seen or heard from again until they reached Sierra Leone. Five days later on 11 February he reported, "This is a day to try men's faith: high seas, sickness, gale and making no headway."[48] Although they were moving again the next day they also spotted a wreck with a ship named *Elizabeth* out of Boston. No one was found aboard. "We believe," Coker wrote, "that there are dangers and trials ahead."[49] Among these were the reported unhealthiness of the African environment. Moreover, Coker observed that the ship would probably arrive during the unfavorable period: the rainy season.

A day of fasting and prayer took place on 24 February. But later that same day an incident severely strained relations between the crew and the black passengers. Peter Small of Philadelphia and the ship's captain "engaged each other" following a fight between their dogs. With some difficulty Rev. Samuel Bacon, one of the colonization agents, parted the two men. The captain still in a "great passion" called for his pistols. Luckily they were not produced and the blacks all retired below decks. In the evening Coker and Bacon held another prayer meeting. The following day peace was made when Coker induced Small and the captain to apologize.

More trouble was not long developing. On 2 March the agents became upset over "improper expressions made use of by some of the immigrants."[50] Coker did not reveal the exact nature of the comments but he was sufficiently troubled and called a meeting of the male passengers. After some discussion Coker proposed signing a statement of confidence in the agents. Two recalcitrant passengers refused to sign.

In his *Journal* that night Coker commented on the ingratitude of suspecting the motives of the agents. They had, he concluded, given proof of their sincerity and had left friends and faced the same dangers as the blacks. Coker may not have appreciated that the blacks with less experience than he in dealing with whites might not only be more suspicious but also more alert to paternalism. Seasickness and the death of a child added to the pressures of the crossing.

Troubled times did not cease once they arrived in port. On Wednesday, 9 March 1820 the *Elizabeth* anchored at Free Town Harbor in Sierra Leone. Ashore the following day Coker and others were scandalized by the nakedness of the population, both male and female. Later he and Bacon were approached and asked to drink rum by a group of Kru men. In paternalistic pidgin they explained that "we no drinkey rum, God no like dat."[51] Coker later congratulated himself for making a good first impression on the "heathens." Unfriendly African chiefs refused to meet with Coker but, perhaps the unkindest cut of all occurred when an African accused of stealing objected to Coker acting as justice of the peace. The accused was vocal about not wishing to be judged by a mulatto. It must have been strangely ironic to Coker to face the same criticism about his racial background in Africa as he faced in America. John Kizzel, a repatriated African, saved the day by asserting that Coker was a descendant of Africa and that the civil authority must and would be obeyed.

Once settled, the overall impression was positive. In a letter to Jeremiah Watts, Coker praised the opportunities for trade, for acquiring land, and for doing "better than you possibly do in America and not work half so hard." Nathaniel Peck of Baltimore wrote his mother to alert her that he would be returning to bring her back. Peck had been a free black and had owned his own mill in Baltimore. He was trying to raise funds through solicitations to set up a much needed mill in the colony. Still Coker's letter issued a warning. He would welcome thousands of black Americans to the colony but the religious divisions must be left in America.

From Coker's *Journal* and his subsequent writings it is difficult to delineate a developed nationalist stance. Instead his focus seemed limited to finding the opportunity for religious tolerance and an atmosphere where blacks could be commercially successful. Some emphasis was given to the acquisition of land but it did not seem a primary interest of Coker and his companions.

Coker's place in the continuum of the back-to-Africa movement must be sought in concerns other than black nationalism. His ventures presented a microcosm of the frustrations of some black Americans and is the perfect example of the minority appeal of back-to-Africa. At the time of Coker's decision to leave, the majority of black Americans had decided to stay in America. Their decisions were not the result of a lessening zeal for things African or a denial of their African connections, nor can their change be interpreted as an assimilationist gesture.

VIII

In the wake of the founding of the ACS most Afro-American leaders were motivated by the necessity to counter the denigrating attacks on black Americans launched by the organization. Having experienced the end of slavery in most of the North, the cessation of the international slave trade, and the enthusiastic role blacks played in defending America's sovereignty most blacks concluded that equal citizenship was possible. In addition, they thought that black Americans had to continue their conscious and consistent fight to broaden their acceptance within the nation. Lacking the resources for total black migration and lacking a fully rationalized nationalist program, the return to Africa was felt to be of limited value. While a black American colony in Africa might relieve the psychological trauma of those individuals lucky enough to emigrate, it would not change the quality of life for the bulk of the black community.

Even with the overwhelming black opposition to an African return after 1817 the idea did not disappear. In fact the virulence of the opposition kept alive not only the continuing attack on ACS but also the attempt to limit the back-to-Africa appeal. Once broached, the question of African emigration could not be completely submerged. Black Americans were not ignorant of the historical importance of migration to oppressed people. Thus, even when African emigration was being opposed other emigration plans were emerging.

In the thirty years between 1820 and 1850 black emigration to Canada, Mexico, Haiti, and the West Indies was discussed, rejected, and revived on a regular basis. Because of its proximity to the United States, its available land, and black Americans' inaccurate perceptions about its antislavery atmosphere, Canada was the most popular choice of relocation after the late 1820s. Other observations about Canada made it attractive for many blacks. There was a feeling that Canada was being the target of choice for fugitive slaves. Whether that mindset reflected reality or not it was a powerful magnet in the black mind. Canada's proximity also lessened the charges of cowardice aimed at those who opted for emigration. It was close enough that one could assist blacks in bondage easily should such assistance be necessary. Finally, northern white philanthropy was more forthcoming in its financial support of blacks who migrated to Canada. Several missionary societies maintained special connections with fugitive communities, black schools, and churches, and financed these projects through fund raising in the United States. The number of whites giving financial support to Haitian relocation or other West Indian projects was almost nonexistent.

No other location was favored as much as Canada. Mexico, for example, was both praised and condemned as a haven for blacks in 1832 in the *Liberator* by a "colored female." She immediately rejected African emigration without stating reasons. She was also against establishing an independent political entity but felt blacks should attach themselves to the United States. If blacks should leave they needed to seek out a locale where they could achieve the following: "we can be received as brothers [and sisters]; our worth will be felt and acknowledged; we may acquire education, wealth, and respectability; a knowledge of the arts and sciences, and the power to enjoy them which the states deny."[52]

The correspondent asserted that Mexico would provide those conditions. In addition, the climate was healthy and warm and the soil rich and fertile. Moreover, the population of Mexico was overwhelmingly colored and amalgamation was occurring. She envisioned colored American merchant ships plying their trade in American ports. The only objection to Mexico was its papist religion. Even Catholicism could be overcome and perhaps black Americans would become the instruments for establishing the Protestant church in Mexico. There is no evidence that the positive assessment of Mexico stimulated much black interest.

Perhaps Mexico stirred so little in the black mind because a group of well-placed black Bostonians lobbied more effectively for the black republic of Haiti. Prince Saunders not only lived in Haiti and England but also traveled to the court of the Russian Czar and was the outstanding proponent of the Haitian Exodus, as it came to be called.[53] Saunders was ably assisted in the enterprise by Rev. Thomas Paul and other members of the Paul family. As early as 1811 Thomas Paul, on the meager resources of the African Baptist Church, visited Haiti on several occasions. He also declared the country as a theater of missionary activity for his Boston congregation. More than a decade later he was writing to extol the virtues of Haiti.[54] His letter attained a degree of legitimacy not found in the writing on Mexico. He had been given, he wrote, permission to promote Haiti for black Americans during an audience with President Boyer.

Although the major portion of his letter is visionary he provided some factual background as well. He listed the country's staple crops as coffee, rice, tobacco, indigo, and corn. There was ample pasturage for herds and the forests abounded with mahogany and other woods. He included price lists for livestock and seafood. Paul made a point of saying his health remained good throughout his visit. In his penultimate paragraph Paul listed a number of labor categories that would find attractive conditions in Haiti: tailors, blacksmiths, painters, cabinetmakers, and bootmakers, among others.

IX

Following the Cuffe and Coker ventures, for a brief period in the 1820s, Haiti emerged as the principal target for black emigrationists. Between 1824 and 1826, a combination of factors gave a brief notoriety to the cause: strong support from President Boyer of Haiti; participation by leading black Philadelphians and New Yorkers; the charisma of Prince Saunders; and the existence of organizations focused on Haiti, gave a brief notoriety to the cause. Among the inducements offered by President Boyer was a rhetorical promise that everyone from farmers to craftsmen would find a place in the Haitian economy. The president announced that land was available for at least six thousand blacks. In addition, the forty-dollar cost of transportation would be borne by the Haitian government. As important as the money was, the dispatching of Jonathan Granville to the United States to assist blacks in their preparations was a boon to black Americans.

Like Prince Saunders, Granville was black. Unlike Saunders he was Haitian and in black American eyes had greater legitimacy than Saunders because of his direct ties to the Boyer regime. Boyer's interest in black Americans was largely dictated by his own political needs. Among his pressing concerns were hoped-for recognition by the United States and manpower to increase agriculture and manufacturing and provide a force against the French military.

Whether they knew of Boyer's hidden agenda or not, black Americans accelerated plans for Haitian emigration. New York and Philadelphia both created Haytian Emigration Societies of Colored People.[55] The New York society aggressively pursued the objectives of providing for black emigrants. Much of this aggressiveness was a reaction to white activities organized by an ACS aide formerly committed to African repartition. The less-than-successful efforts of Cuffe and Coker, and the negative publicity about politics in Liberia, increased the difficulties of ACS agents in trying to attract blacks. Loring D. Dewey, despairing of sending blacks to Liberia, turned in 1824 to a promotion of Haiti. Although he refused to work with blacks, Dewey promoted their separate efforts.[56] Although angered by Dewey's work and connections with President Boyer, who had seized on Dewey's ACS affiliation to further diplomatic designs, blacks were committed to Haiti.

New Yorkers were bombarded with publicity about the Haiti project. Rev. Peter Williams, Jr., chaired the New York organization. The society was a virtual who's who of black New York. Its board of managers included the Reverend Samuel Cornish, Thomas L. Jennings (sometimes Jinnings), and Samuel Ennalls. Other members included Peter Vogelsang, Thomas Sipkins, Benjamin Paul, Boston Crummell, and James Varick. This group in 1824 and 1825 sent hundreds of blacks to the black republic. Peter Williams extended his services and spoke before interested groups in Philadelphia, and also went to Haiti in 1825. His trip, however, was tarnished because more than fifty blacks who had gone earlier to Haiti returned on the same boat.

Philadelphia blacks duplicated the Haitian activities of their New York counterparts. Although Prince Saunders had been in the city as early as 1819, the Philadelphians did not organize their society until 1824. The incentives for the Philadelphians to organize were the visits of Jonathan Granville and, as in the New York case, the machinations of Loring Dewey. Dewey's anxiety about Granville's Philadelphia stop were well-founded. The city had been, after all, the hotbed of opposition to ACS. Two leaders of that opposition, Richard Allen and James Forten, were more optimistic about President Boyer's rhetoric.

At a public meeting on 6 July 1824 Forten and Allen took charge and shared with the assembled blacks correspondence of Thomas Paul and President Boyer to Loring Dewey. By August Forten and Allen had been joined in the society by Allen's son, Quomony Clarkson, and a number of black merchants.[57] Both Philadelphians and New Yorkers responded most favorably to Boyer's economic arguments. By a happy set of circumstances a survey in New York, concluded in 1824, revealed a number of craftsmen desired by Haiti were residents in the city. Even leaders who had adamantly opposed ACS were sounding as though they might emigrate too. Williams remained in Haiti for several months and Allen's son, John, sent back glowing reports of his trip in 1824. Another Philadelphian, Rev. Benjamin F. Hughes, emigrated in 1824 and sent the same positive reports which circulated widely in Philadelphia.[58]

Despite the positive reports from Hughes, Allen, and others, reports of dissatisfaction began drifting back to Philadelphia. Especially hard was the adjustment of unskilled blacks to Haitian agriculture. Haitian officials, too, were annoyed when those blacks who disdained farming began drifting into the cities. President Boyer had no intention of letting the disgruntled minority of new black settlers become a center for criticizing his regime. Loring Dewey went to Haiti to see the situation firsthand. He complimented the Haitian government on its sincerity and its service to black emigrants but his favorable correspondence could not stem the negative publicity.

While being solicitious to the black community Granville also met with white financiers to court their support of the Boyer government. They failed to respond to Granville's overtures.

Thus, by the spring of 1825, less than a year after the program's inauguration, President Boyer began having second thoughts. He had not succeeded any more with the American government than Granville had with white businessmen. Boyer, also learned that Dewey no longer represented ACS and the president had calculated that the influential whites in the organization would assist in his pursuit of diplomatic ties with the United States. Rumors were also rife about white speculation in real estate and overcharging for transportation and services. The outspokenness of some black Americans made Boyer fear that they might become the center of political agitation. Unable to see any advantages to future black emigration, the president withdrew all of the project's remaining funds.

Black American leaders were shocked and embarrassed. The failure of Afro-Americans to be integrated peacefully into the black republic was double-edged. It certainly challenged the oft-stated assertions of black American capacity for self-government. In addition it reintroduced all the negative stereotypes about Haiti. Moreover, in order to contain the potential dangers of the failure, black leaders had to be circumspect in their criticism. Much of the criticism for the failure was placed, unfairly, on working class blacks who had difficulty adjusting.

Several black leaders were sufficiently angered and discouraged that they became adamant foes of all types of emigration.[59] Samuel Cornish never spoke favorably about emigration after 1825. Peter Williams, who had previously assisted Cuffe and Coker with their plans and also served as president of the New York African Institution, became very circumspect about emigration, even within the Western Hemisphere.

The trauma over the Haitian affair was still acute in 1830 when the 1830 convention endorsed emigration to Canada for the victims of the 1829 Cincinnati riots. Despite the embarrassment of the 1824-1826 Haitian debacle and the stepped-up opposition to emigration in Philadelphia and New York, Boston blacks maintained their longstanding connection with Haiti.

By the 1850s the continuing interest of Boston blacks made the city a logical choice as headquarters of James Redpath's Haitian Exodus plans. Although white and holding negative views of blacks, Redpath had legitimacy in the black community: he had lived in Haiti and was the personal envoy of the president.[60] To assist him in the task of stimulating black interest, Redpath established the *Pine and Palm* newspaper. Dedicated solely to the idea of black liberation from slavery and relocation in Haiti, not on achieving political rights in America, the paper had a small but loyal following. The newspaper made possible tenuous connections between like-minded blacks in Boston and Philadelphia. For a period of time Jacob C. White, Jr., served as the Philadelphia agent for the *Pine and Palm*.

This revival of interest in relocation generally and Haiti specifically could be attributed in part to the growth of antiblack sentiments during the 1850s. As part of its collective legislation the Compromise of 1850 contained a new menace for the black community. The New Fugitive Slave Law was perceived as more dangerous than the ACS. Basically, by the 1850s the black community had demonstrated its ability to fight ACS on a rather equal basis. Few blacks free or slave had accepted the society's offer of assistance partly because the price of acceptance was too high: it meant accepting the negative characterizations that the ACS fostered. Due in part to black opposition the society had failed in its task of removing the free black population from the States. Sustained and rational opposition had limited the impact of the society.

The New Fugitive Slave Law, however, was another matter and included a different level of attack on the community. Unlike the ACS the law had the full backing of the federal government and more than a few state governments. It was not aimed principally at free blacks but for a variety of reasons it created havoc among blacks throughout the North. A significant number of blacks in the North were living a fugitive existence. Many had lived long productive lives there and several prominent black leaders were fugitives.

Henry Highland Garnet, Samuel Ringgold Ward, William Wells Brown, and Henry Bibb were among those who had escaped bondage and become leaders in the North. Since the new law had no statute of limitations all were subject to prosecution. Working-class black men such as like the celebrated Anthony Burns of Boston were also subject to prosecution despite an exemplary life in the North.

Blacks who had purchased their liberty were not necessarily safe from the law's grasp. Frederick Douglass had purchased his freedom in 1847 but was still vulnerable, and since he insisted on playing a role in assisting fugitives he was engaging in conduct specifically prohibited by the new law.

Other facts about the law disturbed black life. Any individual could be deputized to assist in the capture of a fugitive. Refusal meant a fine, jail time, or possibly both. Finally, the fee schedule could be manipulated and militated so that blacks did not receive justice in the slave courts. Commissioners were paid five dollars in cases in which the black was declared free. A ten dollar fee was given commissioners who found in favor of the master. The rationale for the fee schedule was that it required more paper work to return a person to slavery than to set him free.

A partial positive impact of the new legislation was the revival of discussion centered on emigration. Africa, however, was not the immediate target of the new black interest. African emigration , in the minds of many, was too closely associated with ACS. Among the leadership group Martin Delany and Henry Highland Garnet expended the most energy in pursuit of the African return. Garnet created a flap in New York between 1858 and 1861 with his African Civilization Society. As early as 1853-1854 in western cities such as Cleveland, Chatham, Ontario, Toronto, and Detroit regional sentiment was growing for a revival of the African return.

In the East the power of Frederick Douglass and others kept discussions of African emigration at a minimum. Despite this opposition the seemingly strong and smooth operation of the western emigrants began having an effect.

The eastern silence on Africa was broken around 1856 in schemes that were local in nature and of short durations. ACS leaders, always attuned to the winds of change in the black community, began to reassert their efforts. Benjamin Coates, John Pinney, and Thomas Bourne seemed more at ease with black leaders than some of their predecessors.[61] A final ingredient in the eastern change was the activity of Henry Highland Garnet. He had been absent from the United States from 1850 until 1856. Upon his return he involved himself more deeply in the slowly emerging African return discussions. Mostly regarded as an antiemigrationist, Garnet had flirted briefly with the African return in

1849. His 1858 founding of the African Civilization Society became the catalyst for bringing together the western and eastern strands of the African exodus.

It was an uneasy fit as the western and eastern forces seemed motivated by different perspectives. Delany and his western cohorts disdained any white support. Publicly, at least, the eastern leaders did the same. Rumors began to circulate, however, that the African Civilization society, and Garnet, J. Sella Martin, and others in Boston, particularly, had accepted financial support from the dreaded American Colonization Society Although no evidence existed to substantiate the charges they were fueled by a number of circumstances. Chief among the reasons for suspicion was the fact that Garnet and others had been staunchly opposed to colonization.

Colonization, emigration, and the virulent antiblack attacks caused much changing of political position among black leaders. Many began to question, perhaps for the first time, whether elevating the race and other actions would lead to inclusion in American political life. Still, the switch to emigration was not simply a kneejerk response to the newest pressures on black life. Garnet had already left the United States once during the crisis surrounding the New Fugitive Slave Law. While resident in England and Jamaica from1856 through 1858 he had maintained contact with black and white promoters of the African return.[62]

Actually, all the emigrationists, Garnet and Delany included, ultimately accepted support from the American Colonization Society. ACS had continued its effort to co-opt black leaders and found some black leaders willing to listen to its overtures. At the time that Delany, for example, was making plans to explore West African locales other than the ACS-sponsored Liberia, Robert Campbell, a lesser-known black leader, was already on the continent under the auspices of the organization.

Martin Delany was the leading exponent of the western revival. From 1853 through 1858, in a series of conventions, speeches, and publications, his rhetoric moved closer to an ideology of political self-determinism and economic development in Africa.[63] In 1858 after he received the authorization to explore the Niger Valley as a possible site for a black polity, his carefully constructed coalition factionalized.[64] Unable to generate funds or continuing support in the West, Delany affected an expedient liaison with Garnet's African Civilization Society.

This group consisting of black activists, white abolitionists, and emigrationists began to receive heavy criticism about its alleged connections with ACS.[65] Newspapers such as the *Weekly Anglo-African* and *Liberator* reported acrimonious meetings in New York and Boston.[66] Fortunately, Delany was spared the unpleasant confrontations among anti-emigrationists George T. Downing, Charles Reason, Douglass, and emigrationists Garnet, and J. Sella Martin of the African Civilization Society. Delany's trip to Africa and his official report was, for him, confirmation of the black man's capacity for governing his own affairs.

Yet Delany's legacy was bittersweet on several levels. First, the Africans with whom he signed accords quickly repudiated the treaties.[67] His explorations did not result in even the selective migration that he had come to prefer. Next, the bitterness among emigrationists and anti-emigrationists did not abate. Their ideological and personal animosities found outlets in 1860 and 1861 over the renewed interest in Haiti and over the choice of a white American, James Redpath, to head the Haytian emigration bureau.[68]

Redpath had been chosen to head this organization and its newspaper, *The Pine and Palm,* over an old Delany foe and veteran promoter of Haiti, James Theodore Holly. The nationalist perception that black men were as capable of leadership as whites spurred Delany's reaction. Self-determination, a nationalist principle, was embodied in Delany's negative response to Redpath and the Haitian exodus. At the same time, however, the continued infighting prevented the accomplishment of another nationalist norm: racial solidarity.

Although the African exploration did not trigger Delany's hoped for response, it and his later activities demonstrated his adherence to nationalist goals and conduct. He continued to stress racial pride and a dedication to deflating myths of white supremacy. Delany pressed demands for economic and social equality and simultaneously continued to promote an aggressive belief in the competence of black leadership. While asking the U.S. government for a redress of grievances Delany also constantly pointed out that blacks were the source of their own salvation. Despite his ideological fights with friends and foes, most of his contemporaries would have agreed with Douglass' assessment. "Delany was," he said, "the intensest embodiment of black nationality to be met with outside the valley of the Niger."[69] Finally, although Delany's formulations and actions have appealed to generations of black activists, like Garnet, Douglass, and most black leaders, he found himself supporting the federal government in the Civil War. Perhaps commitment to nationalist ideals should have led Delany and others to withhold their services from the United States government at the time of war.[70] Their perceptions about the war's beginnings and its ultimate conclusions differed drastically from the official line of the Lincoln administration and most whites.

Blacks knew intuitively that the war was about slavery even in the face of official denials and despite the fact that they were rejected as soldiers in the northern army. Yet perhaps black leaders, including the nationalists, were too willing to suspend their own commitment to their black liberation in one more effort to gain citizenship rights in America.

The flux of political events led to an ambivalence among black leaders vis a vis the African return and the potential of full citizenship.

This ambivalence is also reflected in the frustrations of everyday blacks trying to come to grips with manhood, political rights, and equality. Leaders met, talked, and fired off newspaper and personal salvos about African redemption. The energy of the rhetoric was not matched by fervid volunteering of blacks to return to Africa. Survival needs took precedence over political rhetoric, especially an ideology calling for resources and for travel to a foreign land. Yet the thought of the African return would not die even among the working class.

William Nesbit and William H. Parham exemplified the general dilemmas facing plain black folk seeking solutions to the trauma of living in America and considering one of the solutions to be the African return. Neither Parham nor Nesbit commanded the same attention in the black community as Delany, Garnet, and before them Cuffe, Coker, or Peter Williams, yet their search for a refuge and a nation was equally dedicated and more closely approximates the circumstances of the majority of antebellum black Americans.

In 1855 William Nesbit attained brief notoriety through a pamphlet detailing his four-month stay in Liberia. His comments were more than the orchestrated attacks on ACS conducted by Theodore Wright and Samuel Cornish during the 1830s and 1840s.[71] He had sailed from New York City on 10 November 1853 with fifty-two other northern blacks headed for Africa. Frustrated and unwilling to remain in the United States, Nesbit and his cohorts represented one of several small private black efforts at repatriation. Their transport and other expenses had been met by ACS. His pamphlet is an indictment of everything associated with Liberia: ACS, missionaries, business practices, white attitudes, indigenous politics, and slavery.[72]

Nesbit had taken the trip because he had "keenly felt the persecutions and annoyances to which my race is subject in this country."[73] ACS publicity was persuasive and he believed that it would be possible for him to reap rewards and benefits not available in America. Unlike Daniel Coker's crossing there were no precipitious incidents during Nesbit's voyage. Subsequent to his arrival in December he experienced things that disillusioned him. Concerning the prosperity of the country he claimed "the statements of the colonization agents were egregious falsehoods."[74] He described crowded and inadequate accommodations where new settlers were expected to spend their first six months. Money and patronage could secure better housing or a favorable interpretation of the law because corruption was rife.

According to Nesbit, at the center of this chicanery sat the Liberian president, Joseph J. Roberts. Nesbit characterized President Roberts as an active agent of the Colonization Society. Roberts, he charged, was involved in the activities of the missionaries, all of whom had left the Christian undertaking and had become traders. Some missionaries engaged in trading rum, firearms, and slaves. Even those with legitimate enterprises cheated their customers. Nesbit was told by the Reverend Mr. Hill of Marshall, "These people have no idea of weights and measures, and when we buy from them, we use a gallon measure that holds a gallon and a half and in this way, pay ourselves for our trouble, and in weighing camwood, we always take enough to make it cheap."[75] Nesbit's bitterest indictment was against the authorities for allowing the existence of slavery. Through a variety of legal fictions bondage, sometimes more severe than in the United States, existed universally, according to Nesbit. What was particularly incomprehensible to Nesbit was that the Liberian masters were themselves repatriated and manumitted slaves.

His final damaging assessment of Liberia concerned the country's political strength. He concluded that "Liberia cannot succeed."[76] If British and American support were withdrawn the politicians could not preserve their nationality for one week, Nesbit averred. Despite the black activists' claims, unconsciously perhaps, Nesbit's assessment did not demonstrate a black capacity to govern. The repatriated blacks had not made significant progress in Christianizing and democratizing Liberia. Blacks, according to Nesbit, seemed as motivated by self-interest as their white counterparts.

Martin Delany's eight-page introduction to Nesbit's work carries on the criticism of the white missionaries and politicians but for the most part ignores the charge of black complicity. Delany asserted that the white missionaries were wholly inadequate to the important work that needed to be done in Africa. Their inadequacy stemmed from "the simple reason that they are not the proper representatives of the people for whom they profess to act."[77] Delany was disturbed by the missionary dogma which asserted the superiority of the white race. It was, to him, one of the worst examples of American hypocrisy.

Although giving a negative assessment of Liberia, Delany had uttered the beginnings of his nationalist appraisal of the African return. The introduction does not provide a developed nationalist rationale but several important themes that he would later develop are present. His idea of blacks as the legitimate source of their own political destiny is clearly presaged in his brief introduction. Delany implied that a successful program of African repatriation would be a black undertaking and would be entirely free of white ACS control, influence, or participation. The introduction is not a condemnation of the African return but of Liberia and ACS interference. At the time that Nesbit was completing his unsuccessful tour of Liberia, Delany began holding secret meetings in the west formulating a program of black-controlled African emigration.

Despite Delany's machinations it was William Parham, like William Nesbit, who provided poignant testimony about the attractiveness and the frustration of African emigration. In three letters written over a thirty-year period Parham discussed exodus as an attractive but elusive alternative to living in America. Unlike Delany, Parham never attained leadership status or personal prominence and so his dilemma probably more closely approximated the average black's struggle to resolve the tensions of living in a racist society. Although not a leader himself, Parham was a close personal friend of the Philadelphian Jacob C. White, Jr. From Cincinnati on 9 December 1861 Parham wrote to his good friend Jake. After informing White that his health remained good Parham went to the heart of his concerns:

> I found the pamphlet which you were kind enough to send me, replete with interesting details, from which I derived much valuable knowledge of the country . . . I had previously read the "Guide." I entertain a very favorable opinion of Hayti; and am a hearty advocate of emigration to that beautiful isle. I do not mean emigration en masse but individual emigration. Emigration of men of mind or men of means. Emigration of those who—"Rather than be slaves dread death would brave" You are aware that there are those among us who hesitate not to tell us, that America suits them well enough and that they are perfectly satisfied to remain in it, notwithstanding they are willing to confess that in their own opinion they can be nought but slaves so long as they remain. These I would not have emigrate. I would not have the sacred soil desecrated by their unhallowed tread. Cowper tells us that "patience itself is meanness in a slave." Having derived so much useful information from the perusal of the before mentioned pamphlets I desire to thank you for your kindness in sending it to me, and assure you that all papers, pamphlets, etc. containing information of the modern "Land of Promise" will be thankfully received and carefully read.[78]

The following year in October, Parham wrote again to his friend. Although written in the midst of the Civil War, Parham gives a stirring but fleeting reference to martial events:

> . . .The excitement consequent upon the recent threatened invasion of Ohio's "Sacred Soil" has subsided; and no more is heard that martial strains of the spirit-stirring drum and ear-piercing fire; no longer do our streets echo back the heavy measured tread of armed battalions, but once more things hereabout have assumed wonted appearance.[79]

Like his black leader friends, Parham questioned the propriety of a white man, even one as presumably qualified as James Redpath, leading a black political concern:

> I have seen Mr. Redpath's "extra sheet" and think under the circumstances, he acted rightly, if the Haytian government really desires our people to settle in their country , they must adopt a better system than the present one which is defective throughout. I am rather glad Mr. Redpath has resigned, and hope the Bureau will be reconstructed immediately under the super-intendence of some intelligent, worthy colored man. I do not by this mean to reflect on that gentleman or his administration of affairs; but as there are those among us as well fitted by education, experience and moral worth to fill the position, as he or any other man, why, then, should we not place such a man there . . ..[80]

Doggedly, Parham moves on to his major concern:

> Like you, I too have been devoting much thought to the probable future of my people, but can discern no ground upon which to base the slightest hope. Slavery will die, but its twin, or other self—prejudice will live on. True the north is growing antislavery, but at the same time, it grows more antinegro. This is undeniably obvious. While thousands, aye, millions stand up to do battle for liberty, few or in fact, none can be found with the courage of will to demand or even advocate equality. And without equality we are slaves still. My intention to emigrate remains unchanged notwith-standing I am unable to go this fall. I think that I shall go about the last of the Spring of first of the Summer at the utmost. If I could believe that our condition would shortly become less abject, I should not have recourse to expatriation; but the bitter, deep and abiding prejudice which seems indigenous to American minds precludes not only belief but even hope itself. Each day brings in its train events which unceasing admonish us to go hence, for this is not our abiding place.I know very little of Jamaica but this much I do know that there men are not proscribed by law on account of complexion-color neither makes nor damns the man-the black man may stand shoulder to shoulder with the white and declare and maintain his manhood and equality. This is all we ask. That prejudice exists there to some extent, I do not pretend to doubt, but with political equality, the majority with us, and equitable laws shielding us, we can treat it with the contempt it merits. If you have not yet read it I should like to advise you to read Sewel's "Ordeal of Free Labor in the West Indies." I think it will repay the perusal. Besides giving a very good description of the country it is the most complete and viable argument in vindication of the

working of the free labor system, in those islands ever given to the public.I am still teaching. . . .[81]

The final letter of 27 February 1890 completed a thirty-year cycle of Parham thinking long and deeply on social, personal, and political matters. Ironically and poignantly he ends by asking his friend Jake's opinion of places to emigrate.

I am still doing business at the old stand not withstanding my determination to quit it as expressed to you a year ago. I am heartily tired of it and only remain because it pays better than anything else. This is no doubt a disgraceful admission and I suppose I ought to be ashamed of it, but it is true. On the 22nd of August next I will have been in harness thirty years. Year after year, the same old grind had gone on. Of a rather mercurial temperament I have desired a more active life. I recognize, however, how exceedingly good God has been to me—how much he has blessed me above my deserving. When I wrote you last I thought of going to Virginia with the purpose of making it my future home...There is more caste and the bitterness of prejudice to be encountered in the north than I can well bear without going south in quest of more. . . I am not fully decided yet what I shall do after I quit school work. Of course I must do something. After passing the fiftieth milestone on life's road, it is generally a doubtful experiment to strike out on new lines of effort. My chosen profession is the law; yet I fear it is now too late to win success in it. I like the excitement of politics, but despise the dirty tricks incident to practical politics. I might succeed in business, but the question with me is whether or not it is worth while for me to burden myself with the cares inseparable from it when there is not one but my wife to provide for. When you write, give me your opinion of Oklahoma, Mexico, and Brazil as places of future promise.[82]

Although unable to make the practical decision to leave Parham continued to explore, at least imaginatively, the thoughts of leaving America.

His three letters capture the poignancy and the impediments of emigration for most black Americans. Its attractions were certainly leaving behind overwhelming prejudice in America; achieving equality in a new environment; and exercising political power and responsibility. Yet survival needs for Parham as well as most blacks were equally powerful. He had to keep living, to support his wife, and to find employment commensurate with his skills and interests.

Thus, the years slipped away, conditions did not improve, but emigration maintained its hold on the black American mind. It functioned not only as an abstraction for potential liberty but also as a refuge against personal disintegration. Just as Parham rejected the dirty tricks of practical politics he also, like most blacks, failed to take practical steps incident to emigration. Nonetheless, in periods of intense racial animosity the considerations of leaving gave black Americans some hope. Even when they failed to consider Africa, the emigrationists' focus usually settled on an area where blacks or colored people were the majority.

Perhaps more important, through Delany the emigrationists did provide the initial black nationalist critique of American society. Their perceptions, their rhetoric, and their activity moved significantly beyond the reformist thrust of American politics in general and black political activity specifically.

Notes

1. Sterling Stuckey, *The Ideological Roots of Black Nationalism* (Boston: Beacon Press, 1972), 1-2, 5, 7, 8; Wilson Jeremiah Moses, *The Golden Age of Black Nationalism, 1850-1925* (New York: Oxford University Press, 1978), 9-17; Sterling Stuckey, *Slave Culture: Nationalism Theory and the Foundations of Black America* (New York: Oxford University Press, 1987), note Walker, Garnet, and Delany among free blacks with deep African, hence, nationalist roots. See also John H. Bracey, Jr., August Meier and Elliott Rudwick, eds., *Black Nationalism in America* (Indianapolis: Bobbs-Merrill, 1970), 38-50 in their discussion of colonization the editors characterize Coker, Cuffe, and Thomas Forten with a desire to uplift Africa more than using Africa as the linchpin of black American political advancement; Rodney Carlisle, *The Roots of Black Nationalism* (Port Washington, New York: Kennikat Press, 1975), 16-23, makes an interesting but overstated case for Cuffe's nationalism.

2. Daniel Coker, *Journal of Daniel Coker, A Descendant of Africa, from the Time of Leaving New York, on the Ship Elizabeth, Capt. Sebon, on a Voyage for Sherbo, in Africa in the Company with Three Agents and about Ninety Persons of Color* (Baltimore: Edward T. Coale, 1820).

3. Martin R. Delaney, *Official Report of the Niger Valley Exploring Party* (New York: T. Hamilton, 1861) reprinted in Howard H. Bell, ed., *Search for a Place; Black Separation and Africa* (Ann Arbor: University of Michigan Press, 1969).

4. Thomas F. O'Dea, *The Sociology of Religion* (Englewood Cliffs, New Jersey: Prentice Hall, 1966), 4-6; Monroe Fordham, *Major Themes in Northern Black Religious Thought* (Hicksville, New York: Exposition Press), 5-8; W.E.B. Du Bois, *The Souls of Black Fork* (New York: Avon Books, 1965), 10, 340; Joseph R. Washington, Jr., *Black Religion* (Boston: 1966), 37-38, 253; Clarence E. Walker, *Rock in a Weary Land: The African Methodist Episcopal Church during the Civil War and Reconstruction* (Baton Rouge: Louisiana State University Press, 1982), 1-3; David E. Swift, *Black Prophets of Justice: Activist Clergy before the Civil War* (Baton Rouge: Louisiana State University Press, 1989), 2-9.

5. Quomony Clarkson, *Letter* to committee on education, Pennslyvania Abolitionist Society, 27 July 1802; *Letter* to PAS, 24 December 1809; *Letter* to John Parrish 13 March 1806, and *Letter* to PAS, 4 October 1813.

6. Samuel Ringgold Ward, *Autobiography of a Fugitive Negro* (New York: Arno Press, 1968), 5-14, 3-25; David E. Swift, *Black Prophets*, 2-6; Joel Schor, *Henry Highland Garnet: A Voice of Black Radicalism in the Nineteenth Century* (Westport Conn.: Greenwood Press, 1977), Earl Ofare, *"Let Your Motto be Resistance" The Life and Thought of Henry Highland Garnet* (Boston: Beacon Press, 1972).

7. Henry Highland Garnet *Letter* to Maria Weston Chapman (written 17 November 1843) appeared in *Liberator,* 8 December 1843.

8. Ward, *Autobiography,* 24-25.

9. Melvin H. Buxbaum, "Cyrus Bustill Addresses the Blacks of Philadelphia," *William and Mary Quarterly* 29 (January 1972): 99-103; and Anne Bustill Smith, "The Bustill Family" *Journal of Negro History* 10, no. 4 (October 1925): 638-44.

10. August Meier, *Negro Thought in America, 1880-1915, Racial Ideologies in the Age of Booker T. Washington* (Ann Arbor: University of Michigan Press, 1963), 3-19; Leon Litwack *North of Slavery; The Negro in the Free States, 1790-1860* (Chicago: University of Chicago Press, 1961), 179-82.

11. Isaiah G. De Grass and George W. Allen, *Letters and Poems of the Free African Society, 1826-29,* New York City, housed in the Pennsylvania Abolition Society microfilm.

12. Octavius V. Catto, *Our Alma Mater* (Philadelphia: C. Sherman, Son and Co., 1864), 11-12.

13. Ibid., 18-20.

14. Jacob C. White Jr., *Address to Gov. James Pollock,* May 24, 1855, Jacob C. White, Jr., Papers Historical Society of Pennsylvania. See also Harry C. Silcox, "Philadelphia Negro Education: Jacob C. White Jr., *The Pennsylvania Magazine of History and Biography* 98, no. 1 (January 1973): 80-81, Harry A. Reed, "Not by Protest Alone: Afro-American Activists and the Pythian Baseball Club of Philadelphia 1867-1869, *The Western Journal of Black Studies* 9, no. 3 (Fall 1985): 145-46.

15. Hosea Easton *A Treatise on the Intellectual Character, and Civil and Political Condition of the Colored People of the United States* (Boston: Isaac Knapp, 1837), 18-19; Daniel Coker, *A Dialogue Between a Virginian and an African Minister* (Baltimore: Benjamin Coales, 1810), 20, both pamphlets in Dorothy Porter, ed., *Negro Protest Pamphlets: A Compendium* (New York: Arno Press and the New York Times, 1969); David E. Swift, *Black Prophets,* 7.

16. J. Marcus Mitchell, "The Paul Family" *Old Time New England* 63, no. 3 (Winter 1973): 76; George A. Levesque, "Inherent Reformers—Inherited Orthodoxy: Black Baptists in Boston, 1800-1873" *Journal of Negro History* 60, no. 4 (October 1975): 500-2; Arthur O. White, "Salem's Antebellum Black Community; Seedbed of the School Integration Movement" *Essex Institute Historical Collections* 108, no. 2 (April 1972): 108-10; James Oliver Horton, "Generations of Protest: Black Families and Social Reform in Antebellum Boston," *The New England Quarterly* 49, no. 2 (June 1976): 244.

17. Herbert Aptheker ed., *Documentary History of the Negro People in the United States* (New York: The Citadel Press, 1969), 7-8. Petition signed by Peter Bestes, Felix Holbrook, Chester Joie, and Sambo Freeman.
18. Ibid., 8.
19. Ibid.
20. Ibid.
21. Ibid.
22. Ibid.
23. Prince Hall, *Petition to the General Court of Massachusetts: Return to Africa*, 4 January 1787.
24. Ibid.
25. Ibid.
26. Ibid.
27. Ibid.
28. Charles H. Wesley, *Prince Hall, Life and Legacy* (Washington, D.C.: the United Supreme Council, Prince Hall Affiliation, 1983), 42-43.
29. Prince Hall, *A Charge Delivered to the Brethren of the African Lodge* (Boston: The African Lodge, 1797), 10-12.
30. Lorenzo Johnston Greene, *The Negro in Colonial New England* (New York: Columbia University Press, 1942), 278-79; Henry Noble Sherwood, "Early Negro Deportation Projects," *Mississippi Valley Historical Review* 11, no. 4 (March 1916): 497-500; Floyd J. Miller, *The Search for a Black Nationality: Black Emigration and Colonization, 1787-1863* (Urbana: University of Illinois Press, 1975), 6-13.
31. The account of Newport and Providence as drawn largely from Miller, *Search for a Black Nationality,* 3-20; George E. Brookes, Jr., *Yankee Traders Old Coasters, and African Middlemen: A History of American Legitimate Trade with West Africa in the Nineteenth Century* (Boston: Boston University Press, 1970), 28, 90, 128.
32. Miller, *Search for a Black Nationality,* 20.
33. Sally Loomis, "The Evolution of Paul Cuffe's Black Nationalism" in David W. Wills and Richard Newman, eds. *Black Apostles at Home and Abroad: Afro-Americans and the Christian Mission from the Revolution to Reconstruction* (Boston: G.K. Hall and Co., 1982), (f.17), 194, 201
34. Henry N. Sherwood, "The Formation of the American Colonization Society," *Journal of Negro History* 11, no. 3 (July 1971): 222; Sheldon H. Harris, *Paul Cuffe: Black America and the African Return* (New York: Simon and Schuster, 1972), 90-91; Lamont D. Thomas, *Rise to Be a People: A Biography of Paul Cuffe* (Urbana: University of Illinois Press, 1986), 32-38; Henry N. Sherwood,"Paul Cuffe," *Journal of Negro History* 8, no. 2 (April 1923): 198; and Peter Williams Jr., *A Discourse on the Death of Paul Cuffe* (New York: B. Young and Co., 1817), 10-11.
35. Harris, *Paul Cuffe,* 78; Thomas, *Rise to Be a People,* 28.
36. Paul Cuffe, *A Brief Account of the Settlement and Present Situation of the Colony of Sierra Leone in Africa* (New York: Samuel Wood, 1812), 3-5.
37. Ibid.
38. Ibid.
39. Ibid.
40. Harris, *Paul Cuffe,* 142-43.

41. Ibid., 77-80.
42. James Forten *Letter* to Paul Cuffe, Philadelphia, 15 February. 1815.
43. Harry A. Reed, "Financing an Early Back to Africa Scheme," *The Proceedings of the Massachusetts Historical Society* 90 (1978) 103-5.
44. For accounts of Cuffe's passengers and the experiences of Daniel Coker in the colony, see Christopher Fyfe, *History of Sierra Leone* (New York: Oxford University Press, 1960), 3-14; Floyd J. Miller, *The Search for a Black Nationality*, 6-13; Richard West, *Back to Africa: A History of Sierra Leone and Liberia* (London: Jonathan Cape, 1970), 5-15; and the James St. G. Walker, *The Black Loyalists: The Search for a Promised Land in Nova Scotia and Sierra Leone, 1787-1870* (New York: Africana Publishing Company, 1976), 4-20.
45. Harris, *Paul Cuffe*, 69; Loomis, *Evolution of Pual Cuffe's Black Nationalism*, 199.
46. Harris, *Paul Cuffe*.
47. Josephus R. Coan, "Daniel Coker: 19th Century Black Church Organizer, Education and Missionary," *The Journal of the Interdenominational Center* 111, no. 1 (Fall 1975): 24; Matei Markwe, "The Rev. Daniel Coker of Sierra Leone" in David W. Wills and Richard Newman, eds., *Black Apostles at Home and Abroad: Afro-Americans and the Christian Mission from the Revolution to Reconstruction* (Boston: G.K. Hall and Co., 1982), 205; Daniel Alexander Payne, *Recollections of Seventy Years* (New York: Arno Press, 1968), 100-1.
48. Daniel Coker, *The Journal of Daniel Coker* (Baltimore: Edward J. Coale, 1820), 11.
49. Ibid., 16.
50. Ibid., 18.
51. Ibid., 23.
52. *Liberator,* 7 January 1832, 7.
53. Arthur O. White, "Prince Saunders: An Instance of Social Mobility among Antebellum Blacks," *Journal of Negro History* 60 (October 1975): 535; Earl Leslie Griggs and Clifford H. Prator, eds., *Henry Christophe and Thomas Clarkson: A Correspondence* (Berkeley and Los Angeles: University of California Press, 1952), 45, 91, 125, see especially *Letter* Prince Saunders to Thomas Clarkson, Philadelphia, 2 May 1823, 248-51; Julie Winch, *Philadelphia's Black Elite: Activism, Accommodation, and the Struggle for Autonomy, 1787-1848* (Philadelphia: Temple University Press, 1988), 50-55; Hubert Cole, *Christophe: King of Haiti* (New York: The Viking Press, 1967), 15, 229, 269; and Prince Saunders, *Haytian Papers, A Collection of the Very Interesting Proclamations and other Official Documents; Together with some Account of the Rise, Progress, and Present State of the Kingdom of Haiti,* ([London, 1816] Westport, Conn: Negro Universities Press, 1969). Gary B. Nash, *Forging Freedom: The Formation of Philadelphia's Black Community, 1720-1890* (Cambridge: Harvard University Press, 1988), 241-42.
54. John Edward Baur, "Mulatto Machiavelli, Jean Pierre Boyer, and the Haiti of his Day," *Journal of Negro History* 32, no. 3 (July 1947): 324-25; Griggs and Clifford, *Henry Christophe and Thomas Clarkson*, 141; White, *Prince Saunders,* 125.

55. Rhoda Golden Freeman, *The Free Negro in New York City in the Era before the Civil War* (Ph.D. diss., Columbia University, 1966), 28-30; *Correspondence Relative to the Emigration to Hayti, of the Free People of Color, in the United States Together with the Instructions to the Agents sent out by President Boyer* (New York: Mahlon Day, 1824), 27-28, Nash, *Forgiving Freedom*, 243.

56. Winch, *Philadelphia's Black Elite*, 52-55; Baur, *Mulatto Machiavelli*, 327; Miller, *Search for a Black Nationality*, 77-79; and Peter Williams, *Address of the Board of Managers of the Haytain Emigration Society of Colored People, to the Emigrants intending to Sail to the Island of Hayti in the Brig De Witt Clinton* (New York: Mahlon Day, 1824), 3-5..

57. Benjamin Hunt, *Remarks on Haiti as a Place of Settlement for Afro-Americans* (Philadelphia: T.B. Pugh, 1860); Winch, *Philadelphia's Black Elite*, 55, 189; Nash, *Forging Freedom*, 244.

58. Nash, *Forging Freedom*, 244; Miller, *Search for a Black Nationality*, 80-81; Baur, *Mulatto Machiavelli*, 325.

59. Ibid., 245, Miller, *Search for a Black Nationality*, 82-83; Jane H. Pease and William H. Pease, *Bound with Them in Chains: A Biographical History of the Antislavery Movement* (Westport, Conn.: Greenwood Press, 1972), 155; Swift, *Black Prophets*, 44-6.

60. Charles F. Horner, *The Life of James Redpath and the Development of the Modern Lyceum* (New York: Barse and Hopkins, 1926), A flowery biography of Redpath but it does establish his credentials as a newspaper man and an abolitionist. It, however, avoids any controversial interpretations. Earl Ofari, *Motto*, 99-102; Schor, *Henry Highland Garnet: A Voice of Black Radicalism in the Nineteenth Century* (Wesport, Conn.: Greenwood Press, 1977), 176. Schor refers to Redpath as an abolitionist opportunist. Miller, *Search for a Black Nationality*, 236-44; Victor Ullman, *Martin R. Delany: The Beginnings of Black Nationalism* (Boston: Beacon Press, 1971), 249-52.

61. Benjamin Coates, *Suggestions on the Importance of the Cultivation of Cotton in Africa, in Reference to the Abolition of Slavery in the United States, Through the Organization of an African Civilization Society* (Philadelphia: C. Sherman and Son, 1858). This work had received favorable responses among black leaders because it discussed the commercial aspects of cotton-growing which many blacks saw as an essential component of the African return. Coates was one of the first whites noting the more favorable climate for discussing Africa among eastern blacks. See Miller, *Search for a Black Nationality*, 184-86.

62. Schor, *Henry Highland*, 159-70.

63. Delany's nationalism is fully developed in several secondary sources. See Ullman, *Martin R. Delany*, passim; Miller, *Search for a Black Nationality*, 197-98; M.R. Delany and Robert Campbell, *Official Report of the Niger Valley exploring Party* (New York: Thomas Hamilton, 1861) also in Howard H. Bell, ed., *Search for a Place; Black Separatism and Africa* (Ann Arbor: University of Michigan Press, 1969), passim. For a dissenting view on Delany and nationalism, see Theodore Draper, *The Rediscovery of Black Nationalism* (New York: The Viking Press, 1970), 3-47.

64. For the details of the various splits see Miller, *Search for Black Nationality*, 192-98, Ullman, *Martin R. Delany*, 195-210, Pease and Pease, *Bound with Them in Chains*, 269-72; *Liberator*, 4 May 1860; Howard Brotz, ed., *Negro Social Thought, 1850-1920 Representative texts* (New York: Basic Books, 1966), 191.

65. Stuckey, *Slave Culture*, 197; Miller, *Search for a Black Nationality*, 196; Pease and Pease, *Bound with Them in Chains*, 271-72; Brotz, *Negro Social Thought*, 191.

66. Pease and Pease, *Bound with Them in Chains*, 270; *The Weekly Anglo-African*, 22 October 1859, 1-3; *Frederick Douglass Monthly* October 1859, 1; *Liberator*, 4 May 1860, 1.

67. Copy of treaties in Delany, *Official Report*, 29-35. See Miller, *Search for a Black Nationality*, 213-16 for a discussion of the problems of defining Yoruba land tenure rules that plagued Delany and Campbell. Miller, *Search for a Black Nationality*, 254-55.

68. Delany, *Chatham Planet*, 15 January 1861 in Ullman, *Martin R. Delaney*, 250-51.

69. *Frederick Douglass Monthly*, August 1862, see also Ullman, *Martin R. Delany*, 221.

70. Like black activists throughout American history, nineteenth century black nationalists could not overcome their belief or hopes that America would drop its racist attitudes in return for black support during a crisis. For World War I, see W. E. B. DuBois, "Close Ranks" *Crisis*, 16 July 1918, and "Returning Soldiers" *Crisis*, 17 May 1919. During World War II, the March on Washington Movement and the Double V for Victory campaign displayed the same combination of nationalist assertions and inclusionary hopes. See Harvard Sitkoff, *A New Deal for Blacks: The Emergence of Civil Rights as a National Issue: The Depression Decade* (New York: Oxford University Press, 1978), 314-21.

71. Samuel E. Cornish and Theodore S. Wright, *The Colonization Scheme Considered* (Newark: A. Guest, 1840), 5-12. Thomas C. Brown, *Examination of Mr. Thomas C. Brown, a Free Colored Citizen of South Carolina, as to the Actual State of Things in Liberia in the Years 1833 and 1834* (New York: S.N. Benedict, 1834), 6-15.

72. William Nesbit, *Four Months in Liberia: On African Colonization Explored* (Pittsburgh: J.T. Shyrock, 1855), 1-8.

73. Ibid., 9.

74. Ibid., 12.

75. Ibid., 50.

76. Ibid., 53.

77. Ibid., 6.

78. Ibid., "Introduction."

79. Ibid.

80. William Parham *Letter* to Jacob C. White, Jr., 9 December 1861, JWC Papers, Historical Society of Pennsylvania.

81. Ibid., 6 October 1862.

82. Ibid.

83. Ibid.

84. William Parham *Letter* to Jacob C. White, Jr., 27 February 1890, JWC Papers, HSP.

7

Conclusion

Amomentous transformation occurred in the lives of northern free blacks between the American Revolution and the Civil War. That transformation was made possible by the conscious melding of five elements, identified here as the platform for change. Individually and collectively the independent church impulse, the founding of organizations, the creation of black newspapers, the convention movement, and the ideology of emigration ably assisted blacks in at least three ways. First, they connoted a transformation of black consciousness from an individual/personalized response to an organized community model of new black awareness. For example, blacks who emerged as leading church organizers in the period 1800 to 1830 had experienced their individual conversions in the 1770s and 1780s. Once having achieved either conversion or membership within a white denomination they sought out or came in contact with other blacks like themselves seeking spiritual sustenance within their own prayer assemblies and ultimately within their own churches.

Second, the constellation of the five activities assisted the community through developmental stages and helped to prepare the way for a diversity and maturity of outlook among black leaders. As leaders gained experience, as conditions against blacks changed in some ways and hardened in others, so were churches, newspapers, conventions, organizations, and emigration, updated, modified, and refined to meet new challenges.

The platform for change passed through stages of initial founding and experimentation in the 1780s and the early 1800s, through adjustment in the late 1830s and 1840s, into maturity in the 1850s and 1860s. It should not be interpreted that black leaders and followers before 1850 lacked sophistication but it seems clear that early leaders sought redress of black grievances primarily within the United States. They were always seeking to make America live up to its stated credo of all men being created equal. Even as they sought a black-defined self-determination, they sometimes included relocation but usually as a short term experiment that would take away the most vulnerable portions of the population, and demonstrate to America that blacks could handle the responsibilities of citizenship. The sophistication of their later counterparts embodied protection of blacks but also, perhaps more important, were based on establishing a black polity where blacks would govern themselves.

A feature of the maturity, throughout the entire antebellum period, despite the acrimony of some black on black confrontations, was an adherence to racial solidarity. Differences of opinion did exist and were expressed but those differences accurately reflect the changes in political and social views as blacks gained new experiences, tested new opportunities, obtained better education, developed new visions, and acquired new nerve to explore alternatives. These and other changes speak to the modernization of black political activity.

Third, the platform for change model has continued to serve the black community's needs to the present. In some combination, usually updated because of time, region, or other circumstances, the five elements have been guideposts of black political action and a marker of the black community's efforts to deal with life in America. The platform for change has served more than the particular interests of the black community. The historical legacy continues to affect American life on at least two significant universal levels. First, the foundations for change are ever-present in black political responses. Second, American society has learned that the problems of discrimination are not moribund, have not been solved in previous generations, and that black people, given an opportunity, continue to believe in and provide a main impetus for equality in America.

Despite the struggles of blacks from the revolutionary war to the outbreak of the Civil War they failed, like the abolitionists, to eliminate slavery and discrimination from American life. Their failure, however, cannot be termed an exercise in powerlessness.[1] The intensity with which the free black leadership aligned itself with the Union cause undermines any thought in its own mind about a sense of failure. Moreover, like its contemporaries, the abolitionists, the free black leadership in the antebellum period left a historical legacy that is difficult to ignore.

The elements constituting the platform for change were responsible for initiating change and also for protecting those agents of change whether they were individuals, institutions or, ideologies. A solid protective atmosphere was a necessity if the new collective consciousness was to survive the existing slavery and discrimination but also the new white backlash that confronted black attempts at independence. Black independent churches stimulated initially by a need to worship openly in a nondiscriminatory setting in turn pioneered other secular and non-secular ways of broadening the community's organizational structure, providing the same with necessary leadership, and providing competent protection when the organization or the community came under fire.

Black newspapers, even when short-lived, contributed so over-whelmingly to the new black consciousness of voice and visibility that individuals continued to publish papers although faced with tremen-dous economic and distribution pressures and possibly a limited talent pool. Thus, newspapers continued to be a part of the black community profile. Newspapers shaped the black image, discussed black responses, guided black public opinion and, of course, defended the race. Newspaper editors, with the possible exception of Frederick Douglass, were not as powerful as black clergymen but were influential members of the black leadership cadre. Like the preachers, newspaper editors, some of whom were also clergymen, were not one-dimensional men. As newspaper editors, Samuel Cornish, Phillip A. Bell, William Hamilton, John Brown Russwurm, Charles B. Ray, Henry Highland Garnet, and Thomas Hamilton all engaged in other forms of community action. Moreover, the pages of their papers were opened to a wide-ranging discussion of how best to change the status of black Americans.

Throughout the antebellum period black leaders who were not edi-tors, publishers, or proprietors extolled the benefits of a black newspa-per and worked in various ways to support the black print media. Jacob C. White, Jr., David Walker, Abraham D. Shadd, James McCune Smith, Peter Vogelsang, and Junius C. Morel were distributors, agents, and good old fashioned promoters of black newspapers. For blacks more than for whites, the financial needs of a newspaper presented extraordi-nary obstacles. Although unable to capitalize newspapers heavily and equally unable to attract large advertising revenues, black individuals such as Peter Williams, Boston Crummell, Benjamin Hughes, Benjamin Roberts, James G. Barbadoes, and David Ruggles by various devices attempted to keep papers alive financially. Despite the fact that many failed to survive, their importance was so acute that someone was always ready to take the plunge.

Finally, the importance of papers to the struggle for change was col-lectively keen so that organizations as well as individuals published or considered publishing organs to meet the community's need to be informed. For a brief period the American Moral Reform Society pub-lished its own journal. An essential idea in the later years of the conven-tion movement, although never realized, was the establishment of a national black newspaper. The national paper failed to materialize not because of lack of interest but because several successful black papers existed at the time.

While the convention movement never succeeded in printing a national paper the combination of papers and conventions constituted an essential element in the platform for change. They shared similar profiles in that both were excellent gauges of the elan and vitality of the black engagement in solving America's problems as well as problems more directly facing blacks. They were also the most direct organs of black public opinion. Whether the issue was slavery, discrimination, or leaving the United States, conventions as well as newspapers distributed the views of the race's best and brightest. As newspapers made an individual as well as a collective impact, so too did the convention movement. The primary thrust of conventions was collective and national and it represented the first public gathering of black men from across America to discuss black American solutions.

The convention movement first demonstrated black ability for sustained political deliberation. The conclaves usually met for a minimum of five days and sometimes met for as long as ten days. During that period leaders debated and attempted to resolve the community's most pressing problems. Every shade of opinion was represented, although a greater consensus appeared during the meetings of 1830 through 1835 than in those following 1835. More important than the length of each convention were the almost insurmountable challenges which black leaders attacked with a tenacity that seldom is discussed as part of the black political legacy. The leaders did not abandon a problem simply because it seemed to be insoluble. Instead, they returned year after year to issues such as Canadian relocation and each discussion produced new, if not dramatic, insights and proposals. Since the circumstances of black lives were dynamic and shifting, black leaders could not afford to become routine in their responses to community needs. Out of the annual discussions concerning the need for Canadian relocation one can see the lines of future arguments concerning emigration clearly emerging.

As early as 1830 and 1831 proponents of Canadian relocation were honing the supports that 1850s activists would raise to the level of an ideology. They, in part, argued: Why remain in the United States if citizenship was not forthcoming? Further, they investigated the laws of land acquisition, economic opportunities, legal status of blacks, and governmental access to redress grievances. In these early debates over leaving their country of birth the leaders set two precedents that have since guided blacks in the consideration of emigration. First, they made clear that they deserved and had the capacity for full citizenship and their decision to leave because of overwhelming prejudice in no way negated the positive assessment of themselves. Second, all the debates made clear that leaders envisioned a selective, not collective, emigration. They could not condone free blacks leaving their southern brothers in bondage. Nor did they think all blacks were prepared to go or prepared to make a positive contribution in their new country of origin.

Although tenacity was important, perhaps a greater benefit of the convention movement was closure. The conventions provided an arena where arguments could be pursued without breaking the community apart. In addition the conventions provided black leaders with a security that they could expect an annual meeting where they could explore topics that might not be popular in their local region. If such topics were introduced in Boston they might create a split in the local leadership but among the national leadership they might find a sympathetic ear. For example, a Boston leader interested in emigration to Africa found his activity stifled because of the long history of the Haiti-Boston connection. The convention format offered such a leader a forum where allies might be present to further the resolution of the problem. Although Junius C. Morel's interest in helping Ohio blacks seemed popular in Philadelphia, the convention still provided a broader arena for discussion, fund-raising, fact finding, clarification of issues, and creating a consensus. Closure was equally important in that New Yorkers who were beaten to the call for the first convention did not organize a rump meeting and make public what could have been a debilitating competition. Instead, they salved their pique for one or two years and then let themselves be drawn into the Philadelphia-dominated convention orbit. Later, New Yorkers served as convention presidents and soon succeeded in organizing their clout to be able to host the 1834 meetings.

Even when, on the surface, the consensus appeared to be broken, closure continued to operate as a function of the convention movement. Douglass and Garnet, bitter rivals though they were, did not organize competing conventions built around their own ideological stances until the mid 1850s. In the 1830s there was no crisis in the black convention movement to equal the ideological and physical split in American abolition which resulted in two rival organizations in 1840. Nor did anything like the white Boston Clique, with the brief exception of the moral reformers of 1834-1835, exist within the black convention movement. Instead of availing themselves of the opportunity to set up a rival convention movement, they tried and successfully took over the existing structure. They thus affirmed the convention model while bending it to their own particular ideological focus. When the American Moral Reform Society proved too weak or too narrowly focused to keep the model alive, the convention ceased to exist for eight years.

Even in that break, however, no leader condemned the convention or sought to bury its memory. They continued to meet at the state and local levels through instruments constructed in the very first convention.

Ultimately in 1843 the national convention format was revived and continued to serve the community throughout the antebellum period.

In the mid-1850s convention revival, competing conferences were held. Usually these conclaves met away from those early centers of power—New York, Philadelphia, and Boston. Although meeting outside these original sites, the later congresses confirmed the convention model. The meetings continued to draw together black male and female delegates to speak to the many issues that continued to plague the black community. While not uniformly accepted, black women often served as delegates at conventions during the 1850s.

At these rival conventions, promoters organized around their own particular ideology and screened out or kept the opposition to a minimum. Unable to gain a voice, the compromised faction would circulate its own call for a convention. The organizers would in turn deny credentials to participants of the earlier meeting. As pressures mounted on black American life and the New Fugitive Slave Law began to take a toll on black leadership, rival conventions became the vogue. Still, the convention model was reinforced: no group or leader suggested that the convention format was outmoded or defunct. The coming of the Civil War halted the trend toward rival meetings as black activists turned their attention to the war.

Early in the antebellum period blacks experimented with creating organizations to assist in the desired change of status. The efforts often began quite tentatively. Nevertheless, once founded and operated successfully they stimulated the founding of other complementary organizations. In less than a decade after the first organization was founded, all three cities had created a broad community infrastructure that included mechanics associations, debating societies, women's organizations, fraternal and self-help organizations, as well as groups, clubs, and associations dedicated to all levels of black uplift. Black America did not copy antebellum America's proclivity for creating and joining organizations; it simply made use of an existing historical current and shaped it to fit its own needs.

While some organizations remained local in nature, others became national in scope. Certainly by 1830-1835 black organizations were credibly established and an individual could move from one city to another and find familiar outlets for his or her political, intellectual, and religious energies.

Developmentally, the maturation of black organizations is illustrated in a variety of ways. The black Philadelphian, Jacob White, Sr., corresponded with his counterparts in the New York Vigilance Society such as David Ruggles and Samuel Cornish. White could be certain that the New Yorkers would honor his requests to shelter, feed, and provide transport to fugitives sent on to them by the Philadelphians. The national scope of the AME Church attests to the maturity of black organizational development. By 1831, it had chosen the second bishop with little disruption and the order itself had established branches up and down the East coast and throughout the South; and by 1836, it was beginning to open churches in western cities such as Detroit.

Another feature of the maturity of the national black organizational infrastructure was the incorporation of black females into the political activity. An evolutionary change that took place over a fifty-year span, the process of organizational life gave black women collectively an earlier entry to political life than was true for their white sisters. Black women in Boston as early as 1792 had formed support groups for male political activity. Until the end of the period black females continued to work in the political arena. Still, they did not experience a level of equality with black males. Any black female who found herself making independent public, political statements could suffer the same criticism that Maria W. Stewart received in Boston in 1833. Yet, if she remained within an organization and spoke with a collective voice on male approved topics, her opinions—even if political—were given wide distribution. Only in the 1840s was it possible for an individual black female to receive courteous and interested attention when expressing her political views; but that polite, seemingly equal, treatment could be withdrawn if she ventured into controversial subject matter. Mary Ann Shadd was given the silent treatment in 1852 after she published a pamphlet on emigration. This was quite in contrast to the praise bestowed on her first publication in 1849 which explored the subject of black uplift. While black women made an entry in to the public arena, much of their political life was protected by organizations and the positive valuation of organizational life in antebellum black America.

Of the five elements, the most politically adventurous and therefore the most controversial was emigration. A slowly developing ideology of leaving the United States, it pitted factions of the community against itself. Those who were slowly evolving into nationalists argued for the founding of a black polity that would economically rival the United States, particularly, the slave South. While this polity might not match the political strength of the United States, would demonstrate the capacity of black people to govern themselves. Moreover, a black polity would also show that blacks could create and maintain a Christian commonwealth where neither slavery nor discrimination would be articles of faith. Not all blacks agreed with the emigrationists and the last decade before the Civil War was a time of lively discussion. Although a minority and conflict filled philosophy, within the community emigration was a major force in the platform for change. Not only did it make blacks indict American politics but it stimulated them to begin constructing their own separatist, nationalist politics. It took them beyond being disadvantaged Americans to being articulate promoters of their own political interest. The emphasis on Africa as a central tenet in black nationalist thought has continued into the twentieth century.

During the nineteenth century the elements constituting the platform for change were consistent yet fluid enough to keep pace with the needs of the community and the dictates of the American scene. As access to opportunities became more sharply restrictive or for brief periods more liberalized, black leaders adjusted the emphases of the five elements to maximize the pace of hoped for change. Clearly, the shifting emphasis from church to individual leaders, to organization building, to ideological primacy, demonstrates both the modernization of black political activities and the developmental stages of black consciousness. Individuals, institutions, and ideologies coexisted simultaneously creating a rich, multilayered fabric of black community consciousness.

Until the 1830s the church was the primary developer and incubator of black leadership. By the early 1830s the burgeoning American reform movement was heralded in the black community by a shift away from church to moral but secular reform pursuits. The role of the church was de-emphasized. A move away from sacred activity became the norm for most large black churches. The sacred had never been the primary focus of many churches anyway because they had to provide so much of the community's leadership. Reform societies, secular social uplift activities, and a proliferation of organizations moved into the vacuum that resulted from the church's lessening primacy. This new activity relieved some of the strain on the church while simultaneously ensuring it had an honored position in the community infrastructure. Although de-emphasized, the church as an instrument for black change was not abandoned. It was able to carry out two specific functions, both of which had a developmental impact. First, the church continued to produce leaders for the community. From 1830 through 1865 these new leaders were hyphenated clergymen. In short, they made their mark as clergymen/activists either in journalism, by conventioneering, as emigrationists, or as agitators committed as much to political as to moral change. Second, the church became the keystone of the black community. It anchored blacks in the present and in the hereafter.

Rather than destroying the church or negating its good works, the 1830s de-emphasis was a positive step in the developmental maturation of black community consciousness. Blacks could speak to the religious concerns of nineteenth-century life and could simultaneously comprehend and act on the growing political concerns. Like reformers elsewhere in the nineteenth century, blacks used the prevailing religious language and symbol; while doing so, however, they were also moving toward solutions grounded in the practical, the here and now. The results of such a move were immediately manifest. Articulation of black problems was free of the hint of divine intervention as the only solution.

Once freed of biblical connections, black solutions became more liberal, even radical politically. Since the American church had never been radical in its social or political perceptions, it was necessary for blacks to drop the religious rhetoric in order to give their vision a grounding in the political realities of nineteenth-century America.

When this freedom from religious rhetoric was realized blacks began to think more politically in terms of changing their status. It was possible then in the late 1830s and early 1840s to heed the courting of blacks by new American third parties. Unlike the early nineteenth-century adherence of blacks to several state federalist machines, this later development demonstrated that blacks did not simply have to wait for the largess of their political benefactors.

By the 1840s several influential black leaders were seeking to end slavery by way of political party participation and through the legislative process. This would not have been possible during the era of church dominance.

A further developmental stage followed naturally from the participation in political parties and self-interested politics. By the 1850s the more sophisticated black leaders tired of the intransigence of American racism began to fashion a politics of self-determination based on nationalist precepts, not on inclusion. When we reflect that black emigration had been around since the Newport African Union of the late 1780s, the 1850s incarnation displays the maturation of black political thought.

When citizenship was not offered to blacks, although they felt they had demonstrated the capacity for it, many found emigration a worthwhile alternative. Theoretically emigration was quite attractive. As articulated by Henry Highland Garnet, James Theodore Holly, Martin Delany, and others, it was a call for blacks to govern themselves in their own nation-state. The way to achieve this, in its broadest outline, was to organize a selective migration of hard-working, upwardly mobile, skilled, and democratically imbued blacks to depart America. Their task would be to transform an existing black polity into an economic and political challenger to slave-holding America. Thus black political thought had passed through stages of seeking religious separation, of relying on moral suasion, of achieving redress through political party participation, to full-blown calls to create black nation-states.

The elements making up the platform for change represented possibilities. The platform for change allowed blacks to do more than simply arraign American society. It provided a framework in which a community consciousness emerged and grew into a sophisticated expression of nationalist self-determination. The activities generated, articulated, and pursued in New York, Boston, and Philadelphia gave expression to the national conscious. They opened to black people and by extension to white Americans the power of possibilities: the vision of an egalitarian society free of the stigmas of slavery, discrimination, and oppression.

The platform represents more than power or the triumph of the human spirit; it represents the legitimate attempts of blacks to contribute to and force America to live up to its ideals. The failure of blacks to achieve that vision says more about the inability of whites to operationalize the democratic American creed than about black shortcomings.

Societies seem to be transformed by either wars or revolutions. Blacks did not have the resources to create either, but their activities through the platform for change challenge any interpretation that black agitation in antebellum America was an exercise in powerlessness. The intensity of the black commitment to the Union cause during the Civil War is an illustration of their perception that they possessed some power to create change. Arraigning American society, creating alternatives to the status quo, and trying to effect positive change are evidence of the power of antebellum black political activity; that power emerged in its public manifestation in the five elements here called the platform for change.

For blacks the five elements delineated as the platform for change have been present since the end of Reconstruction to guide leaders and followers toward their political and social goals. Reconstruction itself provides the first test of the efficacy of the five elements. As the Civil War was drawing to a close, newly liberated blacks immediately began putting into practice several activities that had originated during the antebellum period. Northern black leaders began holding conventions to celebrate the war's successful conclusion but also to signal their willingness to support the new order and their expectations about change in the reconstructed nation. Southern blacks, who had not been totally absent from the platform for change process, began holding conventions that harkened back to the antebellum national and state conventions.[2]

Like the conventions of the 1830s, those immediately following the Civil War tended to be conciliatory in their demands. Seemingly sensitive to the uncertainties of the immediate postwar period, blacks were willing to place a great deal of confidence in the radical republicans.

Perhaps the confidence in Lincoln and later the radical republicans was unwarranted, but it was a logical direction on the part of leaders of the black community. For more than three decades black leaders had attempted to balance the tensions between idealism and practical politics. Their struggles had taught them the politics of the possible, more in keeping with America's ability to make needed social/political change.

Conclusion

As the promises of Reconstruction began to dissipate and the white backlash became more prominent, for a brief period blacks flirted with more radical solutions to their disabilities. The conventions began discussing the establishment of a black third party, the founding of a national trade union movement, the founding of an all-black state and, finally, to new calls for emigration.

Blacks thus raised the level of American political discourse while simultaneously reshaping their inherited historical past. When the backlash became entrenched and Jim Crow became the direction of American life, the black community adjusted accordingly. No longer able to utilize the mode of direct challenge, the convention movement changed much as it had in the 1840s. The new incarnation involved northern or state conclaves that discussed the virulence of the new race relations and acknowledged that southern blacks again had a new peculiar institution. Although the new institution severely restricted, it did not obliterate the convention movement as a viable part of the black political struggle.

Southern black women, for example, used the convention movement both to organize their own concerns and also to push for state organizations that would address issues ranging from education to women's franchise. By the 1890s the leaders, some of whom had been active in the antebellum period, began working toward combining the various state and regional women's groups into one or more national organizations.[3]

It has been argued that the late nineteenth- and early twentieth-century black women's movement espoused a black bourgeois feminism.[4] The important consideration here is not the accuracy of the observation about black women's political philosophy but the method of activism: the convention movement. In the most virulent period, 1870 to 1915, the convention movement transformed itself once more. Again, the beneficiaries of this change were blacks and the American political process at large. What the black club women demonstrated was the efficacy of elements of the platform for change to order the priorities of making life in America bearable. They took an inherited black historical heritage from the antebellum period to challenge and enhance the quality of black life. In doing so they, like blacks down to the present, paid homage to the platform for change.

Notes

1. Jane H. Pease and William H. Pease, *They Who Would Be Free: Black's Struggle for Freedom, 1830 to 1861* (New York: Antheneum, 1974), 68-94, 281-99.
2. August Meier, *Negro Thought in America, 1895 to 1915: Racial Ideologies in the Age of Booker T. Washington* (Ann Arbor: The University of Michigan Press, 1963), 3-84; John Hope Franklin, *Reconstruction After the Civil War* (Chicago: University of Chicago Press, 1961), 105, 133-38.
3. N.F. [Mrs. Gertrude] Mossell, *The Work of the Afro-American Woman* (Philadelphia: G.S. Ferguson, 1894; Reprint, Freeport, NY: Books For Libraries Press, 1971), 9-47, 104-14; Gerda Lerner, "Early Club Work Among Negro Women," *Journal of Negro History* 59, no. 2 (April 1974): 158-68.
4. Wilson Jeremiah Moses, *The Golden Age of Black Nationalism, 1850-1925* (New York: Oxford University Press, 1978), 103-31.

Bibliography

Manuscript Collections

Andover, Massachussetts
  Andover-Newton Theological Center
Boston, Massachussetts
  Atheneum
  Massachussetts Historical Society (MHS)
  Massachussetts State Archives (MSA)
  Public Library. Department of Rare Books and Manuscripts.
  Antislavery Collection (BPL)
New Bedford, Massachussetts
  Free Public Library. Paul Cuffe Papers (FPL)
New York, New York
  Public Library. The Schomberg Collection (NYPL)
  New York Historical Society (NYHS)
Philadelphia, Pennsylvania
  American Philosophical Society (APS)
  Atheneum
  Historical Society of Pennsylvania (HSP)

Printed Matter: Primary Sources

African Education and Civilization Society. New York: The Executive
    Committee, 1845.
African Episcopal Church. *Act of Incorporation, Causes and Motives of
    the African Episcopal Church of Philadelphia.* Philadelphia:
    White-Hall, 1810

African Methodist Episcopal Church. *Articles of Association of the City of Philadelphia in the Commonwealth of Pennsylvania.* Philadelphia: John Ormrod, 1799

African Institution. *Second Annual Report.* London: W. Phillips, 1808
_____. *Twelfth Annual Report.* London: Ellerton and Henderson, 1818.

African Protestant Episcopal Church *Broadside.* " A Fund Raised By Subscription for the Maintenance Of Another Colored Minister." Philadelphia: n.p., 1810.

African Zoar Methodist Episcopal Church. *Constitution.* Philadelphia: Manly, Orr, and Lippincott, 1842

Agricultural and Mechanics Association of Pennsylvania and New Jersey. *List of Subscribers and List of Stockholders.* 6 May 1839.

Allen, Richard, and Absalom Jones. *A Narrative of the Proceedings of the Black People during the late awful calamity in Philadelphia, in the year 1793 and the refutation of some censures thrown upon them in some late publications.* Philadelphia: William Woodward, 1794.

Allen Richard and Jacob Tapsico. *The Doctrines and Discipline of The African Methodist Episcopal Church.* Philadelphia: John H. Cunningham, 1817.

Allen, Rt. Rev. Richard. *The Life Experiences and Gospel Labors of the Rt. Rev. Richard Allen.* New York: Abington Press, 1960.

American Negro Historical Society. *Collection of Quotations Showing Attitudes of Black Groups Toward Colonization.* Philadelphia: n.p., 1831-1832.

Anderson, Dr. James. *Observations on Slavery.* Manchester: J. Harrap, 1789.

Andrews, Charles C. *The History of the New York African Free School.* New York: Mahlon Day, 1830.

Anonymous. *Colored American National Society: Address To The Free Colored People of These United States of America.* Philadelphia: n.p. 1845 (HSP)
_____. *Laws of the African Society Instituted at Boston, 1796,* (MHS).
_____. *Opinion: Robert Green vs The African Church called Bethel,* 1815, (HSP).
_____. *Proceedings of the Anti-Slavery Convention of American Women Held in Philadelphia.* Philadelphia: Merrihew and Gunn, 1838.
_____. *The Abolitionist: Or Record of the New England Anti-Slavery Society.* Boston: Garrison and Knapp, 1833.

Anonymous. *The Appendix: Or, Observations on the Expediency of the Petition of the Africans, Living in Boston and Lately Presented to the General Assembly of this Province to Which is Annexed the Petition Referred to Likewise Thoughts on Slavery With a Useful Extract from the Massachussetts Spy of Jan. 28 1773, By Way of an Address to the Members of the Assembly.* Boston: E. Russell, 1773.

Baldwin, Thomas. *The Eternal Purpose of God, the Foundation of Effectual Calling.* Boston: Manning and Loring, 1804.

Boston Gazette. "Dedications." 8 December 1806.

Brown, Levi. *Letter* to Absalom Jones, 26 September 1801, (HSP).

Brown, Robert. *Docket Book.* Philadelphia, n.p., 1831.

Brown, Thomas. *Examination of Mr Thomas Brown, A Free Colored Citizen Of South Carolina, As To The Actual State of Things In Liberia in the Years 1833 and 1834.* New York: S.W. Benedict and Company, 1834.

Brown, William Wells. *A Lecture Delivered Before the Female Anti-Slavery Society of Salem.* Boston: Massachussetts Anti-Slavery Society, 1847.

Burch, Robert. *Letter* to S. Shoemaker, Esq., 15 December 1815, (HSP).

Bustill, Joseph C. *Letter* to William Still, 31 June 1856, (HSP).

Cabot, S. *Letter* to Dr. George Shattuck, 27 December 1839, (MHS).

Carey, Matthew. *A Short Account of tHe Malignant Fever, Lately Prevelant in Philadelphia: With a Statement of the Proceedings That Took Place on the Subject in Different Parts of the United States.* Philadelphia: The Author, 1793

Carey, Matthew. *Account of Schools for Colored Persons.* Philadelphia: n.p., 1822.

Catto, Octavius V. *Our Alma Mater.* Philadelphia: C. Sherman, Son and Company, 1864.

Catto, William T. *A Semi-Centenary Discourse, Delivered in the First African Presbyterian Church Philadelphia, On the Fourth Sabbath of May 1857: With a History of the Church From Its First Organization Also, An Appendix Containing Sketches of All the Colored Churches in Philadelphia.* Philadelphia: Joseph M. Wilson, 1857.

Chapman, Maria Weston. "The Buffalo Convention of Men of Color." *The Liberator,* 22 September 1843.

Clarkson, Quomony. *Letter* to Committee on Education Pennsylvania Anti-Slavery Society, 27 July 1802.

_____. *Letter* to The President and Members of the Pennsylvania Anti-Slavery Society, 24 December 1804.

_____. *Letter* to John Parrish, 13 March 1806, (HSP).

_____. *Letter* School for Black Children, 4 October 1813, (HSP).

Coates, Benjamin. *Suggestions on the Importance of the Cultivation of Cotton in Africa in Reference to the Abolition of Slavery in the*

United States Through the Organization of an African Civilization Society. Philadelphia: C. Sherman and Son, 1858.

Coker, Daniel. *A Dialogue Between A Virginian and an African Minister.* Baltimore: Benjamin Edes, 1810.

Coker, Daniel. *Journal of Daniel Coker, A Descendent of Africa, From the Time of Leaving New York in the Ship Elizabeth. Capt. Sebor, on a Voyage for Sherbro, in Africa in the Company with Three Agents and About Ninety Persons of Colour.* Baltimore: Edward J. Coale, 1820.

Cornish, Samuel, and John Brown Russwurm, *Letter* to Isaac Barton, 2 October 1827, (MHS).

Cornish, Samuel. "An African Association for Mutual Relief." *Freedom's Journal,* 30 March 1827.

Cornish, Samuel, and Theodore S. Wright. *The Colonization Scheme Considered.* Newark: A. Guest, 1840.

Correspondence Relative to the Emigration to Hayti, of the Free People of Color, in the United States. Together with the Instructions to the Agents Sent Out by President Boyer. New York: Mahlon Day, 1824.

Cuffe, Paul. *Petition of Paul Cuffe and Several Poor Negroes and Mulattoes Who Are Inhabitants of the Town of Dartmouth.* 1780.

_____. *A Brief Account of the Settlement and Present Situation of The Colony of Sierra Leone, in Africa; as Communicated by Paul Cuffe (A Man of Colour) to his Friend in New York; also an Explanation of the Object of his Visit; and Some Advice ti the People of Colour in the United States. To Which is Subjoined, An Address to the people of colour from the Convention of Delegates from the Abolition Societies in the U. States.* New York: Samuel Wood, 1812.

Davidson, Amelia. *Letter* to Betsey Stockton, 18 February 1828, (NYPL).

_____. *Letter* to John B. Russwurm, 1 April 1828, (HSP).

Delany, Martin R. *Official Report of The Niger Valley Exploring Party.* New York: Thomas Hamilton, 1861.

Dillwyn, William. *Letter* to Susanna and Samuel Emlen, 19 August 1810, (HSP).

Douglass, William. *Sermons Preached in the African Protestant Episcopal Church of St. Thomas, Philadelphia.* Philadelphia: King and Baird, 1854.

Douglass, William. *Annals Of the First African Protestant Episcopal Church of St. Thomas, Philadelphia, Noe Styled The African Episcopal Church of St. Thomas, Philadelphia.* Philadelphia: King and Baird, 1862.

Draper, Charlotte. *For the Presbyterian Female if Color's Enterprising Society in Baltimore.* Baltimore: Frederick Hanzschee, 1860.

Drinker, Elizabeth. *Diary* 1799-1807, (HSP).

Easton, Rev. Hosea. *A Treatise on the Intellectual Character and Civil and Political Condition of the Colored People of the United States and the Prejudice Excerised Toward Them.* Boston: Isaac Knapp, 1837.

First African Baptist Church, Philadelphia. *Brief or Title of Land,* 1833.

_____. *Booklet,* 1834.

_____. *Agreement Between First African Baptist Church and Martha Simmons,* 1848.

_____. *Petition,* 1848.

_____. *Documents Concerning the Court Case Involving the Legality of the Expulsion of One of Their Members, Robert Green,* 1815.

_____. *Documents Supplement to Original Articles of Incorporation,* 1815.

Fitler, Jacob. *Deed,* 22 June 1815.

_____. "Sheriff's Sale" *Broadside,* 22 June 1815.

Fletcher, Hon. Richard. "Opinion on the Rights of Colored Children in Common Schools" *The Common School Journal,* 6, no. 20 (15 October 1844): 326-28.

Fowle, William B. *Letter* to Hon. Horace Mann, 11 July 1844, (MHS).

Freedom's Journal. "African Dorcas Association," 15 February 1828.

Friendly Society of St. Thomas's African Church. *Constitution and Rules To Be Observed And Kept.* Philadelphia: W.W. Woodward, 1797.

Gardiner, John S. J. *A Sermon, Preached Before the African Society on the 14th of July 1810, the Anniversary of the Abolition of the Slave Trade.* Boston: Munroe and Francis, 1810.

Garnet, Henry Highland. *The Liberator,* 19 April 1834.

_____. "Letter to Maria Weston Chapman." *The Liberator,* 3 December 1843.

_____. *An Address to the Slaves of the United States of America.* New York: J. H. Tobitt, 1848.

_____. *The Past and Present Condition and the Destiny of the Colored Race.* Troy: J. C. Kneeland and Company, 1848.

_____. "African Civilization Society." New Haven, 1861, (BPL).

_____. *Letter* to Jacob C. White Sr., 8 May 1865, (HSP).

Garrison, William Lloyd. *Thoughts on African Colonization.* Boston: Garrison and Knapp, 1832.

_____. *An Address on the Progress of the Abolition Cause.* Boston: Garrison and Knapp, 1832.

_____. "An Address Delivered Before the African-American Female Intelligence Society of Boston." *The Liberator,* 28 April 1832.

_____. *Letter* to Nathaniel Paul, 17 August 1833, (BPL).

George, David. "An Account of the Life of Mr. David George from Sierra Leone in Africa" *The Baptist Annual Register* 1793, (BPL).

Gray, William. *Letter* to Benjamin Rush, 24 October 1792, (HSP).

_____. *Letter* to Joseph G. Bend, 12 August 1793, (HSP).

_____. *Letter* to James Rush, 1820, (HSP).

_____. *Letter* to Mary Still, 17 September 1873, (HSP).

Green, Agustus. *A Treatise On the Episcopacy of the African M.E. Church: Duty of Parents and Churches to Baptize Children An Examination of the Mother Church.* Pittsburgh: H. M. Poindexter, 1845.

Guinn, William. *Subscription Paper Circulated in Behalf of a Group of Boston Negroes,* 15 November 1815, (MHS).

Hall, Prince. *Petition to the General Court of Massachussetts: Return to Africa,* 4 January 1787, (MHS).

_____. *A Charge Delivered to the Brethren of the African Lodge.* Boston: Bible and Heart, 1792.

_____. *A Charge Delivered to the Brethren of the African Lodge.* Boston: African Lodge, 1797.

Hodgson, Adam. "Letter to Jean Baptiste." *Freedom's Journal,* 10, 17, 24, and 31 August 1827.

_____. "Compares South American Slavery to Feudalism." *Freedom's Journal,* 7 and 14 September 1828.

Holmes, David, and J.E. Davis. "Letter and Narrative of Peter Hook," *Democratic Press* (Natchez), 23 December 1826.

Holly, James Theodore. "Thoughts on Hayti." *The Anglo-African Magazine,* 1, 6, June 1859.

Hopkinson, Joseph. *Opinion on Bethel Church,* 24 April 1815, (HSP).

Howard, Edward. *Letter* to Jacob C. White, Jr., 28 June 1862, (HSP).

Hume, David. "Slave Labor." *Freedom's Journal,* 17 August 1827.

Hunt, Benjamin. *Remarks on Hayti as a Place of Settlement for Afric-Americans.* Philadelphia: T. B. Pugh, 1860.

Hurst, A. *Account of the Lombard Street Colored School,* 20 December 1827, (HSP).

Jones, Absalom. *A Thanksgiving Sermon.* Philadelphia: Fry and Kammerer Printers, 1808.

Lawrence, Jr., George. *Letter* to Jacob C. White, Jr., 25 June 1862, (HSP).

_____. *Letter* to Henry J. Lombard, Esq., 30 September 1862, (HSP).

Lowell, Charles. *Letter* to Dr. George Shattuck, 31 July 1853, (MHS).

Lundy, Benjamin. *Genius of Universal Emancipation,* 27 November. 1829, (MHS).

Marrant, John. *A Narrative of the Lord's Wonderful Dealings with John Marrant, A Black.* London: Gilbert and Plummer, 1785.

Marrant, John. *A Sermon Preached on the 24th Day of June Being the Festival of St. John the Baptist.* Boston: Bible and Heart, 1789.

Mifflin, Warner. *Letter* to John Parrish, 24 January 1794.(MHS)

Minot, William. *Address, Delivered at the Dedication of the Smith School House in Belknap Street,* 3 March 1835, (MHS).

Minutes and Proceedings of the First Annual Convention. Philadelphia: J.W. Allen, 1831.

Minutes and Proceedings of the Second Annual Convention for the Improvement of the Free People of Color in These United States. Philadelphia: Martin and Boden Printers, 1832.

Minutes and Proceedings of the Fifth Annual Convention for the Improvement of the Free People of Colour. Philadelphia: William P. Gibbons, 1835.

Minutes and Proceedings of the Fourth Annual Convention for the Improvement of the Free People of Colour. New York: By Order of the Convention, 1834

Minutes and Proceedings of the Third Annual Convention for the Improvement of the People of Colour. New York: The Convention, 1833.

Minute Book of the United Daughters of Tapsico, 1823-1847, (HSP).

Minutes of the National Convention of Colored Citizens: Held at Buffalo, on the 15th, 16th, 17th, 18th, 19th of August, 1843 for the Purpose of Considering Their Moral and Political Condition as American Citizens. New York: Pierce and Reed, 1843.

Minutes of the State Convention of the Colored Citizens of Pennsylvania. Philadelphia: Merrihew and Thompson, Printers, 1849.

Minutes of the Union Benevolent Sons of Bethel, 1826-1844, (HSP).

Morse, Jedidiah. *A Discourse Delivered at the African-Meeting House, in Boston, 14 July 1808, in Grateful Celebration of the Abolition of the African Slave Trade by Governments of the United States, Great Britain, and Denmark.* Boston: Lincoln and Edmands, 1808.

Mother Bethel. *Minutes and Trial Book 1822-1835,* (HSP).

Nell, William. *Services of Colored Americans in the Wars of 1776 and 1812.* Boston: Prentiss and Sawyer, 1851.

Nell, William. *The Colored Patriots of the American Revolution, with Sketches of Several Distinquished Colored Persons to Which is Added a Brief Survey of the Condition and Prospects of Colored Americans.* Boston: Robert F. Wallcut, 1855.

Nesbit, William. *Four Months in Liberia: Or African Colonization Exposed.* Pittsburgh: J. T. Shyrock, 1855.

New England Anti-Slavery Society. *First Annual Report of the Board of Managers of the New England Anti-Slavery Society.* Boston: Garrison and Knapp, 1833

Newton, A. E. *Letter* to Jacob C. White Jr., 13 August 1861, (HSP).

Nicholson, John. *Letter* to Absalom Jones and William Gray, 6 August 1798, (HSP).

Parham, William. *Letter* to Jacob C. White Jr., 9 December 1861, (HSP).

_____. *Letter* to Jacob C. White Jr., 6 October 1862, (HSP).

_____. *Letter* to Jacob C. White Jr., 27 February 1890, (HSP).

Pennsylvania Abolition Society. *Facts on Beneficial Societies 1823-1838*, (HSP).

_____. *American Convention Miscellaneous Addresses, Memorials and Related Materials* 1826-1829, (NYPL).

Record Book of the Bethel African M. E. Church. New York: Carleton and Porter, 1864.

Redpath, James. *Letter* to Jacob C. White Jr., 23 August 1862, (HSP).

Right and Wrong in Boston in 1836. Boston: The Society, 1836.

Roberts, Jonathan. *Letter* to Elizabeth Roberts, 19 February 1826, (HSP).

Russwurm, John B. *Letter* to Rev. R. R. Gurley 26 February 1827, (HSP).

_____. *Letter* to Rev. R. R. Gurley 8 May 1829.

Saint Luke's Society, Sisterhood of the Good Angels; and The By-Laws of St. Luke's Society, Of Said Sisterhood New Haven: William H. Stanley, 1856.

Sanders, Prince. *Haytian Papers, A Collection of the Very Interesting Proclamations and Other Official Documents; Together with Some Account of the Rise, Progress and Present State of the Kingdom of Hayti* London: n.p., 1816.

_____. *Letters* 1819-1820, (HSP).

Shadd, Mary Ann *A Plea for Emigration; or Notes on Canada West in its Moral, Social, and Politicasl Aspect: with Suggestions Respecting Mexico, West Indies, and Vancouver's Island for the Information of Colored Emigrants.* Detroit: GeorgeW. Pattison,1852.

Shoemaker, Samuel. *Opinion on Supplement Articles of Incorporation Bethel Church.*7 April 1815, (HSP).

Simms, James M. *The Colored Baptist Church in North American, Constituted At Savannah, Georgia, 20 January 1788, With Biographical Sketches Of The Pastors.* Philadelphia: J. B. Lippincott Company, 1888.

Simpson, R. L. *Letter* to Jacob C. White Jr. 20 November 1861, (HSP).

Sparhawk, E. T. *Letter* to Matthew Carey, Esq. 20 January 1828, (HSP).

_____. *Letter* to Miss Melish 1830, (HSP).

Stewart, Maria W. *Religion and the Pure Principles of Morality, the Sure Foundation on Which We Must Build.* Boston: Isaac Knapp, 1831, (HSP).

Tanner, Benjamin Tucker. *An Appology For African Methodism* Baltimore: n.p., 1867, (HSP).

The Abolitionist July 1833, (NYPL).

The Colored People's Trade Register. Pennsylvania Abolition Society, 1838.

The Liberator. "Meeting in Philadelphia." 12 March 1831, (BPL).

_____. "Death of Bishop Allen." 9 April 1831, (BPL).

_____. "Proposals for Publishing a Weekly Paper in Philadelphia." 2 July 1831, (BPL).

_____. 7 January 1832, (BPL).

_____. 28 September 1833, (BPL).

Vigilant Committee, Philadelphia. 31 May 1839, (HSP).

Thirteenth General Conference of the African M. E. Church. Philadelphia: William S. Young, 1864.

Ward, Samuel Ringgold. *Letter* to The Christian Conference, Cincinnati, 3 April 1850.

Watson, Joseph. *Proclamation,* 9 February 1827, (HSP).

Weaver, Elisha. *The Doctrines and Disciplines of African Methodist Episcopal Church.* Philadelphia: James H. Bryson, 1860.

West, William. *Note* to Jacob C. White Jr., 8 December 1843, (HSP).

Whipper, William. *Letter* to Jacob C. White Jr., 26 April 1839, (HSP).

White, Jacob C. Jr. *Address to the Governor James Pollock,* 24 May 1855, (HSP).

_____. *Advertisements 1860,* (HSP).

_____. *Letters* to Thomas Hamilton, Esq. 5 January and 31 January 1860, (HSP).

_____. *Letters* to George Lawrence Jr. Esq., 2 April, 16 April and 6 May 1861, (HSP).

_____. *Letter* to James Redpath, 3 June 1861, (HSP).

_____. *Letters* to James Redpath, 24 June and 29 July 1861, (HSP).

_____. *Letter* to James Redpath, 21 August 1861, (HSP).

_____. *Letter* to James Redpath, 9 September 1861, (HSP).

_____. *Letter* to James Redpath,16 December 1861, (HSP).

_____. *Letter* to James Redpath, 6 January 1862, (HSP).

_____. *Letter* to Robert Hamilton, Esq., 20 February 1862, (HSP).

_____. *Accounts Book,* 1 January to 30 June 1862, (HSP).

White, Jacob C. Sr. *Miscellaneous Newspaper Clippings,* 1822-1862, (HSP).

_____. *Letter* to David Ruggles 6 December 1838, (HSP).

White, J. S. *Reciept* to Jacob C. White Jr., 1 January 1862, (HSP).

Williams, Peter. *Letter* to Thomas Tucker, New York Manumission Society, 10 June 1816.

_____. *A Discourse Delivered on the death of Paul Cuffe* New York: B. Young and Company, 1817.

Williams, Peter. *Letter* to John H. Hobart, 14 August 1826, (NYHS).

_____. *An Address to the Citizens of New York*, 1830, (NYHS).

Wilson, Joseph. *Sketches of the Higher Classes of Colored Society in Philadelphia.* Philadelphia: Merrihew and Thompson, 1841.

Winchell, James M. *Two Discourses Exhibiting An Historical Sketch of the First Baptist Church in Boston From Its Formation in Charlestown 1665 to the Beginning of 1818.* Boston: James Loring, 1820.

Secondary Sources: Articles

Aptheker, Herbert. "South Carolina Negro Conventions, 1865." *The Journal of Negro History* 31, no. 1 (January 1946): 91-98.

Bailey, Kenneth. "Protestanism and Afro-American in the Old South: Another Look." *Journal of Southerm History* 41 (November 1975): 451-72.

Baur, John Edward. "Mulatto Machiavelli, Jean Pierre Boyer, and the Haiti of His Day." *Journal of Negro History* 32, no. 3 (July 1947): 307-52.

Bell, Howard H. "Negro National Conventions of the Middle 1840s: Moral Suasion vs. Political Action." *Journal of Negro History* 42, no. 4 (October 1957): 247-60.

_____. "Free Negroes of the North 1830-35: A Study of National Cooperation." *The Journal of Negro Education* 26, no. 4 (Fall 1957): 447-52.

_____. "The New Emigration Movement, 1849-1854: A Phase of Negro Nationalism." *Phylon* 20, no. 2 (Summer 1959): 132-42.

_____. "Some Reform Interests of the Negro During the 1850s as Reflected in State Conventions." *Phylon* 21, no. 2 (Summer 1960): 173-81.

Bennett, Robert A. "Black Episcopalians: A History from the Colonial Period to the Present:" *Historical Magazine of the Protestant Episcopal Church* 42, no. 3 (September 1974): 231-45.

Bishop, Shelton H. "A History of St. Phillips Church, New York City." *Historical Magazine of the Protestant Episcopal Church* 15, no. 4 (December 1946): 298-317.

Bogin, Ruth. "Sarah Parker Remond: Black Abolitionist from Salem." *Essex Institute Historical Collections* 110, no. 2 (April 1974): 120-50.

Brewer, William M. "John B. Russwurm." *Journal of Negro History* 13 (1928): 413-22.

Brooks, Walter H. "The Evolution of the Negro Baptist Church." *Journal of Negro History* 7, no. 1 (January 1922): 14-15.

Brown, Delindus R. "Free Blacks Rhetorical Impact of African Colonization." *Journal of Black Studies* 9, no. 3 (March 1974): 251-66.

Buxbaum, Melvin H. "Cyrus Bustill Addresses the Blacks of Philadelphia." *William and Mary Quarterly* 29 (January 1972): 99-108.

Coan, Josephus R. "Daniel Coker: 19th Century Black Church Organizer, Educator, and Missionary." *Journal of the Interdenominational Theological Center* 3, no. 1(Fall 1976): 17-31.

Cooper, Frederick. "Elevating the Race: The Social Thought of Black Leaders, 1827-50" *American Quarterly* 24, no. 5 (December 1972): 604-25.

Crawford, Paul. "A Footnote on Courts for Trial of Negroes in Colonial Pennsylvania." *Journal of Black Studies* 5, no. 2 (December 1974): 167-74.

Davis, John W. "George Liele and Andrew Bryan, Pioneer Negro Baptist Preachers." *Journal of Negro History* 3, no. 2 (April 1918): 119-27.

Fisher, Miles Mark. "Lott Cary, The Colonizing Missionary." *Journal of Negro History* 7, no. 4 (October 1922): 380-418.

Foner, Phillip S. "John Browne Russwurm, A Document." *Journal of Negro History* 54, no. 4 (October 1969): 393-97.

Fox, Dixon Ryan. "The Negro Vote in Old New York." *Political Science Quarterly* 32, no. 4 (June 1917): 252-75.

Friedman, Lee M. "A Beacon Hill Synagogue." *Old-Time New England* 33, no. 1 (June 1942): 1-5.

Friedman, Lawrence, and Arthur H. Shaffer. "Mercy Otis Warren and the Politics of Historical Nationalism." *The New England Quarterly* 48, no. 2 (June 1975): 194-215.

Friedman, Lawrence J. "Antebellum American Abolition and the Problem of Violent Means." *The Psychohistory Review* 9, no. 1(Fall 1980): 23-58.

_____. "William Lloyd Garrison and the Boston Clique." *The Psychohistory Review* 7, no. 1 (Fall 1978): 6-19.

Gliozzo, Charles. "John Jones and the Black Convention Movement, 1848-1856." *Journal of Black Studies* 3, no. 2 (1972-1973): 227-36.

Gravely, Will. "The Rise of African Churches in America (1768-1822): Re-examining the Contexts." *Journal of Religious Thought* 41, no. 1 (1984).

Greene, Lorenzo J. "Prince Hall: Massachusetts Leader in Crisis." *Freedomways* 1, no. 3 (Fall 1961): 238-58.

Gross, Bella. "Freedom's Journal and The Rights Of All." *Journal of Negro History* 18, no. 3 (July 1932): 241-86.

Gross, Bella. "Life and Times of Theodore S. Wright, 1797-1847." *Negro History Bulletin* 111, no. 9 (June 1940): 133-38, 144.

_____. "The First National Negro Convention." *Journal of Negro History* 21, no. 4 (October 1946): 435-43.

Harding, Vincent. "Religion and Resistance Among Antebellum Negroes, 1800-1860," Edited by Augus Meier, and Elliot Rudwick in *The Making of Black America: Essays in Negro Life* (New York: Atheneum, 1969), 179-97.

Hewitt, John H. "New York's Black Episcopalians: In the Beginning, 1704-1722." *Afro-Americans in New York Life and History* 3 (January 1979): 9-22.

Hewitt, John H. "The Sacking of St. Phillips Church, New York." *Historical Magazine of the Protestant Episcopal Church* 46, no. 1 (March 1980): 9-22

Hood, R. E. "From a Headstart to a Deadstart: Historical Basis for Black Indifference Toward the Episcopal Church 1800-1860." *Historical Magazine of the Protestant Episcopal Church* 51, no. 3 (September 1982): 269-96.

Horton, James Oliver. "Generations of Protest: Black Families and Social Reform in Antebellum Boston." *New England Quarterly* 49, no. 2 (June 1976): 242-56.

Johnston, Norman C. "Caste and Class of the Urban Form of Historic Philadelphia." *Journal of the American Institute of Planners,* (November 1966).

Jacobs, Donald M. "William Lloyd Garrison's *Liberator* and Boston's Blacks, 1830-1865." *The New England Quarterly* 49, no. 2 (June 1971): 259-78.

Jacobs, Donald M. "David Walker: Boston Race Leader, 1825-1830." *Essex Institute Historical Collections* 107, no. 1 (January 1971): 94-107.

Lammers, Ann C. "The Rev. Absalom Jones and the Episcopal Church: Christian Theology and Black Consciousness in a New Alliance." *Historical Magazine of the Protestant Episcopalian Church* 51, no. 3 (September 1982): 159-84.

Lapsansky, Emma Jones. "Since They Got Those Separate Churches: Afro-Americans and Racism in Jacksonian Philadelphia." *American Quarterly* 32, no. 1 (Spring 1980): 54-78.

Lerner, Gerda. "Early Club Work Among Negro Women." *Journal of Negro History* 59, no. 2 (April 1974): 158-67.

Levesque, George A. "Black Abolitionists in the Age of Jackson: Catalysts in the Radicalization of American Abolitionism." *Journal of Black Studies* 1, no. 2 (December 1970): 187-202.

Levesque, George A. "Inherent Reformers-Inherited Orthodoxy: Black Baptists in Boston, 1800-1873." *Journal of Negro History* 60, no. 4 (October 1975): 491-525.

McMaster, Richard K. "Henry Highland Garnet and the African Civilization Society" in David W. Wills and Richard Newman, eds.,

Black Apostles at Home and Abroad: Afro-Americans and the Christian Mission from the Revolution to Reconstruction (Boston: G. K. Hall and Company, 1982), 265-82.

Mabee, Carlton. "A Negro Boycott to Integrate Boston Schools." *The New England Quarterly* 41, no. 3 (September 1968): 341-61.

Markwei, Matei. "The Rev. Daniel Coker of Sierra Leone" in David W. Wills and Richard Newman, eds., *Black Apostles at Home and Abroad: Afro-Americans and the Christian Mission from the Revolution to Reconstruction* (Boston: G. K. Hall and Company, 1982), 203-20.

Murray, Alexander. "The Provincial Freeman: A New Source for the History of the Negro in Canada and the United States" *Journal of Negro History* 44, no. 2 (April 1959): 123-35.

Loomis, Sally. "The Evolution of Paul Cuffe's Black Nationalism" in David W. Wills and Richard Newman, eds, *Black Apostles at Home and Abroad: Afro-Americans and the Christiam Mission from the Revolution to Reconstruction*. Boston: G. K. Hall and Company, 1982, 191-202.

Mehlinger, Louis. "The Attitude of the Free Negro Toward African Colonization." *Journal of Negro History* 1, no. 1 (January 1916): 276-301.

Meyer, Michael. "Thoreau and Black Emigration." *American Literature* 53, no. 3 (November 1981): 380-96.

Mitchell, J. Marcus. "The Paul Family." *Old Time New England* 63, no. 3 (Winter 1973): 73-77.

Payne, Aaron Hamlet. "The Negro in New York Prior to 1860." *The Howard Review* 1, no. 1 (June 1923): 1-64.

Pease, Jane H. and William H. Pease. "Negro Conventions and the Problem of Black Leadership." *Journal of Black Studies* 2, no. 1 (September 1971): 29-44.

Pease, William H. and Jane H. Pease. "Boston Garrisonians and the Problem of Frederick Douglass." *Canadian Journal of History* 11, no. 2 (September 1967): 29-48.

Perlman, Daniel. "Organizations of the Free Negro in New York City, 1800-1860." *Journal of Negro History* 56, no. 3 (July 1971): 181-98.

Pride, Armistead. "Negro Newspapers: Yesterday, Today and Tomorrow." *Journalism Quarterly* 28 (Spring 1951): 179-88.

Quarles, Benjamin. "The Breach Between Douglass and Garrison." *Journal of Negro History* 23, no. 2 (April 1938): 139-54.

Reed, Harry. "Not By Protest Alone: Afro-American Activists and the Pythian Baseball Club of Philadelphia, 1867-1869." *The Western Journal of Black Studies* 9, no. 3 (Fall 1985): 144-51.

Sernett, Milton C. "First Honor: Oneida Institute's Role in the Fight Against American Racism and Slavery." *New York History* 66, no. 2 (April 1985): 101-22.

Sherwood, Henry Noble. "Early Negro Deportation Projects." *Mississippi Valley Historical Review* 11, no. 4 (March 1916): 484-508.

_____. "The Formation of the American Colonization Society." *Journal of Negro History* 2, no. 3 (July 1917): 209-28.

_____. "Paul Cuffe" *Journal of Negro History* 8, no. 2 (April 1923): 153-230.

Shiffrin, Steven H. "The Rhetoric of Black Violence in the Ante-Bellum Period: Henry Highland Garnet." *Journal of Black Studies* 2, no. 1 (September 1971): 45-56.

Silcox, Harry C. "Philadelphia Negro Educator: Jacob C. White, Jr." *The Pennsylvania Magazine of History and Biography* 51, no. 1 (January 1973):75-98.

Smith, Anne Bustill. "The Bustill Family." *Journal of Negro History* 10, no. 4 (October 1925): 638-44.

Smith, Timothy. "Slavery and Theology: The Emergence of Black Christian Consciousness in Nineteenth Century America." *Church History* 41, no. 4 (December 1972): 497-512.

Swift, David C. "Black Presbyterian Attacks on Racism: Samuel Cornish, Theodore Wright and Their Contemporaries." *Journal of Presbyterian History* 51, no. 4 (Winter 1973): 433-70.

Taylor, Henry L. "On Slavery's Fringe: City-Building and Black Community Development in Cincinnati, 1800-1850." *Ohio History* 95 (Winter-Spring 1986): 5-33.

Twombly, Robert C., and Richard H. Moore. "Black Puritan: The Negro in Seventeenth Century Massachussetts." *The William and Mary Quarterly* 24, no. 2 (April 1967): 224-42.

Usrey, Miriam L. "Charles Lenox Remond: Garrison's Ebony Echo at the World Antislavery Convention, 1840." *Essex Institute Historical Collections* 106, no. 2 (April 1970): 112-25.

Wade, Richard C. "The Negro in Cincinnati, 1800-1830." *Journal of Negro History* 39, no. 1 (January 1939): 43-55.

Walters, Ronald G. "The Erotic South: Civilization and Sexuality in American Abolitionism." *American Quarterly* 25, no. 2 (May 1973): 177-201.

Warner, Robert A. "Amos Gerry Beman, 1812-1874; A Memoir on a Forgotten Leader." *Journal of Negro History* 22, no. 2 (April 1937): 200-21.

Washington, James Melvin. " The Origins of Black Evangelicalism and the Ethical Function of Evangelical Cosmology." *Union Seminary Quarterly Review* 32, no. 2 (Winter 1977): 104-16.

Wesley, Charles H. "The Negroes of New York in the Emancipation Movement." *Journal of Negro History* 34, no. 1 (January 1939): 65-103.

White, Arthur O. "Salem's Antebellum Black Community: Seedbed of the School Integration Movement." *Essex Institute Historical Collections* 108, no. 2 (April 1972): 99-118.

White, Arthur O. "Prince Saunders: An Instance of Social Mobility Among Antebellum Blacks." *Journal of Negro History* 60, no. 4 (October 1975): 526-35.

Woodson, Carter G. "The Negro in Cincinnati Prior to the Civil War." *Journal of Negro History* 1, no. 1 (January 1916): 1-22.

Zanger, Jules. "The Tragic Octoroon in Pre-Civil War Fiction." *American Quarterly* 18, no. 1 (Spring 1966): 63-70.

Secondary Sources: Books

Allen, Robert L. *Reluctant Reformers: Racism and the Social Reform Movements in the United States.* Washington, D. C.: Howard University Press, 1983.

Aptheker, Herbert. *One Continual Cry; David Walker's Appeal to the Colored Citizens of the World 1829, 1830, Its Setting, Its Meaning, Together with the Full Text of the Third and Last Edition of the Appeal.* New York: Humanities Press, 1965.

Aptheker, Herbert. *Documentary History of the Negro People in the United States (1661-1910).* New York: Citadel Press, 1961.

Banks, William L. *A History of Black Baptists in the United States.* Philadelphia: The Continental Press, 1987.

Bearden, Jim, and Linda Jean Butler. *Shadd: The Life and Times of Mary Shadd Cary.* Toronto: NC Press, 1977.

Bell, Howard Holman. *Minutes of the Proceedings of the National Negro Conventions 1830-1864.* New York: Arno Press, 1969.

Blackett, R. J. M. *Building An Antislavery Wall: Blacks in the Atlantic Abolitionist Movement, 1830-1860.* Baton Rouge, Louisiana: Louisiana State University Press, 1983.

Blassingame, John ed. *The Frederick Douglass Papers: Speeches, Debates, and Interviews, 1847-1854.* vol.2. New Haven: Yale University Press, 1982.

Boone, Theodore S. *From George Lisle to L. K. Williams: Short Visits to the Tombs of Negro Baptists.* Detroit: A. P. Publishing, 1941.

Bragg, George Freeman. *Richard Allen and Absalom Jones.* Baltimore: Church Advocate Press, 1915.

Bragg, George Freeman. *The History of the Afro-American Group of the Episcopal Church.* Baltimore: The Church Advocate Press, 1922.

Carlisle, Rodney. *The Roots of Black Nationalism.* Port Washington, New York: Kennikat Press, 1975.

Childs, John Brown. *The Political Black Minister: A Study in Afro-American Politics and Religion.* Boston: G. K. Hall and Company, 1980.

Cole, Bill. *Coltrane: A Biography.* New York: De Capo Press, 1976.

Coleman, Charles L. *A History of the Negro Baptist in Boston.* MA thesis, Andover Newton Theological School, 1956.

Crummell, Alexander. *Africa and America: Addresses and Discourses.* New York: Negro Universities Press, 1969.

Curry, Leonard P. *The Free Black in Urban America: The Shadow of the Dream.* Chicago: University of Chicago Press, 1981.

Daniels, John. *In Freedom's Birthplace: A Study of the Boston Negroes.* Boston: Houghton Mifflin Company, 1914.

Dann. Martin E. *The Black Press, 1827-1890.* New York: Capricorn Books, 1971.

Dean, David M. *Defender of the Race: James Theodore Holly Black Nationalist Bihop.* Boston: Lambeth Press, 1979.

Detweiler, Frederick G. *The Negro Press in the United States.* Chicago: University of Chicago Press, 1922.

Dick, Robert C. *Black Protest; Issues and Tactics.* Westport, Conn.: Greenwood Press, 1974.

DuBois, W. E. B. *The Souls of Black Folk.* New York: Fawcett, 1961.

_____. *The Philadelphia Negro.* Philadelphia: University of Pennsylvania, 1899.

Dunbar, Alice Moore. *Masterpieces of Negro Eloquence: The Best Speeches Delivered by the Negro from the Days of Slavery to the Present.* New York: The Bookery Publishing Company, 1914.

Finkle, Lee. *Forum For Protest: The Black Press During World War II.* Rutherford, New Jersey: Fairleigh Dickinson University Press, 1975.

Fisher, Paul L., and Ralph L. Lowenstein, eds. *Race and News Media.* New York: Frederick A. Praeger, Inc., 1967.

Foner, Phillip S. *The Life and Writings of Frederick Douglass.* New York: International Publishers, 1950.

Fordham, Monroe. *Major Themes in Northern Black Religious Thought, 1800-1860.* Hicksville, New York: Exposition Press, 1975.

Frazier, E. Franklin. *Black Bourgeosie.* New York: The Free Press, 1957.

Frazier, E. Franklin. *The Negro Church in America.* New York: Schoken Books, 1964.

Freeman, Rhoda Golden. *The Free Negro in New York City in the Era Before the Civil War.* Ph.D. diss., Columbia University, 1966.

George, Carol V. R. *Segregated Sabbaths: Richard Allen and the Emergence of Independent Black Churches, 1765-1840.* New York: Oxford University Press, 1973.

Griggs, Earl Leslie and Clifford H. Prator, eds. *Henri Christophe and Thomas Clarkson: A Correspondence.* Berkeley: University of California Press, 1952.

Grimshaw, William. *Official History of Freemasonary Among the Colorado People in North America.* New York: np, 1903.

Harris, Joseph. *Africans and Their History.* New York: New American Library, 1972.

Harris, Sheldon H. *Paul Cuffe: Black America and the African Return.* New York: Simon and Schuster, 1972.

Hood, Bishop James Walker. *One Hundred Years of the African Methodist Episcopal Zion Church, or The Centennial of African Methodism.* New York: AMEZ Book Concern, 1895.

Horner, Charles. *The Life of James Redpath and the Development of the Modern Lyceum.* New York: Barse and Hopkins, 1926.

Horton, James Oliver and Lois E. Horton. *Black Bostonians: Family Life and Community Struggle in the Antebellum North.* New York: Holmes and Meier Publishers, Inc., 1979.

Jacobs, Donald M., ed. *Antebellum Black Newspapers: Indices to Freedom's Journal (1827-29), The Rights of All (1829), and The Colored American (1834-41).* Westport, Conn.: Greenwood Press, 1976.

Jernegan, Marcus Wilson. *Laboring and Dependent Classes in Colonial America, 1607-1783; Studies of the Economic, Educational, and Social Significance of Slaves, Servants, Apprentices, and Poor Folk.* Chicago: University of Chicago Press, 1931.

Johnson, Ruby F. *The Development of Negro Religion.* New York: Philosophical Library, 1954.

Kaplan, Sidney. *The Black Presence in the Era of the American Revolution 1770-1800.* Washington, D.C.: Smithsonian Institution, 1973.

Katz, William Loren. *Negro Protest Pamphlets.* New York: Arno Press and The New York Times, 1969.

Kraditor, Aileen S. *The Ideas of the Women Suffrage Movement.* Garden City, New York: Doubleday and Company Inc., 1971.

LaBrie, Henry G. *Perspectives of the Black Press: 1974.* Kennebunkport, Maine: Mercer House Press, 1974.

Leffall, Delores C. *The Black Church: An Annotated Bibliography.* Washington: Minority Research Center, 1973.

Levine, Lawrence. *Black Culture, Black Consciousness.* New York: Oxford University Press, 1970.

Lerner, Gerda ed. *Black Women in White America: A Documentary History.* New York: Pantheon Books, 1972.

Loewenberg, Bert James, and Ruth Bogin, eds. *Black Women in Nineteenth Century American Life: Their Words, Their Thoughts,*

Their Feelings. University Park: Pennsylvania State University Press, 1976.

Malone, Dumas ed. *Dictionary of American Biography*, 18. New York: Charles Scribner's Sons, 1936.

McCoy, Drew. *The Elusive Republic: Political Economy in Jeffersonian America.* Chapel Hill: The University of North Carolina Press, 1980.

McPherson, James. *The Abolitionist Legacy: From Reconstruction to the NAACP.* Princeton: Princeton University Press, 1975.

Matthews, Marcia M. *Richard Allen.* Baltimore: Helicon, 1963.

Mays, Benjamin Elijah, and Joseph William Nicholson. *The Negro's Church.* New York: Negro Universities Press, 1933.

Miller, Floyd J. *The Search for a Black Nationality: Black Emigration and Colonization 1787-1863.* Urbana: University of Illinois, 1975.

Montague, Ludwell Lee. *Haiti and The United States, 1714-1938.* New York: Russell and Russell, 1966.

Moses, Wilson Jeremiah. *The Golden Age of Black Nationalism, 1850-1925.* New York: Oxford University Press, 1978.

Myrdal, Gunnar. *An American Dilemma.* New York: Harper and Brothers, 1944.

Nash, Gary B. *Forging Freedom: The Formation of Philadelphia's Black Community 1720-1840.* Cambridge: Harvard University Press, 1988.

Nelson, Hart M. and Raytha L. Yokely, and Anne K. Nelson, eds. *The Black Church in America.* New York: Basic Books, Inc. Publishers,

Nelson, Truman, ed. *Documents of Upheaval: Selections from William Lloyd Garrison's The Liberator, 1831-1865.* New York: Hill and Wang, 1966.

O'Dea, Thomas F. *The Sociology of Religion.* Englewood Cliffs, N.J.: Prentice Hall, 1966.

Ofari, Earl. *Let Your Motto Be Resistance: The Life and Thought of Henry Highland Gannet.* Boston: Beacon Press, 1972.

Ottley, Roi and William J. Weatherby. *The Negro In New York: An Informal History.* Dobbs Ferry, N.Y.: Oceana Publishers, Inc., 1967.

Payne, Daniel Alexander. *Recollections of Seventy Years.* New York: Arno Press, 1968.

_____. *History of the African Methodist Episcopal Church.* New York: Arno Press, 1969,

Pease, Jane H., and William H. Pease. *Bound With Them in Chains: A Biographical History of the Antislavery Movement.* Westport, Conn.: Greenwood Press, 1972.

Pease, William H., and Jane H. Pease. *They Who Would Be Free: Blacks' Search For Freedom, 1830-1861.* New York: Atheneum. 1974.

Penn, I. Garland. *The Afro-American Press and Its Editors.* New York: Arno Press, 1969.

Porter, Dorothy. *Early Negro Writing 1760-1837.* Boston: Beacon Press, 1971.

Quarles, Benjamin. *Black Abolitionists.* New York: Oxford University Press, 1969.

Richardson, Harry V. *Dark Salvation: The Story of Methodism as it Developed Among Blacks in America.* Garden City, N. Y.: Anchor-Press/Doubleday, 1976.

Richardson, Marilyn. *Black Women and Religion, A Bibliography.* Boston: G. K. Hall, 1980.

_____. *Maria W. Stewart: America's First Black Woman Political Writer.* Bloomington: Indiana University Press, 1987.

Richmond, M.A. *Bid the Vassal Soar: Interpretive Essays on the Life and Poetry of Phillis Wheatley (c1753-1784) and George Moses Horton (c1797-1883).* Washington, D.C.: Howard University Press, 1974.

Rigsby, Gregory U. *Alexander Crummell: Pioneer in Nineteenth Century Pan-African Thought.* Westport, Conn.: Greenwood Press, 1987.

Robinson, William. *Black New England Letters: The Uses of Writing in Black New England.* Boston: Trustees of the Public Library of the City of Boston, 1977.

_____. *Phillis Wheatley and Her Writings.* New York: Garland Publishing, Inc., 1984.

Schor, Joel. *Henry Highland Garnet: A Voice of Black Radicalism in the Nineteenth Century.* Westport, Conn.: Greenwood Press, 1977.

Sernett, Milton C. *Black Religion and American Evangelicalism 1787-1865.* Metuchen, N. J.: The Scarecrow Press, 1975.

_____. *Afro-American Religious History: A Documentary Witness.* Durham, N.C.: Duke University Press, 1985.

Simms, James M. *The Colored Baptist Church in North America Constituted at Savannah, Georgia, 20 January 1788 With Biographical Sketches of the Pastors.* Philadelphia: J. B. Lippincott Company, 1888.

Simpson, George. *The Negro in Philadelphia Press.* Philadelphia: University of Pennsylvania Press, 1936.

Singleton, George. A. *The Romance of African Methodism: A Study of the African Methodist Episcopal Church.* New York: Exposition Press, 1952.

Staudenraus, P. J. *The African Colonization Movement 1816-1895.* New York: Columbia University Press, 1961.

Stuckey, Sterling. *The Ideological Roots of Black Nationalism.* Boston: Beacon Press, 1972.

_____. *Slave Culture: Nationalist Theory and the Foundations of Black America.* New York: Oxford University Press, 1987.

Swift, David E. *Black Prophets of Justice: Activist Clergy Before The Civil War*. Baton Rouge: Louisiana State University Press, 1989.

Thomas, Lamont. *Rise To Be A People: A Biography of Paul Cuffe*. Urbana: University of Illinios Press, 1986.

Tyler, Alice Felt. *Freedom's Ferment: Phases of American Social History from the Colonial Period to the Outbreak of the Civil War*. New York: Harper and Row, 1944.

Ullman, Victor. *Martin R. Delany: The Beginnings of Black Nationalism*. Boston: Beacon Press, 1971.

Wade, Richard C. *The Urban Frontier: The Rise of Western Cities, 1790-1830*. Cambridge: Harvard University Press, 1959.

Walker, Clarence E. *A Rock in a Weary Land: The African Methodist Episcopal Church During the Civil War and Reconstruction*. Baton Rouge: Louisiana State University Press, 1982.

Walker, James W. St. G. *The Black Loyalists: The Search For A Promised Land in Nova Scotia and Sierra Leone, 1783-1870*. New York: Africana Publishing Company, 1976.

Walls, William J. *The African Episcopal Zion Church: Reality of the Black Church*. Charlotte, N.C.: AMEZ Publishing House, 1974.

Washington, James Melvin. *Frustrated Fellowship: The Black Baptist Quest for Social Power*. Macon, Georgia: Mercer University Press, 1986.

Washington, Joseph. *Black Religion*. Boston: Beacon Press, 1966.

Wesley, Charles H. *Richard Allen: Apostle of Freedom*. Washington, D.C.: The Associated Publishers, Inc., 1935.

West, Richard. *Back to Africa: A History of Sierra Leone and Liberia*. London: Jonathan Cape, 1970.

Williams, Melvin D. *Community in a Black Pentecostal Church: An Anthropological Study*. Pittsburgh: University of Pittsburgh Press, 1974.

Willis, David W. and Richard Newman, eds. *Black Apostles at Home and Abroad: Afro-Americans and the Christian Mission from the Revolution to Revolution*. Boston: G. K. Hall and Company, 1982.

Wilmore, Gayraud. *Black Religion and Black Radicalism*. New York: Doubleday, 1972.

Wilson, Ellen Gibson. *The Loyal Blacks*. New York: G.P. Putnam's Sons, 1976.

Wiltse, Charles M. *David Walker's Appeal*. New York: Hill and Wang, 1965.

Winch, Julie. *The Leaders of Phildelphia's Black Community 1787-1848* Ph. d. diss., Bryn Mawr, 1982.

_____. *Philadelphia's Black Elite, Activism, Accomodation, and the Struggle for Autonomy*. Philadelphia: Temple University Press, 1988.

Wolseley, Roland E. *The Black Press U.S.A.* Ames, Iowa: The Iowa State University Press, 1971.

Wood, Nathan. *The History of the First Baptist Church of Boston 1665-1899.* Philadelphia: American Baptist Publication Society, 1899.

Woodson, Carter G. *The Education of the Negro Prior to 1861.* New York: Arno Press, 1968.

_____. *The History of the Negro Church.* Washington D.C.: Associated Publishers, 1921.

_____. *The Mind of the Negro as Reflected in Letters Written During the Crisis 1800-1860.* New York: New American Library, 1970.

Ziversmit, Arthur. *The First Emancipation: The Abolition of Slavery in the North.* Chicago: University of Chicago Press.

Index

A

Abysinian Babtist Church, the, 82
Adams, Joseph, 138
African Baptist Church, the, 120
African Civilization Society, the, 84, 85, 157, 199, 200
African Institution, the, 129, 132, 181, 182, 185, 187
African Masonic Lodge: establishment of, 7, 60-61, 63; role in black community, 64-67
African Methodist Episcopal Church (AME): and African religious practices, 13, 19; of Boston, 27; establishment of national body, 32; and Richard Allen, 14; role of women in, 33-34, 37
African Methodist Episcopal Zion Church (AMEZ), 43-44
African Society, the, 67-68
Agricultural and Mechanics Association, the, 89
Alexander, Daniel Payne, 13
Allen, John, 138, 197
Allen, Rev. Richard: and the African Methodist Episcopal Church, 14-15, 28-32; and the

African Methodist Episcopal Zion Church, 43, 44; and the American Colonization Society, 54n.54, 132; and the Bethel court system, 34; and the black convention movement, 5, 127, 135-36, 137, 138; and the Committee for the Education of Colored Youth, 75; death of, 140; and emigrationism, 141, 181, 196-97; employment of, 74; and the Free African Society, 23, 30-31, 71; and *Freedom's Journal*, 107-8; and Philadelphia yellow fever epidemic, 31, 71-72; and St. George Church, 29-32; and the Second African Masonic Lodge, 73; and the social action gospel, 167-68; and women's rights, 33, 37
Allen, William, 185, 187
American, The, 125n.56
American Colonization Society, the (ACS): and the back-to-Africa movement, 190-91, 193-94, 199, 200; and the black convention movement, 128, 133-35,